COLUMBIA CRITICAL GUIDES

James Joyce

Ulysses
A Portrait of the Artist as a Young Man

EDITED BY JOHN COYLE

Series editor: Richard Beynon

COLUMBIA UNIVERSITY PRESS ▲ NEW YORK

Columbia University Press
Publishers Since 1893
New York
Editor's text copyright © 1998 John Coyle
All rights reserved

First published in the Icon Critical Guides series in 1998
by Icon Books Ltd.

Library of Congress Cataloging-in-Publication Data
James Joyce, Ulysses, A portrait of the artist as a young man / edited
    by John Coyle.
            p.   cm. — (Columbia critical guides)
    Originally published: Duxford, England : Icon Books, 1997, in
series: Icon critical guides.
    Includes bibliographical references and index.
    ISBN 0–231–11530–x (cloth : alk. paper). —
    ISBN 0–231–11531–8 (phk.)
    1. Joyce, James, 1882–1941.   Portrait of the artist as a young
man.   2. Joyce, James, 1882–1941.   Ulysses.   3. Dublin
(Ireland)—In literature.   I. Coyle, John (John G.)   II. Series.
PR6019.09P6454   1998
823'.912—dc21   98–39510

c 10 9 8 7 6 5 4 3 2 1
p 10 9 8 7 6 5 4 3 2 1

Contents

Introduction

No twentieth century writer is as justifiably famous as Joyce, yet he could never be introduced by saying that he requires no introduction. Indeed one is never done with introducing Joyce, such is the myth of his difficulty and encyclopaedic inexhaustibility.

This is not the only problem. *A Portrait* and *Ulysses* are also notoriously resistant to classification: since they both question and transcend generic boundaries, it has traditionally been difficult to know how to place them, and efforts to classify usually say as much about the preconceptions of critics as they do about the works themselves. This last point is of course to some extent true about the relation of criticism to any literature, but Joyce presents an unusually difficult case. Both Joyce's novels (and a question in parenthesis – should we call them novels?) seemed to appeal equally to symbolism and to naturalism, to a gorgeousness of textual artifice and to an unremitting attention to documentary realism. The author is as obtrusive in calling attention to his art as any writer before or since, and yet, in other respects, he is invisible, refusing not only judgement but even guidance to his readers. The reader is given no clear signal whether he or she is to respect, despise or remain indifferent to the central characters. The author asserts more control than any other over his material, and yet admits readily to the role of contingency in his work. Styles shift constantly, but there is no obvious hierarchy among them, so that the solace of an authoritative literary language is lost. Joyce is credited with inventing, or at least popularising the technique of the interior monologue or stream of consciousness, and as such is celebrated for his psychological realism, but he is also hailed as the poet of mythic archetypes. Both novels conclude on a note of resounding celebration, but they could equally be said to end in bathos. Championed variously by modernist aesthetes, realists, humanists, formalists, new critics, structuralists, post-structuralists, post-modernists, post-colonialists, all reading the same books and all seeing different things in them, rejected variously by the country, church and literary tradition which his works addressed, Joyce has prompted more critical commentary than any writer in English outside Shakespeare, but is still one of those few writers (Proust is another) whom members of an educated reading public can acceptably boast about not having read.

Without recourse to the shrugs of relativism or the apotheosising of Joyce-as-enigma, how does one account for so many contradictory or irreconcilable readings? A recent editor of Joyce[1] suggests that his work is allotropic, taking her metaphor from the property of certain chemical elements to exist in more than one distinct form, as carbon exists in coal,

5

graphite and diamond. Another recent critic, resorting to a more traditional ocular metaphor, writes of 'oscillating perspectives'[2] at work in Joyce's writing. A third possibility advanced by Hugh Kenner is that of 'parallax'; a word used by Joyce's hero Leopold Bloom which refers to the possibility of the same object appearing differently according to various perspectives.[3] Any account of the history of Joyce criticism would have to amalgamate these metaphors, recognising a set of oscillating perspectives on a Protean text. So much has been published on Joyce that one must adopt ruthless, and I hope not arbitrary principles of selection in a volume such as this one. The present book is organised around the idea that the two novels are mutually interdependent, so that critical material ostensibly based on *A Portrait* will give the reader something to think about *Ulysses*, and vice-versa. In particular this guide will concentrate on the matter of Joyce's stylistic variations and how these, by throwing into question accepted relations between author, narrator and characters, determine how the novels are read and received.

It is possible to construct a rough and provisional narrative of Joyce's critical reception, and such a narrative will guide the selections and discussions of this book. The movement, broadly speaking, begins with a concentration on Joyce's formal scaffolding (Stephen's aesthetic theories, the Homeric correspondences around which *Ulysses* is constructed), and moves on to a recognition of Joyce's place in the history of the novel (reasserting questions of character, plot and narrative perspective). This in turn involves and leads on to an increasing of attention paid to the nature of Joyce's language and how it throws into question the conventions of linguistic representation. The final stage recognises how Joyce's example extends beyond the literary and informs theories of textuality and contextuality, throwing into question the very discourses, literary and non-literary, by which we address issues of politics, gender and the subject.

None of these phases can be demarcated with definite ease, and of course there will be leakages from one to another, but I hope to bring out the governing preconceptions and informing metaphors of each of the critics cited. If occasionally the reader might be driven to expostulate, as Byron did of Coleridge, 'I wish he would explain his explanations,' it might be useful to reflect that all criticism speaks of its time and of the systems of value proper to that time, and that what is obvious to one generation is puzzling to another.

This book is, then, both another introduction to Joyce and a guide to the outlines of Joyce's critical reception. As such it aims to familiarise the reader with the main developments of Joyce criticism, and in doing so wishes to make the following points. First, that the history of Joyce criticism anticipates and exemplifies the development of criticism itself in this century; second, that this pattern of development is explored and questioned in the relation of the early novel to the later one. Beginners to Joyce are most often put off by the implicit suggestion that besides reading the text in hand they should also be reading or have in mind something else as well; most famously in the case of *Ulysses*, where Homer's *Odyssey* is perceived as the necessary supplement. This Icon Guide tackles this problem head on, by making the point that the reading of *A Portrait* makes a lot more sense, and makes for a lot more fun, when complemented by a knowledge of *Ulysses*, and vice-versa. It helps, to say the least, to know that the confident surge of Stephen's ambition at the end of *A Portrait* is thrown into question by the bathos of his subsequent situation in the opening chapters of *Ulysses*. It helps even more to realise that the pattern of development from innocence to maturity, from 'Once upon a time' to 'Old Father, old artificer, stand me now and ever in good stead' exemplifies the maturing conscience of the reader who is, however, led eventually to wonder what innocence there ever was to be lost. Every reader of Joyce starts out innocent, wishing to be otherwise, aware that there is a world of words out there waiting to be mastered, and that there are meanings already somewhere presupposed. *A Portrait* begins with the frail babytalk of a character assailed by the language of others, and ends with the spectacle of his assumed mastery over language; in the interim, however, the whole idea of mastery of language has been turned inside-out by Joyce's exploitation of narrative voice and perspective and of rhetorical effects. This process is continued exponentially in *Ulysses*, by the end of which a paradigm has been created which in turn projects itself onto the history of critical response to Joyce. This also moves from an innocent biographical narrative of victimhood triumphant to a complex retrospective awareness of authorial ironies, based on the idea that language, or rather the clash of discourses, is never innocent. If the central focus of the novels moves from Stephen to Bloom to Molly, the same might be said for Joyce criticism, provided that we take these characters' names as representing a set of presumptions and narrative expectations about what is desired from the texts. There are versions of the Joyce story which are centred around the struggling artist undervalued in his country and time, others which stress the importance of the representative modern man, and then those insistent on the disruptive force of new or as yet unrecognised forms and voices. Behind them all of course is the figure of what Hugh Kenner, for all his fondness for the pun, could never quite bring himself to call 'The Lone Arranger', Joyce himself, silent, exiled and punning.

Joyce always played with the idea of the innocent, unmediated reading, not least by directing in the early stages the reading of his work; and the publishing history and initial reception of both *A Portrait* and

Ulysses are bound up with the history of Modernism as a concerted exercise in publicity by its protagonists. If there is such as thing as a Joyce industry then it was founded and fuelled by Joyce, and the status of his novels as classics, perhaps the classics of the twentieth century, has much to do with his promotion of the books as such. Some readers will approach this work through *A Portrait*, some through *Ulysses*; the latter being the most celebrated, the former being the most read. Both are enshrined in the canon, and as such demand to be read. One of the pleasures of this book will be to lead neophytes to imagine what it must have been like to read them for the first time. The history of criticism of Joyce is similarly structured; beginning with fellow writers and creators, continuing with licensed exegetes, moving on to institutional explicators and ending (continuing) with readers. All of this again replicates the developmental pattern of the two novels.

CHAPTER ONE

First Reactions

A Portrait was first published in serial form in *The Egoist* between February 1914 and September 1915, and after many rejections first came to light as a book in New York at the very end of 1916, eventually being published in Britain by the Egoist Press on 2nd February 1917, Joyce's 35th birthday. The dateline 'Dublin 1904 – Trieste 1914' indicates a long gestation period including the false start of *Stephen Hero*, but this volume is less concerned with the evolution of either novel than with the fact that the dateline suggests an itinerary which is completed by that of *Ulysses*; 'Trieste–Zurich–Paris, 1914–1921'. The first copies of *Ulysses* arrived in Paris, hot from the Dijon printers, on 2nd February 1922, Joyce's 40th birthday. There is more to this than superstition: Joyce seems to insist on lending to his life, or rather his life's work, the symmetries and coincidences of art. Whether the pattern of Stephen Dedalus' career matches that of Joyce's life is, like all questions of autobiography, largely indeterminate and beside the point. What matters is that this pattern, of the struggle against hostile circumstances to achieve aesthetic autonomy, is that which Joyce was very anxious to engineer for his books. The first chapters of *A Portrait* show Stephen assailed by and trying to come to terms with the uncomprehending voices and voiced misrecognitions of his family, teachers and fellows:

■ – Tell us Dedalus, do you kiss your mother before you go to bed?
Stephen answered:
– I do.
Wells turned to the other fellows and said:
– O, I say, here's a fellow says he kisses his mother every night before he goes to bed.
The other fellows stopped their game and turned round, laughing. Stephen blushed under their eyes and said:
– I do not.
Wells said:
– O I say, here's a fellow says he doesn't kiss his mother before he goes to bed. (pp. 10–11) □

Not knowing at this stage what is the right answer, Stephen is primed to resolve to take control of his self-definition. If one turns to the reception of *A Portrait*, one sees a similar dynamic at work. Modernist art's perverse

9

dependence on a climate of neglect and victimhood in order to confirm its claims to originality was well served by the initial reactions to *A Portrait*, most notably by Edward Garnett's report which prompted Duckworth's rejection. In complaining about the novel's *'longueurs'*, Garnett claimed to be speaking not so much for himself but for 'the ordinary man' among the reading public. That public will call the book, as it stands at present, realistic, unprepossessing, unattractive. We call it ably written. The picture is 'curious', it arouses interest and attention. But the author must revise it and let us see it again. It is too discursive, formless, unrestrained, and ugly things, ugly words are too prominent; indeed at times they seem to be shoved in one's face, on purpose, unnecessarily. The point of view will be voted 'a little sordid' ... it is too 'unconventional'. ... Unless the author uses restraint and proportion he will not gain readers. His pen and his thoughts seem to have run away with him sometimes. ... The author shows us that he has art, strength and originality, but this MS. wants time and trouble spent on it, to make it a more finished piece of work, to shape it more carefully as the product of the craftsmanship, mind and imagination of the artist.'[1]

It is easy to mock Garnett's cagey presumptuousness from the vantage point of the present day, but his report set the tone for public debate about Joyce's work along the two lines of obscenity and form-lessness. For the Moderns, Ezra Pound leapt to the defence, gleefully heaping 'ugly words' on the hapless Garnett as he asserted the novel's formal perfections in the face of mass-market philistinism.

■ Hark to his puling squeak. Too 'unconventional'. What in hell do we want but some change from the unbearable monotony of the weekly six shilling pears soap annual novel. ... 'Carelessly written', this of the sole, or almost sole piece of contemporary prose that one can enjoy sentence by sentence and re-read with pleasure ... if this louse will specify exactly what verbal changes he wants made I will approach Joyce in the matter. But I most emphatically will not forward the insults of an imbecile to one of the very few men for whom I have the faintest respect. ... God! 'A more finished piece of work'. ... as for altering Joyce to suit Duckworth's readers – I would like trying to fit the Venus de Milo into a piss-pot. – a few changes required.[2] □

Pound elsewhere hailed the work as 'the nearest thing to Flaubertian prose that we have now in English... It will remain a permanent part of English literature written by an Irishman in Trieste and first published in New York City.'[3] Joyce is hailed as the inheritor of Flaubertian realism in terms of pure, spare style, and, without the word Modernism being used, is welcomed into the vanguard of anglophone modernism, comprising

10

Wyndham Lewis, T.S. Eliot, and Pound himself. All of these writers would have further things to say about *Ulysses*.

As for *A Portrait*, much of the critical reception was respectful, if occasionally impercipient, and fellow writers especially warmed to some if not all of Joyce's qualities. An exception to this was the unsigned review in *Everyman* of 21st Feb, 1917, entitled 'A Study in Garbage', which complained that 'Mr Joyce's new book … is an astonishingly powerful and extraordinarily dirty study of the upbringing of a young man by Jesuits, which ends so far as we have been at all able to unravel the meaning of the impressionist ending – with his insanity … Mr Joyce is a clever novelist, but we feel he would really be at his best in a treaty on drains.'[4] All this of course would help Joyce and Joyceans in setting up the master as the enemy of prudery and philistinism, as would the reactions of the *Manchester Guardian*'s essayist who complained of Stephen's 'passion for foul-smelling things'[5] or *The Freeman's Journal*'s insistence that 'Mr. Joyce plunges and drags his readers after him into the slime of foul sewers', such criticisms, it seems, prompted by the (for today's reader innocuous) mention of bedwetting on the first page. H.G. Wells, in an otherwise enthusiastic review,[6] had cause to mention Joyce's 'cloacal obsession'. Thus was born Joyce's reputation as a writer of 'dirty books', employing a conflation of the scatological and the sexual not altogether unencouraged by the texts themselves. Pound took up Wells' criticism in his 1918 review of Joyce's early works, pointing out that 'there is nothing in life so beautiful that Joyce cannot touch it with profanation – without, above all, the profanations of sentiment and sentimentality – and there is nothing so sordid that he cannot treat it with his metallic exactitude.'[7] And yet Wells also noted formal properties in *A Portrait* which were skirted by Pound: the aurality of Joyce's writing, how he was moved by sounds as much as by smell. H.G. Wells recognises bold experiments with paragraph and punctuation and sees in them a link with the new technology of representation: 'most of the talk flickers blindingly with these dashes, one has the same wincing feeling of being flicked at that one used to have in the early cinema shows'. (Joyce, let it be remembered, opened the first cinema in Dublin.) Another common thread in negative reactions to Joyce, that of distrust of the alien Irish, emerges in Wells' criticism. 'One believes in Stephen Dedalus as one believes in few characters in fiction. And the peculiar lie of the interest for the intelligent reader is the convincing revelation it makes of the limitations of a great mass of Irishmen.'

From the beginning acknowledgement of Joyce's realism is torn between definitions of realism itself, either as a form of anthropological slumming or as a concern with representation *per se*. Certainly the novel's treatment of the body, of poverty, of Catholicism and nationalism was presumed to alienate various readerships. Seen as belonging to the tradition of Flaubert and/or Zola, this French novel about the Irish, first published in New York, disturbed presumptions of cultural allegiance and managed to exile itself both from the English tradition and from Irish nationalism.

Critical reception of *A Portrait* gradually became subsumed into that of *Ulysses*, which began appearing in the *Little Review* in March 1918. In a now-famous essay entitled 'Modern Novels' that appeared in 1919, Virginia Woolf hails Joyce as an example of a revolutionary sort of fiction that does away with outmoded conventions. 'Let us record the atoms as they fall upon the mind in the order in which they fall, let us trace the pattern, however disconnected and incoherent in appearance, which each sight or incident scores upon the consciousness,' she urges. In doing this – in shifting the focus inward, toward momentary perceptions and a 'spiritual' dimension of consciousness – Woolf feels the artist will produce something closer to 'life itself'.[8] Ford Madox Ford pays tribute to the earlier novel in 1922, calling it 'a book of such beauty of writing, such clarity of perception, such a serene love of and interest in life, and such charity that, … one was inclined to say: "This surely must be a peak! It is unlikely that this man will climb higher!"' Yet Ford goes on to even more resonant anticipation of *Ulysses*, a 'new continent' which contains 'the undiscovered mind of man'.[9] As we shall see, the novel *Ulysses*, written and received within the death throes of colonisation, is itself a work which sets out to colonise the realm of literature. Writing of and in the midst of the closing stages of the novel, Joyce wrote to Harriet Shaw Weaver on 20th June 1919 that 'each specific episode, dealing with some province of artistic culture, leaves behind it a burnt-up field.'[10] The violence of this metaphor turns 1922 into Year Zero, and makes of *A Portrait* so much scorched earth. The glamour of *Ulysses* is such as to eclipse any previous novel, including Joyce's own.

In a letter to Carlos Linati of September 1920 Joyce wrote:

■ ' It is an epic of two races (Israelite = Irish) and at the same time the cycle of the human body as well as a little story of a day (life). The character of Ulysses always fascinated me – even when a boy. Imagine, fifteen years ago I started writing it as a short story for *Dubliners*! For seven years I have been working at this book – blast it! It is also a sort of encyclopaedia. My intention is to transpose the myth *sub specie temporis nostri*. Each adventure (that is, every hour, every organ, every art being interrelated in the structural scheme of the whole) should not only condition but even create its own technique. Each adventure is so to say one person although it is composed of persons – as Aquinas relates of the angelic hosts. No English printer wanted to print a word of it. In America the review was suppressed four times. Now, as I hear, a great movement is being prepared against the publication, initiated by Puritans, English, Imperialists, Irish Republicans, Catholics – what an alliance! Gosh, I ought to be awarded the Nobel prize for peace!'[11] □

Enclosed with this letter was Joyce's schema for the novel. Prejudices against the novel were real, as will be seen, but Joyce's ironic celebration of the unholy alliance he had created didn't deter him from another tactic later to be adopted by Nobel peace laureates, that of the pre-emptive strike. Letters show Joyce bombarding his friends with explanatory and exegetical material, and the first major piece of criticism on *Ulysses*, Valéry Larbaud's long article in the *Nouvelle Revue Française*, owed much to Joyce's own input. Discussion of *Ulysses* is prefaced by a presentation of *A Portrait* which rejects definitions of the novel as either naturalism or 'pure' autobiography and stresses the symbolism of Joyce's work, and the substitution of dialogue and interior monologue for narration. 'We are more frequently carried to the essence of the thought of the characters: we see the thoughts forming, we follow them, we assist at their arrival at the level of conscience and it is through what the character thinks that we learn who he is, what he does, or where he is and what happens around him. The number of images, of analogies and of symbols increases ... all the symbolism of the church, the different meanings of each object used in the cult, of each gesture made by the priest, without speaking of prefigurations, of prophesies and of concordances. ... All that, furthermore, applies even better to *Ulysses* than to *Portrait of the Artist*.' Besides insisting on the need to understand the achievement of *A Portrait*, and in particular its relinquishment of conventional narrative, before *Ulysses* can be approached, Larbaud stresses the importance of the cultivated reader; since those uncultivated or only half cultivated will not be able to make any sense either of the mythic framework or pattern of allusion which informs the novel, or of the way in which both form and story are a continuation of that achieved in *A Portrait*. The key to the novel is seen to be in the title, in the Homeric correspondences, and in the recreation of Ulysses and all the attendant characters in Homer's epic in our time, amidst the complexities of modern life. The question of Bloom's Jewishness is skirted, and the novel's supposed obscenity excused in similar terms to those used by Pound.[12]

■ ... In this book, which has the form of a novel, Joyce proposed to reconstruct the infancy and adolescence of an artist ... At the same time, the title tells us that this is also, in a certain sense, the story of the youth of the artist, that is of all men gifted with the artistic temperament.

The hero – the artist – is called Stephen Dedalus. And here we approach one of the difficulties of Joyce's work: his symbolism, which we will encounter again in *Ulysses* and which will actually be the plot of that extraordinary book.

First of all, the name of Stephen Dedalus is symbolic: his patron saint is St. Stephen, the proto-martyr, and his family name is Dedalus, the name of the architect of the Labyrinth and of the father of Icarus. But, according to the author, he also has two other names; he is the symbol of two other persons. One of these is James Joyce ... But he is also – we shall see it again in *Ulysses* – Telemachus, the man whose Greek name means Far from the War, the artist who remains apart from the mêlée of interests and desires which motivate men of action; he is the man of science and the man of dreams who remains on the defensive, all his forces absorbed by the task of knowing, of understanding and of expressing. Thus the hero of the novel is both a symbolic character and a real one, as will be all the characters of *Ulysses*.

... The English critics who are concerned with the *Portrait of the Artist* have, again, spoken of the naturalism, in a realisation that is almost as if it were a question of such and such novel by Mirabeau. It was not that writer. They could equally well have spoken of Samuel Butler. In fact, I spoke of this resemblance the other day with a friend who had arrived at the same conclusion: there are certain fortuitous resemblances, commanded by the situation and by the genius of the two writers, between the religious crisis of Ernest Pontifex [in Butler's *The Way of All Flesh*] and that of Stephen Dedalus, and also between the long monologues of Christina and the interior monologue which takes place in Joyce. But it is too much to consider Butler as the precursor of Joyce on only these particular points.

No, the critics are misled. From the *Portrait of the Artist* forward, Joyce is himself and nothing but himself.

They are also deceived who only wanted to see in this book an autobiography ... It is not that, for Joyce has drawn Stephen Dedalus from himself but at the same time he has created him...

The success of this book has been great, and since its publication Joyce has become known to the lettered public. It has been '*un succès de scandale*'. The critics, for the most part English and Protestant, were shocked by its frankness, and the absence of human decency which these 'confessions' bear witness to ... It is certain that in a Catholic country the tone of the press would have been very different ... In fact, the best article dedicated to the *Portrait* was that in the Dublin Review, one of the great reviews of the Catholic world, directed or at least inspired by some priests.

The style of the *Portrait* is a great advance over that of *Dubliners*; the interior monologue and dialogue are substituted more and more for narration. We are more frequently carried to the essence of the thought of the characters: we see these thoughts forming, we follow them, we assist at their arrival at the level of conscience and it is through what the character thinks that we learn who he is, what he does, or where he is and what happens around him. The number of images, of analogies, and of symbols increases ... all the symbolism of the Church, the different meanings of each object used in the cult, of each gesture made by the priest, without speaking of prefigurations, of prophecies and of concordances ... All that, furthermore, applies even better to *Ulysses* than to the *Portrait of the Artist*.

I must, to my great regret, leave out ... the beautiful drama published in 1918, entitled *Exiles*, and I now proceed to *Ulysses*.

The reader who approaches this book without the *Odyssey* clearly in mind will be thrown into dismay. I refer, of course, to the cultivated reader who can fully appreciate such authors as Rabelais, Montaigne, and Descartes; for the uncultivated or half-cultivated reader will throw *Ulysses* aside after the first three pages. I say that the reader is at first dismayed: for he is plunged into the middle of a conversation which will seem to him incoherent, between people whom he cannot distinguish, in a place which is neither named nor described; and from this conversation he is to learn little by little where he is and who the interlocuters are. Furthermore, here is a book which is entitled *Ulysses*, and no character in it bears this name; the name of Ulysses only appears four times. But gradually the reader begins to see his way. Incidentally, he learns that he is in Dublin. He identifies the hero of the *Portrait of the Artist*, Stephen Dedalus, returned from Paris and living among the intellectuals of the Irish capital ... Accordingly this huge book chronicles a single day; or, to be exact, begins at eight o'clock in the morning and ends towards three in the next morning.

As we have indicated, the reader follows the course of Bloom through his long day; for even if much eludes him at the first reading he will perceive enough to keep his curiosity and interest constantly awake. He remarks that, with the appearance of Bloom, the action begins again at eight o'clock, and that the three first chapters of Bloom's progress through his day are synchronous with the three first chapters of the book in which he has followed Stephen Dedalus ... None of this, as I have already said, is told us in narrative form, and the book is a great deal more than the detailed history of Stephen's and Bloom's day in Dublin. It contains a vast number of other things, characters, incidents, descriptions, conversations, visions. But for us the readers, Bloom and Stephen are, so to speak, the vehicles in which we pass across the book. Stationed in the intimacy of their minds, and sometimes in the minds of the other characters, we see through their eyes and hear through their ears what happens and what is said around them. In this way, in this book, all the elements are constantly melting into each other, and the illusion of life, of the thing in the act, is complete: the whole is movement.

But the cultivated reader whom I have postulated will not let himself be wholly carried along by this movement. With the habit of reading and a long experience of books, he looks for the method and the material of what he reads. He will analyse *Ulysses* as he reads. And this is what will certainly be the result of his analysis after a first reading. He will say: This is still the society of *Dubliners*, and the eighteen parts of *Ulysses* can provisionally be considered as eighteen tales with different aspects of the life of the Irish capital as their subjects. Nevertheless, each of these eighteen parts from any of the fifteen tales of *Dubliners* on many points, and particularly by its scope, by its form, and by the distinction of the characters. Thus, the characters who take the principal rôles in the tales of *Dubliners* would be in *Ulysses* only supers, minor characters, or – it comes to the same thing – people seen by the author from the outside. In *Ulysses* the protagonists are all (in a literary sense) princes, characters who emerge from the depths of the author's inner life, constructed with his experience and his sensibility, and endowed by him with his own emotion, his own intelligence, and his own lyricism. Here, the conversations are something more than typical of individuals of such and such social classes; some of them are genuine essays in philosophy, theology, literary criticism, political satire, history. Scientific theories are expounded or debated. These pieces, which we might treat as digressions, or rather as appendices, essays composed outside of the book and artificially interpolated into all of the 'tales', are so exquisitely adapted to the plot, the movement, and the atmosphere of the different parts in which they appear that we are obliged to admit that they belong to the book, by the same rights as the characters in whose mouths or whose minds they are put. But already we can no longer consider these eighteen parts as detached tales: Bloom, Stephen, and a few other characters remain, sometimes together and sometimes apart, the principal figures; and the story, the drama, and the comedy of their day are enacted through them. It must be acknowledged that, although each of these eighteen parts differs from all of the others in form and language, the whole forms none the less an organism, a book.

As we arrive at this conclusion, all sorts of coincidences, analogies, and correspondences between these parts come to light; just as, in looking fixedly at the sky at night, we find that the number of stars appears to increase. We begin to discover and to anticipate symbols, a design, a plan, in what appeared to us at first a brilliant but confused mass of notations, phrases, data, profound thoughts, fantasticalities, splendid images, absurdities, comic or dramatic situations; and we realise that we are before a much more complicated book than we had supposed, that everything which appeared arbitrary and sometimes extravagant is really deliberate and premeditated; in short, that we are before a book which has a key.

Where then is the key? It is, I venture to say, in the door, or rather on the cover. It is the title: *Ulysses*.

Is it possible that this Leopold Bloom, this personage whom the author handles with so little consideration, whom he exhibits in all sorts of ridiculous or humiliating postures, is the son of Laertes, the subtle Ulysses?

We shall see. Meantime, I return to the *un*cultivated reader who was put off by the first pages of the book, too difficult for him; and I imagine that after reading him several passages taken from different episodes, we tell him: 'You understand that Stephen Dedalus is Telemachus, and Bloom is *Ulysses*.' He will now think that he understands; the work of Joyce will no longer seem to him disconcerting or shocking. He will say: 'I see! it's a parody of the *Odyssey*!' For indeed, to such a reader the *Odyssey* is a great awe-inspiring machine, and *Ulysses* and Telemachus are *heroes*, men of marble invented by the chilly ancient world to serve as moral examples and subjects for scholastic theses ... The only distinction between him and the uncultivated reader is that for him the *Odyssey* is not majestic and pompous, but simply uninteresting; and consequently he will not be so ingenuous as to laugh when he sees it burlesqued. The parody will bore him as much as the work itself.

... Joyce extricated Ulysses from the text, and still more from the mighty fortifications which criticism and learning have erected about the text; and instead of trying to return to Ulysses in time, to reascend the stream of history, he made Ulysses his own contemporary, his ideal companion, his spiritual father.

What, then, in the *Odyssey*, is the moral figure of Ulysses? ... He is a man, and the most completely human of all the heroes of the epic cycle: it is this characteristic which first endeared him to the schoolboy. Then, little by little, always bringing Ulysses nearer to himself, the young poet recreated this humanity, this human, comic, and pathetic character of his hero. And recreating him, he has set him among the circumstances of life which the author had before his own eyes – in Dublin, in our time, in the complexity of modern life, and amidst the beliefs, the sciences, and problems of our time.

From the moment that he recreates Ulysses he must logically recreate all the characters who have, in the *Odyssey*, more or less to do with Ulysses. From this point, to recreate an Odyssey on the same plane, a modern Odyssey, was only a step to take ... Accordingly, in

Ulysses, the three first episodes correspond to the Telemachy; Stephen Dedalus, the spiritual son and heir of Ulysses, is constantly on the scene.

From Book V to Book XIII are unfolded the adventures of Ulysses. Joyce distinguishes twelve chief adventures, to which correspond the twelve central chapters or episodes of his book...

Naturally, Joyce has traced for himself, and not for the reader, this minutely detailed scheme, these eighteen sub-divided panels, this close web. There is no explanatory heading or sub-heading. It is for us to decipher, if we care to take the trouble. On this web, or rather in the compartments thus prepared, Joyce has arranged his text. It is a genuine example of the art of mosaic ... This plan, which cannot be detached from the book, because it is the very web of it, constitutes one of its most curious and fascinating features. If one reads *Ulysses* with attention, one cannot fail to discover this plan in time. But when one considers its rigidity, and the discipline which the author imposed upon himself, one asks how it can be that out of such a formidable labour of manipulation so living and moving a work could issue.

The manifest reason is that the author has never lost sight of the humanity of his characters, of their whole composition of virtues and faults, turpitude, and greatness; man, the creature of flesh, living out his day. And this is what one finds in reading *Ulysses*.

Among all the points which I ought to deal with, and have not space to deal with here, there are two on which it is indispensable to say a few words. One is the supposedly licentious character of certain passages – passages which in America provoked the intervention of the Society for the Suppression of Vice. The word 'licentious' is inappropriate; it is both vague and weak: it should be *obscene*. In *Ulysses* Joyce wished to display moral, intellectual, and physical man entire, and in order to do so he was forced to find a place, in the moral sphere, for the sexual instinct and its various manifestations and perversions; and, in the physiological sphere, for the reproductive organs and their functions. He does not hesitate to handle this subject any more than the great casuists do, and he handles it in English in the same way that they handled it in Latin, without respect for the conventions and scruples of the laity. His intention is neither salacious nor lewd; he simply describes and represents; and in his book the manifestations of sexual instinct do not occupy more or less place, and have neither more nor less importance, than such emotions as pity or scientific curiosity. It is of course especially in the interior monologues, the trains of thought, of the characters, and not in their conversations, that sexual instinct and erotic reverie emerge; for example, in the long interior monologue of Penelope – that is to say, Bloom's wife, who is also the symbol of Gæa, the Earth. The English language has a very great store of obscene words and expressions, and the author of *Ulysses* has enriched his book generously and boldly from this vocabulary.

The other point is this: why is Bloom a Jew? There are symbolical, mystical, and ethnological reasons which limitations of space prevent me from examining here – but which should be quite clear to readers of the book. All that I can say is that if Joyce has made his chosen hero, the spiritual father of this Stephen Dedalus who is his second self, a Jew – it is not because of anti-Semitism. □

It is ironic that Larbaud should insist that Joyce extricated Ulysses (the character) from Homer's text, and from the mighty fortifications which criticism and learning have erected about the text, because his stressing of the Homeric plan laid the ground for a whole school of Joyce criticism which insisted on tracing every possible correspondence or allusion, often in a way which treated the rest of the text and all its other aspects as being incidental to the task of source-hunting. What begins as ladder or scaffolding then ends as an impenetrable bristle of fortification. A similar phenomenon is at work in those readings of *A Portrait* which treat the novel exclusively as a source for reconstructing the aesthetic doctrine advocated by Stephen Dedalus, or the reading of *Dubliners* exhaustively in terms of paralysis. All of this, of course, derived eventually from Joyce's habit of leaving clues and providing keys, but as Italo Calvino remarked about his own works, no one key will open all the locks. The danger of such an approach is that it is based on an aesthetic of reconstitution, whereby the true text is elsewhere, in the well-stocked mind and library of the ideal reader or in the schematic paradise of the author's intentions. No one would deny the usefulness of knowing about the original Homeric story, and the complexity of its translation onto the Dublin streets of June 1904, but when critical attention is deflected from Joyce's actual writing and its many innovations the result can be to deny Joyce's revolutionary place in literature. This becomes clear if we look at T. S. Eliot's defence of Joyce in 'Ulysses, Order and Myth', published in *The Dial* in 1923.[13]

■ Mr Joyce's book has been out long enough for no more general expression of praise, or expostulation with its detractors, to be necessary; and it has not been out long enough for any attempt at a complete measurement of its place and significance to be possible. All that one can usefully do at this time, and it is a great deal to do, for such a book, is to elucidate any aspect of the book – and the number of aspects is indefinite – which has not yet been fixed. I hold this book to be the most important expression which the present age has found; it is a book to which we are all indebted, and from which none of us can escape. These are postulates for anything that I have to say about it, and I have no wish to waste the reader's time by elaborating my eulogies; it has given me all the surprise, delight, and terror that I can require, and I will leave it at that.

Amongst all the criticism I have seen of the book, I have nothing – unless we except, in its way, M. Valéry Larbaud's valuable paper which is rather an Introduction than a criticism – which seemed to me to appreciate the significance of the method employed – the parallel to the *Odyssey*, and the use of appropriate styles and symbols to each division. Yet one might expect this to be the first peculiarity to attract attention; but it has been treated as an amusing dodge, or scaffolding erected by the author for the purpose of disposing his realistic tale, of no interest in the completed structure. The criticism which Mr Aldington directed upon *Ulysses* several years ago seems to me to fail by this oversight – but, as Mr Aldington wrote before the complete work had appeared, fails more honourably than the attempts of those who had the whole book before them. Mr Aldington treated Mr Joyce as a prophet of chaos; and wailed at the flood of Dadaism which his prescient eye saw bursting forth at the tap of the magician's rod. Of course, the influence which Mr Joyce's book may have is from my point of view an irrelevance. A very great book may have a very bad influence indeed; and a mediocre book may be in the event most salutary. The next generation is responsible for its own soul; a man of genius is responsible to his peers, not to a studio full of uneducated and undisciplined coxcombs. Still, Mr Aldington's pathetic solicitude for the half-witted seems to me to carry certain implications about the nature of the book itself to which I cannot assent; and this is the important issue. He finds the book, if I understand him, to be an invitation to chaos, and an expression of feelings which are perverse, partial, and a distortion of reality.

> *Ulysses* is more bitter, more sordid, more ferociously satirical than anything Mr Joyce has yet written. It is a tremendous libel on humanity which I at least am not clever enough to refute, but which I am convinced is a libel. There is laughter in *Ulysses*, but it is a harsh, sneering kind, very different from the *gros rire* of Rabelais.

... Whether it is possible to libel humanity (in distinction to libel in the usual sense, which is libelling an individual or a group in contrast with the rest of humanity) is a question for philosophical societies to discuss; but of course if *Ulysses* were a 'libel' it would simply be a forged document, a powerless fraud, which would never have extracted from Mr Aldington a moment's attention. I do not wish to linger over this point: the interesting question is that begged by Mr Aldington when he refers to Mr Joyce's 'great *undisciplined* talent'.

I think that Mr Aldington and I are more or less agreed as to what we want in principle, and agreed to call it classicism. It is because of this agreement that I have chosen Mr Aldington to attack on the present issue. We are agreed as to what we want, but not as to how to get it, or as to what contemporary writing exhibits a tendency in that direction. We agree, I hope, that 'classicism' is not an alternative to 'romanticism', as of political parties, Conservative and Liberal, Republican and Democrat, on a 'turn-the-rascals-out' platform. It is a goal toward which all good literature strives, so far as it is good, according to the possibilities of its place and time. One can be 'classical', in a sense, by turning away from nine-tenths of the material which lies at hand, and selecting only mummified stuff from a museum – like some contemporary writers, about whom one could say some nasty things in this connection, if it were worthwhile (Mr Aldington is not one of them). Or one can be classical in tendency by doing the best one can with the material at hand. The confusion springs from the fact that the term is applied to literature and to the whole complex of interests and modes of behaviour and society of which literature is a part; and it has not the same bearing in both applications. It is much easier to be a classicist in literary criticism than in creative art – because in criticism you are responsible only for what you want, and in creation you are responsible for what you can do with the material which you must simply accept. And in this material I include the motions and feelings of the writer himself, which, for that writer, are simply material which he must accept – not virtues to be enlarged or vices to be diminished. The question, then, about Mr Joyce, is: how much living material does he deal with, and how does he deal with it: deal with, not as a legislator or exhorter, but as an artist?

It is here that Mr Joyce's parallel use of the *Odyssey* has a great importance. It has the importance of a scientific discovery. No one else has built a novel upon such a foundation before: it has never before been necessary. I am not begging the question in calling *Ulysses* a 'novel'; and if you call it an epic it will not matter. If it is not a novel, that is simply because the novel is a form which will no longer serve; it is because the novel, instead of being a form, was simply the expression of an age which had not sufficiently lost all form to feel the need of something stricter. Mr Joyce has written one novel – the *Portrait*; Mr Wyndham Lewis has written one novel – *Tarr*. I do not suppose that either of them will ever write another 'novel'. The novel ended with Flaubert and with James. It is, I think, because Mr Joyce and Mr Lewis, being 'in advance' of their time, felt a conscious or probably unconscious dissatisfaction with the form, that their novels are more formless than those of a dozen clever writers who are unaware of its obsolescence.

In using the myth, in manipulating a continuous parallel between contemporaneity and antiquity, Mr Joyce is pursuing a method which others must pursue after him. They will not be imitators, any more than the scientist who uses the discoveries of Einstein in pursuing his own, independent, further investigations. It is simply a way of controlling, of ordering, of giving a shape and a significance to the immense panorama of futility and anarchy which is contemporary history. It is a method already adumbrated by Mr Yeats, and of the need for which I believe Mr Yeats to have been the first contemporary to be conscious. It is a method for which the horoscope is auspicious. Psychology (such as it is, and whether our reaction to it be comic or serious), ethnology, and *The Golden Bough* have concurred to make possible what was impossible even a few years ago. Instead of narrative method, we may now use the mythical method. It is, I seriously believe, a step toward making the modern world possible for art, toward that order and form which Mr Aldington so earnestly desires. And only those who have won their own discipline in secret and without aid, in a world which offers very little assistance to that end, can be of any use in furthering this advance. □

Leaving aside the astounding claim that *Ulysses* makes the modern world possible for art (it's surely not philistine to suggest that it should be the other way round). Eliot's defence of Joyce is stout enough but conducted largely on Eliot's own terms, even to the extent that it serves better as a description of 'The Waste Land' than of *Ulysses*. The mentions of anthropology, psychology, horoscopes, and most notably the nostalgia for past order are all elements of the other great monument of anglophone modernism. This alerts us at once to the similarities and the differences between the two works. Both are highly allusive, urban, employing mythic parallels to link past and present, but as regards the most salient apparent similarity there is in fact a difference. While both might appear to be polyphonic texts, never settling on one governing voice or register, Eliot's work privileges the language of the past, whereas with Joyce it is much more a matter of two-way traffic, with the polyphony of *Ulysses* denying the existence of any one privileged, authoritative or unifying discourse.

Pound's defence of *Ulysses* in 'James Joyce and Pécuchet' is conditioned by a similarly interventionist agenda; although it makes less of the Homeric parallels it still reads the novel as a reaction against the perceived idiocies of contemporary life. *Ulysses* is taken to be in the satiric tradition of Flaubert's *Bouvard and Pécuchet*, where the illstocked and pretentious 'bourgeois' mind is set up for ridicule in a fastidiously irritated 'Dictionary of Received Ideas'.

■ There are some pages of Flaubert which reveal their matter as rapidly as pages of Joyce, but Joyce has perfected the great collection of objects for ridicule. In a single chapter he discharges all the clichés of the English language like an uninterrupted river...

Bloom's advertising agent, the *Ulysses* of the novel, the sensual average man, the basis – like Bouvard and Pécuchet – of democracy, the man who believes what he reads in the papers, suffers *after his soul's desire*. He is interested in everything, wants to explain everything, to impress everybody. Not only does his celerity and aptness for picking up what is said and thought everywhere, chewed over by everyone a hundred times a week, serve Joyce as a literary device, but the other characters are chosen to support him, in order to pick up the vanities of circles other than his.[14] □

As Eliot's characterising of *Ulysses* was reminiscent of 'The Waste Land', so is Pound's of 'Hugh Selwyn Mauberley', where the proud but defeated artist, whose 'true Penelope was Flaubert', looks with impotent disdain on the money-driven mediocrity of contemporary society. Pound notes, as does Eliot, the variation of styles and voices, but projects his own lordly bitterness onto Joyce, suggesting that Joyce's achievement is to show 'universal imbecility'.

Among reviews by Joyce's contemporaries two others stand out, not least because rather than carry on their own business by means of skewed espousal they acknowledge difficulties with both novels and thus open up critical debate. One of them, Wyndham Lewis, was very much of the Modernist camp, the other, Arnold Bennett, continues to be viewed as the apostle of the middlebrow rearguard which held up the understanding and acceptance of Joyce and his fellow innovators (the word 'middlebrow' is used by the editors of the *Critical Heritage* volume, who offer him a condescending pat on the head by pointing out that he had 'even' (sic.) read *Ulysses*). Bennett, who as 'Mr Nixon' bears the brunt of Pound's satire in 'Mauberley' and who was the whipping boy for Virginia Woolf's modernist manifesto in 'Mr Bennett and Mrs Brown', tells how he had read *A Portrait* [15]

■ under the hypnotic influence of H. G. Wells. Indeed he commanded me to read it and to admire it extremely. I did both. I said 'Yes, it is great stuff.' But in the horrid inaccessible thickets of my mind I heard a voice saying: 'On the whole the book has bored you.' And on the whole it had; and with the efflux of time I began to announce this truth. There are scenes of genius in this novel; from end to end it

23

shows a sense of style, but large portions of it are dull, pompous, absurd, confused and undirected. □

How Bennett reconciles a ubiquitous sense of style with the faults enumerated is not clear: but perhaps this in itself is indicative of what I take to be the central critical problem with Joyce: the relation between author and character, voice and perspective. As we have seen, it was noticed from the beginning that Joyce allotted different styles to different characters, but readers found it difficult to determine whether the styles or the characters were to be approved of or condemned. This is the question raised in different ways by both Pound and Bennett. Was Joyce writing mimetically about Stephen's pomposity and Bloom's vulgarity, or was he himself indulging in pompous and boring language? Decades of critical formulation was still required before even a provisional answer could be offered to this question, and in the interim much time was wasted trying to shoehorn his texts into categories which his example had in fact exploded. In this as in other matters Bennett looked in vain for guidance, damning Joyce for his wilfulness and lack of manners in offering no help to the reader. 'After all, to comprehend *Ulysses* is not one of the learned professions, and nobody should give his entire existence to the job.' The object of the first generation of Joyce critics, abetted by the author, was to demonstrate exactly the converse to be the case. *Ulysses*, like *A Portrait*, had to be learned to be read, and all contemporary readings could be found wanting. Although Bennett praised the Circe and Penelope sections, for their Rabelaisian virtuosity and utterly convincing psychological realism respectively, he could still find in the pages of *Ulysses* 'no geographical sense, little sense of environment, no sense of the general purpose of human nature, and not much poetical sense. Worse than this, he has no sense of perspective.' What is remarkable about Bennett's criticism is not so much its acuity but the fact that the first major works of Joyce scholarship sought to confute his objections one by one. Similarly, Wyndham Lewis's much more sophisticated attack in *Time and Western Man*[16] raised by its adversarial intelligence two crucial objections about Joyce's work which were ironically to prove in the long term the most interesting questions: namely why is Stephen Dedalus so unpleasant, and what motivates Joyce's changes of style? More immediately, it prompted Joyce's collaboration with Stuart Gilbert, to be discussed in the next chapter.

■ I cannot see that any work of Joyce – except *Ulysses* – is very significant. It was about six or seven years ago that I first became acquainted with his writing. The *Portrait of the Artist* seemed to me a rather cold and priggish book. It was well done, like the *Dubliners*, which I have just read; and that was all that I could discover. *Chamber*

24

Music would certainly not have secured its author a place 'among English poets' – it would hardly even have set the Liffey on fire for five minutes. No writing of his before *Ulysses* would have given him anything but an honourable position as the inevitable naturalist-French-influenced member of the romantic Irish Revival – a Maupassant of Dublin, but without the sinister force of Flaubert's disciple.

Ulysses was in a sense a different thing altogether. How far that is an effect of a merely technical order, resulting from stylistic complications and intensified display, with a *Dubliners* base unchanged, or, further, a question of scale, and mechanical heaping up of detail, I should have only partly to decide here. But it places him – on that point every one is in agreement – very high in contemporary letters.

Its evident importance, its success, induced people to go outside the contemporary field for their analogies; and, to start with, it may be as well to remove from our path a few of the unnecessary names at that time, in the first generous flush of praise, injudiciously imported. Ireland, of course, furnished the most obvious comparisons.

So, to start with, Joyce is not a homologue of Swift. That is a strange mistake. There is very little of the specific power of that terrible personage, that *terribilitá*, in the amiable author of *Ulysses*. Another writer with whom he has been compared, and whom he is peculiarly unlike, is Flaubert. But to mention all the authors with whom Joyce has been matched would take an appreciable time. So I will rather attempt to find his true affinities. The choice would lie, to my mind, somewhere between Robert Louis Stevenson and Laurence Sterne, if you imagine those writers transplanted into a heavily-freudianised milieu, and subjected to all the influences resulting in the rich, confused ferment of *Ulysses*.

Contact with any of his writing must, to begin with, show that we are not in the presence of a tragic writer, of the description of Dostoievsky or of Flaubert. He is genial and comic; a humorous writer of the traditional English School – a temper, at his best, very like Sterne. But he has the technical itch of the 'sedulous ape' – the figure under which Stevenson (with peculiar modesty, it is true) revealed himself to his readers. The impression produced by his earlier books, merely as writing, is very like that of a page of Stevenson – not of Stevenson's 'aping', but of the finished, a little too finished, article.

Ulysses, on the technical side, is an immense exercise in style, an orgy of 'apeishness', decidedly 'sedulous'. It is an encyclopaedia of English literary technique, as well as a general-knowledge paper. The schoolmaster in Joyce is in great evidence throughout its pages.

Next, as to his position among the celebrated group of Irishmen contemporary with himself, or his immediate predecessors, that is now fairly well defined. What has distinguished all the famous Irish literary figures of recent years, whether Wilde, Shaw or Yeats, has been the possession of what we call 'personality'. This really amounts to a vein of picturesqueness, an instinct for the value of the person in the picture, which dominates them, externally at all events. And they have probably always been led into making a freer use of this than would a Frenchman, for instance, of the same calibre, owing to the self-effacing, unassuming, over-plain habits of the English background, against which they have had to perform. Or it may have been that, as isolated adventurers – when they had passed from Ireland and descended into Piccadilly Circus, thenceforth watched by an Empire on which the sun never sets – they were as a matter of course mere *persons*, as contrasted with the new alien *crowds* they were amongst. This florid personal aplomb is, however, now expected of the Irishman by his English audience – although, owing to the political separation of the two countries, probably those times of genial interplay are passed.

Mr Joyce is by no means without the 'personal touch'. But in a sense he is not the 'personality' that Shaw or Yeats is, or that Wilde was. But that is in conformity with his rôle, which is a very different one from theirs. Joyce is the poet of the shabby-genteel, impoverished intellectualism of Dublin. His world is a small middle-class one, decorated with a little futile 'culture', of the supper and dance-party in *The Dead*. Wilde, more brilliantly situated, was an extremely metropolitan personage, a man of the great social world, a great lion of the London drawing-room. Joyce is steeped in the sadness and the shabbiness of the pathetic gentility of the upper shopkeeping class, slumbering at the bottom of a neglected province; never far, in its snobbishly circumscribed despair, from the pawn-shop and the 'pub'.

Shaw, again, escaped early from his provincial surroundings. Joyce resembles him in some striking particulars; but the more recent figure, this quiet, very positive, self-collected Irish schoolmaster, with that well-known air of genteel decorum and *bienséance* of the Irish middle class, with his 'if you pleases' and 'thank-yous', his ceremonious Mister-this and Mister-that, is remote from what must have been the strapping, dashing George Bernard Shaw of the shavian heyday. He is also quite unlike the romantic, aristocratic, magic-loving William Butler Yeats.

Shaw is much more a world-figure; but Joyce and Yeats are the prose and poetry respectively of the Ireland that culminated in the Rebellion. Yeats is the chivalrous embodiment of 'Celtic' romance, more of St Brandon than of Ossian, with all the grand manners of a spiritual past that cannot be obliterated, though it wears thin, and of a dispossessed and persecuted people. Joyce is the cold and stagnant reality at which people had at last arrived in its civilised Reservation, with all the snobbish pathos of such a condition, the intense desire to keep-up-appearances at all costs, to be ladylike and gentlemanly, in spite of a beggared position – above which that yeatsian emanation floats.

But on the purely personal side, Joyce possesses a good deal of the intolerant arrogance of the dominie, veiled with an elaborate decency beneath the formal calm of the Jesuit, left over as a handy property from his early years of catholic romance – of that Irish variety that is so English that it seems stranger to a continental almost than its English protestant counterpart.

The Ireland that culminated in the Rebellion reached that event, however, in a very divided state. There was an artificial, pseudo-historical air about the Rebellion, as there was inevitably about the movement of 'Celtic' revival; it seemed to be forced and vamped up long after its poignant occasion has passed. As elsewhere in Europe, the fanatic 'nationalist' consciousness invoked seemed belated and unreal. Joyce was, I understand, against Sinn Fein. In his auto-biographical books you obtain an unambiguous expression of his attitude in the matter. In the *Portrait of the Artist*, where the nationalist, Davin, is talking to him, Stephen (the author, of whom that is a self-portrait as a young man) says:–

'My ancestors threw off their language and took another. They allowed a handful of foreigners to subject them. Do you fancy I am going to pay in my own life and person debts they made? What for?'

'For our freedom,' said Davin.

'No honourable and sincere man,' said Stephen, 'has given up to you his life and his affections from the days of Tone to those of Parnell but you sold him to the enemy or filed him in need or reviled him and left him for another. And you invite me to be one of you. I'd see you damned first.' (220)

A little later Stephen remarks: 'You talk to me of nationality, language, religion. I shall try to fly by those nets.' So from the start the answer of Joyce to the militant nationalist was plain enough. And he showed himself in that a very shrewd realist indeed, beset as Irishmen have been for so long with every romantic temptation, always being invited by this interested party or that, to jump back into 'history'. So Joyce is neither of the militant 'patriot' type, nor yet a historical romancer. In spite of that he is very 'Irish'. He is ready enough, as a literary artist, to stand for Ireland, and has wrapped himself up in a gigantic cocoon of local colour in *Ulysses*.

It is at this point that we reach one of the fundamental questions of value brought out by his work. Although entertaining the most studied contempt for his compatriots – individually and in the mass – whom he did not regard at all as exceptionally brilliant and sympathetic creatures (in a green historical costume, with a fairy hovering near), but as average human cattle with an Irish accent instead of a Scotch or Welsh, it will yet be insisted on that his Irishness is an important feature of his talent; and he certainly also does exploit his Irishness and theirs.

The appreciation of any author is, of course, largely composed of adventitious sentiment. For his vogue to last, or ever to be a serious one, he must have some unusual literary gift. With that he reaches a considerable renown. But then people proceed to admire him for something equally possessed by a quantity of other people, or for reasons that have nothing to do, or even contradict, his gifts. So Englishmen or Frenchmen who are inclined to virulent 'nationalism', and disposed to sentiment where local colour is concerned, will admire Joyce for his alleged identity with what he detached himself from and even repudiated, when it took the militant, Sinn Fein form. And Joyce, like a shrewd sensible man, will no doubt encourage them. That, however, will not at all help us to be clear about this very confused issue. Nor should we be very certain, if we left the matter in that state, in our valuation of Joyce. We should find ourselves substituting orthodox political reactions to the idea of fanatical 'nationalism' (which it is quite evident holds little reality for Joyce) for direct reactions to what is in his work a considerable achievement of art ...

... there is not very much reflection going on at any time inside the head of Mr James Joyce. That is indeed the characteristic condition of the *craftsman*, pure and simple.

And that is what Joyce is above all things, essentially the craftsman. It is a thing more common, perhaps, in painting or the plastic arts than in literature. I do not mean by this that he works harder or more thoroughly than other people, but that he is not so much an inventive intelligence as an executant. He is certainly very 'shoppy', and professional to a fault, though in the midst of the amateurisms of the day it is a fault that can easily be forgiven.

What stimulates him is *ways of doing things*, and technical processes, and not *things to be done*. Between the various things to be done he shows a true craftsman's impartiality. He is become so much a writing-specialist that it matters very little to him *what* he writes, or what idea or world-view he expresses, so long as he is trying his hand at this manner and that, and displaying his enjoyable virtuosity. Strictly speaking, he has none at all, no special point of view, or none worth mentioning. It is such people that the creative intelligence fecundates and uses; and at present that intelligence is political, and its stimuli are masked ideologies. He is only a tool, an instrument, in short. That is why such a sensitive medium as Joyce, working in such a period, requires the attention of the independent critic.

So perhaps it is easy to see how, without much realising what was happening, Joyce arrived where he did. We can regard it as a diathetic phenomenon partly – the craftsman is susceptible and unprotected. There are even slight, though not very grave, symptoms of disorder in his art. The painful preoccupation with the exact place of things in a room, for instance, could be mildly matched in his writing. The *things themselves* by which he is surrounded lose, for the hysterical subject, their importance, or even meaning. Their *position* absorbs all the attention of his mind. Some such uneasy pedantry, in a mild form, is likely to assail any conscientious craftsman – especially in an intensive 'space-time' atmosphere, surrounded by fanatical space-timeists. The poor craftsman has never been in such peril as to-day, for it is a frantic hornpipe indeed that his obedient legs are compelled to execute. But otherwise Joyce, with his highly-developed *physical* basis, is essentially sane.

The method that underlies *Ulysses* is known as the 'telling from the inside'. As that description denotes, it is psychological. Carried out in the particular manner used in *Ulysses*, it lands the reader inside an Aladdin's cave of incredible bric-à-brac in which a dense mass of dead stuff is collected, from 1901 toothpaste, a bar or two of Sweet Rosie O'Grady, to pre-Nordic architecture. An immense *nature-morte* is the result. This ensues from the method of confining the reader in a circumscribed psychological space into which several encyclopaedias have been emptied. It results from the constipation induced in the movement of the narrative.

The amount of *stuff* – unorganised brute material – that the more active principle of drama has to wade through, under the circum-stances, slows it down to the pace at which, inevitably, the sluggish tide of the author's bric-à-brac passes the observer, at the saluting post, or in this case, the reader. It is a suffocating, moeotic expanse of objects, all of them lifeless, the sewage of a Past twenty years old, all neatly arranged in a meticulous sequence. The newspaper in which Mr Bloom's bloater is wrapped up, say, must press on to the cold body of the fish, reversed, the account of the bicycle accident that was reported on the fated day chosen for this Odyssey; or that at least is the idea.

At the end of a long reading of *Ulysses* you feel that it is the very nightmare of the naturalistic method that you have been experiencing. Much as you may cherish the merely physical enthusiasm that expresses itself in this stupendous outpouring of *matter*, or *stuff*, you wish, on the spot, to be transported to some more abstract region for a time, where the dates of the various toothpastes, the brewery and laundry receipts, the growing pile of punched 'bus-tickets, the growing holes in the baby's socks and the darn that repairs them, assume less importance. It is your impulse perhaps quickly to get your mind where there is nothing but air and rock, however inhospitable and featureless, and a little timeless, too. You will have had a glut, for the moment (if you have really persevered), of *matter*, procured you by the turning on of all this river of what now is rubbish, but which was not *then*, by the obsessional application of the naturalistic method associated with the exacerbated time-sense. And the fact that you were not in the open air, but closed up inside somebody else's head, will not make things any better. It will have been your catharsis of the objective accumulations that obstinately collect in even the most active mind.

Now in the graphic and plastic arts that stage of fanatic naturalism long ago has been passed. All the machinery appropriate to its production has long since been discarded, luckily for the pure creative impulse of the artist. The nineteenth-century naturalism of that obsessional, fanatical order is what you find on the one hand in *Ulysses*. On the other, you have a great variety of recent influences enabling Mr Joyce to use it in the way that he did.

The effect of this rather fortunate confusion was highly stimulating to Joyce, who really got the maximum out of it, with an appetite that certainly will never be matched again for the actual *matter* revealed in his composition, or proved to have been lengthily secreted there. It is like a gigantic Victorian quilt or antimacassar. Or it is the voluminous curtain that fell, belated (with the alarming momentum of a ton or two of personally organised rubbish), upon the Victorian scene. So rich was its delivery, its pent-up outpouring so vehement, that it will remain, eternally cathartic, a monument like a record diarrhoea. No one who looks *at* it will ever want to look *behind* it. It is the sardonic catafalque of the Victorian world.

Two opposite things were required for this result. Mr Joyce could never have performed this particular feat if he had not been, in his make-up, extremely immobile; and yet, in contradiction to that, very open to new technical influences. It is the *craftsman* in Joyce that is progressive; but the *man* has not moved since his early days in Dublin. He is on that side a 'young man' in some way embalmed. His technical adventures do not, apparently, stimulate him to think. On the contrary, what he thinks seems to be of a conventional and fixed order, as though perhaps not to embarrass the neighbouring evolution of his highly progressive and eclectic craftsmanship.

So he collected like a cistern in his youth the last stagnant pumpings of Victorian Anglo-Irish life. This he held steadfastly intact for fifteen years or more – then when he was ripe, as it were, he discharged it, in a dense mass, to his eternal glory. That was *Ulysses*. Had the twenty-year-old Joyce of the *Dubliners* not remained almost miraculously intact, we should have never witnessed this peculiar spectacle.

That is, I believe, the true account of how this creative event occurred with Joyce; and, if that is so, it will be evident that we are in the presence of a very different phenomenon from Proust. Proust *returned* to the *temps perdu*. Joyce never left them. He discharged it as freshly as though the time he wrote about were still present, because it was *his* present. It rolled out with all the aplomb and vivacity of a contemporary experience, assisted in its slick discharge by the latest technical devices.

I will now turn to the scandalous element in *Ulysses*, its supposed obscenity. Actually it appears to me that the mind of Joyce is more chaste than most. Once you admit the licence that, at the start, Joyce set out to profit by, it is surprising how very little 'sex' matter there is in his pages. What is there is largely either freudian echoes (they had to enter into it), or else it is horse-play of a schoolboy or public-house order. The motif of the house-drain is once and for all put in its place, and not mentioned again. It is the fault of the reader if that page or two dealing with it assume, in retrospect, proportions it has not, as a fact, in Joyce's pages. That passage can be regarded in the light of the reply of Antigonus to the poet Hermodorus, when the latter had described him as the son of the Sun.

I will next take up in turn a few further items of importance, expiscating them one by one. Joyce is not a moralist, but he has a great relish, on the other hand, for politics. Indeed, Lady Bolingbroke's remark about Pope, that he 'played the politician about cabbages and turnips' (or as somebody else remarked, 'he hardly drank tea without a stratagem'), could be applied to the author of *Ulysses* – the mere name suggests a romantic predilection for guile.

He could claim another affinity with Pope – namely, that although a witty writer, he is, as far as his private and personal legend is concerned, a man of one story. 'One apothegm only stands upon record,' Johnson writes of Pope; it was directed at Patrick. Joyce has one story to his credit, and it is at the expense of Yeats. As it is the general custom, even in the briefest account of Joyce, to tell this story, lest I should be regarded as imperfectly documented, I will give it here. When Joyce was about twenty years old he was very hard up, we are told, and he decided to go to Yeats and see if that gentleman would do anything to help him. He seems to have foreboded the result, and provided himself with a plan of action in the event of a rebuff. The appointed time arrived. As he entered the room, sure enough he read on the face of Mr Yeats the determination *not* to help him. Thereupon he bore down on Yeats, bade him good morning, and immediately inquired how old he was. On learning the extent of Yeats's seniority, with a start of shocked surprise, he mournfully shook his head, exclaimed, 'I fear I have come too late! I can do nothing to help you!' and, turning on his heel, left the apartment, the tables neatly turned ...

... It would be difficult, I think, to find a more lifeless, irritating, principal figure than the deplorable hero of the *Portrait of the Artist* and *Ulysses* ...

... The method of the growth of these books may be partly responsible for it, the imperfect assimilation of the matter-of-fact naturalism of the *Dubliners* to the more complex *Ulysses* ...

What induced Joyce to place in the centre of his very large canvas this grotesque figure, Stephan (sic) Dedalus? Or, having done so, to make it worse by contrasting it the whole time (as typifying 'the ideal') with the gross 'materialism' of the Jew, Bloom? Again, the answer to that, I think, is that things *grew* in that way, quite outside of Joyce's control; and it is an effect, merely, of a confusion of method. □

Wyndham Lewis is the first critic to show strong reservations about the character of Stephen Dedalus, and to question whether such a character can be taken seriously. He is to be linked with Hugh Kenner as co-founders of the 'Stephen-hating school', although one of Kenner's finest articles is prompted by disagreement with Lewis. His reservations concerning *Ulysses* are just as interesting. 'What stimulates him', suggests Lewis 'is *ways of doing things,* and technical processes, and not *things to be done,*' a reservation which would appear to future generations as the finest example one could wish for of praising with faint damns.

CHAPTER TWO

Joyce's Industry

It is widely accepted among critics[1] that Eliot and Pound set the terms for succeeding critical debate on *Ulysses*. Either it was to be read as systematic symbolic epic or as the apotheosis of unflinching realism. Behind both of them was Larbaud, and, behind Larbaud, Joyce. When the first full-length critical studies began to appear in the 1930s they were highly indebted to Joyce for two reasons. Not only did they retrospectively acknowledge Bennett's criticism that help was needed, and obligingly supply the reader with keys to the book's elaborate system of references, allusions and corrrespondences, keys which could only be supplied by Joyce himself: they also relied on extensive quotation from *Ulysses*, quotation so extensive that Stuart Gilbert's *James Joyce's 'Ulysses'* and Frank Budgen's *James Joyce and the Making of Ulysses* almost function as abridged samplers for the novel, in the meantime guiding the reader though the novel episode by episode and clarifying the narrative line. While pointing out that *Ulysses* was much more than a novel, they still helped it to be read much more *as* a novel. There was another reason behind this, of course. Censorship of Joyce's work was still so widespread, and copies of *Ulysses* so rare that for many the only way to read Joyce was in the pages cited by Gilbert and Budgen; only by reading and judging Joyce by the extracts thus provided could one decide whether the effort and expense involved in circumventing censorship by procuring a copy was justified. By offering his support for these projects, and for Herbert Gorman's 1939 biography, Joyce was being at once Stephen Dedalus, purveyor of aesthetic theories and builder of myths, and Leopold Bloom, advertising canvasser.

Gilbert's study borrows heavily from the schema provided for Larbaud, and as a result suffers from being, well, too schematic. Like Eliot, Gilbert wishes to defend the novel from charges of formlessness, and this defensiveness extends to an overstated appeal to Joyce's authority, and an unwillingness to attend to Joyce's multiple ironies (his discussion of the Nausicaa episode is a case in point). This is not to deny Gilbert's usefulness and readability, and one of the consequences of his study is that critics were henceforth to use the episode titles included in the schema but excised from the novel itself. I will not reproduce the schema here, since it is so widely available, not least within the critical apparatus of both the recommended texts of *Ulysses*. As a structural map it does have its uses, but it no more helps one's reading than a map of the

33

London Underground would help one on a walking tour. Harry Levin[2] suggests that the schema seems much more important to Joyce than it could possibly be to any reader, adding that it is best regarded as a scaffold useful for the construction of the novel but which obscures as well as marginalises the non-mythic aspects of the work. Even more damningly, a conversation with Vladimir Nabokov reported by Ellmann suggests that Joyce came to regret the whole enterprise.

■ Joyce's attitude towards the book gradually altered. Vladimir Nabokov recalled a conversation with him at dinner in the Léon's flat about 1937. Joyce said something disparaging about the use of mythology in modern literature. Nabokov replied in amazement, 'But you employed Homer!' 'A whim', was Joyce's comment. 'But you collaborated with Gilbert,' Nabokov persisted. 'A terrible mistake,' said Joyce. 'An advertisement for the book. I regret it very much.'[3] □

Gilbert's study is also interesting in how it reads and uses *A Portrait*. The following extract shows how the aesthetic theory adumbrated by Stephen is taken unequivocally as providing the clue to understanding Joyce.

■ It cannot be too strongly emphasised that the object of the author of *Ulysses* was to present an *aesthetic* image of the world, a sublimation of that *cri de coeur* in which the art of creation begins.

The personality of the artist, at first a cry or a cadence or a mood and then a fluent and lambent narrative, finally refines itself out of existence, impersonalises itself so to speak. ... The mystery of the aesthetic like that of material creation is accomplished. The artist, like the God of creation, remains within or behind or beyond or above his handiwork, invisible, refined out of existence, indifferent, paring his fingernails. (*Portrait*, p. 233) □

This last sentence is one of the most frequently quoted in all of Joyce, and remains a classic statement of the modernist ideal of impersonality. But what is the relation of the invisible author (Joyce) to the visible and voluble Stephen? If Joyce is more apparent in Stephen, what price his invisibility? Furthermore, what is the function of the seldom quoted riposte by Lynch which immediately follows this sentence?

■ – Trying to refine them also out of existence, said Lynch. □

Is Lynch merely the vulgar foil in a pseudo-Socratic dialogue, or is he part of a contrapuntal and polyphonic play of voices in which Stephen's dominant role must be questioned? Here, as elsewhere in the novel, Lynch speaks for the body which Stephen, not Joyce, attempts to deny. Gilbert, though, like most early commentators, took Stephen's voice to be unequivocally authoritative:

■ Aesthetic emotion is *static*. 'The mind is arrested and raised above fear and loathing.' 'The feelings excited by improper art are kinetic, desire and loathing. Desire urges us to possess, to go to something; loathing urges us to abandon, to go from something. The arts which excite them, pornographical or didactic, are therefore improper arts.' Such a conception of the function of the artist presided over the creation of *Ulysses*. The instant when the supreme quality of beauty, the clear radiance of the aesthetic image,

> is apprehended luminously by the mind which has been arrested by its wholeness and fascinated by its harmony is the luminous silent stasis of aesthetic pleasure, a spiritual state very like to that cardiac condition which the Italian physiologist Luigi Galvani, using a phrase almost as beautiful as Shelley's, called the enchantment of the heart.

The artist's aim, then, is to ban kinetic feelings from his readers' minds, and in Ulysses we find the ideal silent stasis of the artist nearly realised, his personality almost impersonalised. The feeling of desire, which urges us to possess, is absent; there is not the least pornographical appeal; but the loathing, which urges us to abandon – that aversion from the sordid which made of Stephen Dedalus an exile in his own country – is, one can but feel, active in certain passages... □

Although Gilbert does go on to admit that Stephen Dedalus might not have attained the ideal complete indifference, this is taken as a possible sign of aesthetic immaturity on Joyce's part (in both novels) rather than an indication of ironic distance between author and hero. In Gilbert's interpretation, the various distances and ambiguities implicit in the very title *A Portrait of the Artist as a Young Man* [my emphasis] are ignored in favour of a reading which insists on the didactic import of a sermon against didacticism and the static nature of a novel of development, desire and loathing.

The Cornish sculptor Frank Budgen was befriended by Joyce in Zurich in 1918, and his *James Joyce and the Making of Ulysses* remains the most engaging of introductions, bringing Joyce's humour and humanism into the foreground while offering new insights into his artistry and ambition. A short quotation from the beginning of the work gives an idea of the range of its qualities; at once biography, anthology, critical commentary and publicity document. The whole benefits greatly from Budgen's bluff and witty espousal of the Boswell role.

■ When I first called on Joyce and his family they were living at No. 38 Universitätsstrasse. There were two guests besides myself. It was after these had gone and Joyce had asked me to stay for a final half-hour's chat that we fell to talking about religion. Being an orthodox agnostic I saw nothing illogical in admitting that what are called miracles might occur. I had no satisfactory evidence that any ever had occurred, but on my limited experience I felt I couldn't rule them out. Perhaps I didn't succeed in defining my position too well, for when I rose to go Joyce laughed and said:

'You are really more of a believer than is many a good catholic.'

The next day I found a packet and a letter awaiting me in my little room in the Schipfe. The packet contained a copy of *A Portrait of the Artist as a Young Man* and the letter extracts from press notices of *A Portrait of the Artist*, *Dubliners* and *Exiles*. I read the book and then the praises of Ezra Pound, H. G. Wells and others, quoted on the many-coloured leaflets. H. G. Wells wrote: 'Its claim to be literature is as good as the claim of the last book of *Gulliver's Travels* ... Like Swift and another living Irish writer, Mr Joyce has a cloacal obsession ... Like some of the best stories in the world, it is the story of an education ... One conversation in this book is a superb success. I write with all due deliberation that Sterne himself could not have done it better.' And Ezra Pound and a dozen others to the same purpose, each in his own way. I remember very well my own impression. The affirmative young man, the terror-stricken and suffering adolescent were but timebound faces of a personality the essence of which is in the boy Stephen Dedalus. He is like a young inquisitive cat taking stock of the world and of himself: climbing, hiding, testing his claws. This bold, tenacious, clear-seeing boy is the essential artist. There comes a moment when hostile forces – cramping poverty and the tyrannies of Church, nation and family – threaten him with loss of freedom, with extinction as an artist, and he must mobilise all his forces of defence and attack to save himself. 'Silence, exile and cunning', says Stephen himself, and he uses these arms and more besides before the battle is won.

A cold wind was blowing when I met Joyce one evening on the Bahnhofstrasse. The brown overcoat buttoned up to his chin lent him a somewhat military appearance.

'I'm glad you liked the "Portrait",' said Joyce. I had returned the book with a letter recording some of my impressions of it.

'That simile of yours, "a young cat sharpening his claws on the tree of life," seems to me to be very just applied to young Stephen.'

I enquired after *Ulysses*. Was it progressing?

'I have been working hard on it all day,' said Joyce.

'Does that mean that you have written a great deal?' I said.

'Two sentences,' said Joyce.

I looked sideways but Joyce was not smiling. I thought of Flaubert.

'You have been seeking the *mot juste*?' I said.

'No,' said Joyce. 'I have the words already. What I am seeking is the perfect order of words in the sentence. There is an order in every way appropriate. I think I have it.'

'What are the words?' I asked.

'I believe I told you,' said Joyce, 'that my book is a modern *Odyssey*. Every episode in it corresponds to an adventure of Ulysses. I am now writing the *Lestrygonians* episode, which corresponds to the adventures of Ulysses with the cannibals. My hero is going to lunch. But there is a seduction motive in the *Odyssey*, the cannibal king's daughter. Seduction appears in my book as women's silk petticoats hanging in a shop window. The words through which I express the effect of it in my hungry hero are: "Perfume of embraces all him assailed. With hungered flesh obscurely, he mutely craved to adore." You can see for yourself in how many different ways they might be arranged.'

A painter is, perhaps, more originality proof than any other artist, seeing that all recent experimental innovations in the arts have first been tried out on his own. And many a painter can labour for a day or for many days on one or two square inches of canvas so that labour expended on achieving precious material is not likely to surprise him. What impressed me, I remember, when Joyce repeated the words of Bloom's hungrily abject amorousness to me, was neither the originality of the words themselves nor the labour expended on composing them. It was the sense they gave me that a new province of material had been found. Where that province lay I could not guess, but as our talk proceeded Joyce spoke of it himself without question of mine. We were by this time sitting in the Astoria Café.

'Among other things,' he said, 'my book is the epic of the human body. The only man I know who has attempted the same thing is Phineas Fletcher. But then his *Purple Island* is purely descriptive, a kind of coloured anatomical chart of the human body. In my book the body lives in and moves through space and is the home of a full human personality. The words I write are adapted to express first one of its functions then another. In *Lestrygonians* the stomach dominates and the rhythm of the episode is that of the peristaltic movement.'

'But the minds, the thoughts of the characters,' I began.

'If they had no body they would have no mind,' said Joyce. 'It's all one. Walking towards his lunch my hero, Leopold Bloom, thinks of his wife, and says to himself, "Molly's legs are out of plumb." At another time of the day he might have expressed the same thought without any underthought of food. But I want the reader to understand always through the suggestion rather than direct statement.'

'That's the painter's form of leverage,' I said.

We talked of words again, and I mentioned one that had always pleased me for its shape and colour. It was Chatterton's 'acale' for freeze.

'It is a good word,' said Joyce. 'I shall probably use it.'

He does use it. The word occurs in 'The Oxen of the Sun' episode of *Ulysses* in a passage written in early English, describing the death and burial of Bloom's son Rudolph: '... and as he was minded of his good lady Marion that had borne him an only manchild which on this eleventh day on live had died and no man of art could save so dark is destiny. And she was wondrous stricken of heart for this evil hap and for his burial did lay him on a fair corselet of lamb's wool, the flower of the flock, lest he might perish utterly and lie akeled ...'

In leaving the café I asked Joyce how long he had been working on Ulysses.

'About five years,' he said. 'But in a sense all my life.'

'Some of your contemporaries,' I said, 'think two books a year an average output.'

'Yes,' said Joyce. 'But how do they do it? They talk them into a typewriter. I feel quite capable of doing that if I wanted to do it. But what's the use? It isn't worth doing.'[4] □

Budgen's work retains, at Joyce's prompting, the insistence on Homeric correspondences, but there is also, as there is not in Gilbert, a desire to present the characters as basically sympathetic. Allied with this of course is the promulgation of the ideal of Joyce as the artist who excelled Flaubert in his devotion to his work, and some of its anecdotes are hence a bit too pat. But, as Hugh Kenner has argued, it is still unsurpassed as an introduction to *Ulysses*.[5] Not only does it humanise Joyce by bringing Bloom to the centre of attention, thus inaugurating a liberal-humanist tradition of Joyce commentary which persisted until very recently; it also allows, by virtue of its extensive quotation, for close reading of Joyce's text, giving scope for analysis rather than just description, extrapolation and summary. The moment when primary attention would be devoted to a properly textual reading of Joyce was still, however, a long way off.

Joyce would surely have welcomed with ironic relish the fact that the first fully independent and comprehensive study of his work, Harry

Levin's *James Joyce: A Critical Introduction*, appeared in the year of his death. Levin's study is noteworthy for its achievement in placing both *Ulysses* and *A Portrait* in the context of modern European literature, although Edmund Wilson's still-readable 1932 essay in *Axel's Castle*[6] also deserves mention in this regard. Levin astutely and helpfully mediates between both symbolist and naturalist, or, as he puts it, art-for-art's-sake and slice-of life interpretations of the novels, pointing out the value and limitations of both, and although much of the book is still devoted to exposition, it attains a level of critical sophistication hitherto rare in the field. His discussion of *A Portrait* notes the stylistic departures from *Stephen Hero* but otherwise stresses the autobiographical nature of the work, insisting that it is based on a literal transcript of the first twenty years of Joyce's life and that it is, by reason of its concentration on the emotional and intellectual life of its protagonist, if anything more candid than most autobiographies. It is noticed that most of the other characters have been consigned to the background or refined out of existence, and dramatic elements replaced by meditation, *tableau* or soliloquy. Crucially, Levin attends to that aspect which I have been arguing as central to the developing debate on Joyce's writing; the oscillations of style in the novel.

■ [Stephen] is marked by the aureole of the Romantic hero, like Thomas Mann's outsiders, pressing their noses against the window panes of a bourgeois society from which they feel excluded. 'To merge his life in the common tide of other lives was harder for him than any fasting or prayer, and it was his constant failure to do this to his own satisfaction which caused in his soul at last a sensation of spiritual dryness together with a growth of doubts and scruples.' At school he takes an equivocal position, 'a free boy, a leader afraid of his own authority, proud and sensitive and suspicious, battling against the squalor of his life and against the riot of his mind.' At home he feels his own 'futile isolation'. He feels that he is scarcely of the same blood as his mother and brother and sister, but stands to them 'rather in the mystical kinship of foster-age, foster child and foster-brother'.

Joyce's prose is the register of this intellectual and emotional cleavage. It preserves the contrast between his rather lush verse and his rather dry criticism, between the pathetic children and the ironic politicians of *Dubliners*. All his sensibility is reserved for himself; his attitude towards others is consistently caustic. The claims to objectivity of a subjective novel, however, must be based on its rendering of intimate experience. If Joyce's treatment of Stephen is true to himself, we have no right to interpose any other criteria. Mr Eliot has made the plausible suggestion that Joyce's two masters in prose were Newman and Pater. Their alternating influence would account for the oscillations in style in the *Portrait of the Artist*. The sustaining tone, which it adopts towards the outside world, is that of precise and mordant description. Interpolated, at strategic points in Stephen's development, are a number of purple passages that have faded considerably.

Joyce's own contribution to English prose is to provide a more fluid medium for refracting sensations and impressions through the author's mind – to facilitate the transition from photographic realism to aesthetic impressionism. In the introductory pages of the *Portrait of the Artist*, the reader is faced with nothing less than the primary impact of life itself, a presentational continuum of the tastes and smells and sights and sounds of earliest infancy. Emotion is integrated, from first to last, by words. Feelings, as they filter through Stephen's sensory apparatus, become associated with phrases. His conditioned reflexes are literary. In one of the later dialogues of the book, he is comparing his theory to a trimmed lamp. The dean of studies, taking up the metaphor, mentions the lamp of Epictetus, and Stephen's reply is a further allusion to the stoic doctrine that the soul is like a bucketful of water. In his mind this far-fetched chain of literary associations becomes attached to the sense impressions of the moment: 'A smell of molten tallow came up from the dean's candle butts and fused itself in Stephen's consciousness with the jingle of the words, bucket and lamp and lamp and bucket.'

This is the state of mind that confers upon language a magical potency. It exalts the habit of verbal association into a principle for the arrangement of human experience. You gain power over a thing by naming it; you become master of a situation by putting it into words. It is psychological need, and not hyperfastidious taste, that goads the writer on to search for the *mot juste*, to loot the thesaurus. Stephen, in the more explicit manuscript, finds a treasure house in Skeat's *Etymological Dictionary*. The crucial moment of the book, which leads to the revelation of his name and calling, is a moment he tries to make his own by drawing forth a phrase of his treasure:

– A day of dappled seaborne clouds.

The phrase and the day and the scene harmonised in a chord. Words. Was it their colours? He allowed them to glow and fade, hue after hue: sunrise gold, the russet and green of apple orchards, azure of waves, the greyfringed fleece of clouds. No, it was not their colours: it was the poise and balance of the period itself. Did he then love the rhythmic rise and fall of words better than their associations of legend and colour? Or was it that, being as weak of sight as he was shy of mind, he drew less pleasure from the reflection of the glowing sensible world through the prism of a language many coloured and richly storied than from the contemplation of an inner world of individual emotions mirrored perfectly in a lucid supple periodic prose? (181)

The strength and weakness of his style, by Joyce's own diagnosis, are those of his mind and body. A few pages later he offers a cogent illustration, when Stephen dips self-consciously into his word-hoard for suitable epithets to describe a girl who is wading along the beach. We are given a paragraph of word-painting which is not easy to visualise. 'Her bosom was as a bird's, soft and slight, slight and soft as the breast of some dark-plumaged dove,' it concludes. 'But her long fair hair was girlish: and girlish, and touched with the wonder of mortal beauty, her face.' This is incantation, and not description. Joyce is thinking in rhythms rather than metaphors. Specification of the bird appeals to the sense of touch rather than to the sense of sight. What is said about the hair and face is intended to produce an effect without presenting a picture. The most striking effects in Joyce's imagery are those of coldness, whiteness, and dampness, like the bodies of the bathers who shout Stephen's name. □

Levin goes on here to pay tribute to Joyce's gift for realistic rendering of conversation. Oddly enough, given his insights into the novelty of Joyce's technique as detailed above, he calls this 'the most vital element in Joyce's writing'.

■ The *Portrait of the Artist*, as Joyce's remembrance finally shaped it, is a volume of three hundred pages, symmetrically constructed around three undramatic climaxes, intimate crises of Stephen's youth. The first hundred pages, in two chapters, trace the awakening of religious doubts and sexual instincts, leading up to Stephen's carnal sin at the age of sixteen. The central portion, in two more chapters, continues the cycle of sin and repentance to the moment of Stephen's private apocalypse. The external setting for the education of the artist is, in the first chapter, Clongowes Wood College; in the second, third and fourth, Belvedere College, Dublin. The fifth and final chapter, which is twice as long as the others, develops the theories and projects of Stephen's student days in University College, and brings him to the verge of exile. As the book advances, it becomes less sensitive to outside impressions, and more intent upon speculations of its own. Friends figure mainly as interlocutors to draw Stephen out upon various themes. Each epiphany – awakening of the body, literary vocation, farewell to Ireland – leaves him lonelier than the last.[7] □

Levin's study is valuable both in its own right and for the debates engendered by his assertions. It is for him the book, not Stephen, which becomes less sensitive to outside impressions, and throughout there is a conflation of novel, author and hero: they share credit for achievements and blame for lapses. If the prose is too purple in patches it is Joyce's indulgence which is at fault. Later critics would not be so ready to presume such identifications, and would insist on a more ironic reading of *A Portrait*. Levin is willing to see ironic distance in *Ulysses* where the Homeric identifications invite them, but any ironies in *A Portrait* he sees as being endemic to the autobiographical mode, as when Stephen's humourless swoony prose is compared to the plaintive, cloying stanzas of *Chamber Music*.

The relationship between language and point of view also informs Levin's discussion of *Ulysses*, where the proliferation of styles comes to dismay the critic:

■ We know that Joyce, with his unhappy estrangement from society, came to equate language and experience. We wonder whether his confidence in words was not overweening, whether he was not too articulate to achieve a really profound portrayal of human emotion. Could Joyce have apprehended the mute suffering in the eyes of the little princes, dying of childbirth in Tolstoy's *War and Peace*, or – in a different strain – the magnificent incoherence of Peeperkorn's speech, completely drowned out by the sound of a waterfall in Mann's *Der Zauberberg*? How far is language adequate to express the finer shadings and subtler modulations of the mind? □

Well, thanks to language, Levin makes his point and misses the point. The cases cited use language, as they must, as much as Joyce does: muteness, suffering, incoherence and waterfalls can only be conveyed in novels by means of language. Levin's error here lies in assuming that there are two types of language: that which asserts itself as 'style' and that which refers transparently to an outside truth. Joyce's demolition of this distinction was to make him the darling of the post-structuralists.

■ Joyce feels less and less committed to the point of view of either Stephen or Bloom. Having established their respective rhythms in the morning, and brought them together at noon, he feels free to break through their soliloquies and embark upon an independent series of self-conscious stylistic adventures. The episode at the office of the *Irish Freeman*, the cave of the winds, where both heroes put in their mid-day appearance, is punctuated by increasingly animated headlines. Each succeeding chapter becomes more involved in style, more distorted in shape, and more permeated by what Yvor Winters considers 'the fallacy of imitative form.' Joyce meets no serious obstacle in verbalising the atmosphere of a newspaper office, or even in finding half-chewed syllables for the sounds of Bloom's lunch: 'Table talk. I munched hum un thu Unchster Bunk un Munchday. Ha? Did you, faith?' 167 But Joyce's premise, that any given physical effect can be exactly duplicated by means of language, lures him into a confusing *mélange des genres.* □

By adhering to the category of internal monologue, and thus assuming that styles are prompted either by characters' limited point of view or by the author's self indulgence, Levin clearly sets forth a critical position on Joyce which would take a lot of dislodging. His citing of Yvor Winters shows him to be aware of the tenets of what was to be called the New Criticism, but his own work is hardly free of what other new critics were to consider the 'The Intentionalist Fallacy'.

CHAPTER THREE

Years of Consolidation

The four decades following Joyce's death saw the industry go into full production: more than 7,500 studies have been recorded up to 1981, and as it would be impossible even to summarise the best of them within the scope of this guide, the reader is referred to Thomas F. Staley's *Annotated Critical Bibliography of James Joyce* (1988), which offers a selective and intelligent appraisal of the main contributions to criticism within the period. Certain landmark contributions, however, must be mentioned. Foremost of these is that of Richard Ellmann, whose 1959 biography of Joyce is indispensable, and a work admired by a constituency far wider than that of Joyceans. Ellmann's edition of the *Letters* (three volumes, first volume edited by Stuart Gilbert, 1966), the 1976 *Selected Letters*, with some notorious additions, along with his editions of *Joyce's Critical Writings* (1959), and Stanislaus Joyce's at once revealing and sour *My Brother's Keeper* (1958), made him deservedly preeminent among Joyceans, while keeping the professors busy tuning their explications to the newly revealed facts concerning Joyce's life and working methods. One of the dangers of this is that the supplementary material uncovered by Ellmann encourages an overly biographical reading of the works, prompting easy identifications instead of pointing out the text's disjunctures.

This biographical material informed many of the introductory works on Joyce published during the period, but also prompted critics to ask whether *Ulysses* was indeed a novel, or a kind of ragbag of Joyce's personal memories, inspired doodlings, speculations, private jokes, and scattered observations of Dublin life as it was lived in the early nineteen hundreds? In the general view, however, as Cleanth Brooks pointed out, *Ulysses* is an ordered and intricately organised masterpiece. Indeed it is usually accorded the treatment given to a sacred book. A painfully careful exegesis is regarded as appropriate to these Joycean scriptures, which have been diligently searched in order to discover proof texts, to recover hidden meanings, to unravel cryptic allusions, and, more ambitiously, to develop a systematic symbolism.

Thanks largely to the burgeoning institution of literary criticism in the universities, particularly in the United States, Joyce attained the diligent and devoted readership that he wished, but it is important to recognise that this readership was still at the stage where *A Portrait*, and particularly *Ulysses*, required patient explicatory introduction, in the way that few other texts did. (Of course this is still the case for every new generation of readers, but it may be of solace to those presently puzzled to understand the experience of previous generations.) Such works as *A Reader's Guide to James Joyce* (1959) by William York Tindall, and *Here Comes Everybody* by Anthony Burgess are still useful in this way, as are the various volumes of annotation devoted to the novels, and the latest paperback editions are extremely well furnished with notes. One other work which can be highly recommended, and not just to the first-time reader, is Harry Blamires' *The Bloomsday Book*, which, though not in itself a work of criticism, offers a path through the labyrinth of *Ulysses* by sticking doggedly to a construed narrative of events in the novel and ignoring the distractions of linguistic invention. Anyone who wishes to find out the story of *Ulysses*, page by page, is referred to Blamires. *The Bloomsday Book* is however also interesting and profitable as a *reductio ad absurdum* of a particular way of reading Joyce's work, one which held sway in the period under discussion here and which sought to normalise the texts, as it were to translate *A Portrait* and *Ulysses* into something more amenable to readers' expectations. In their various ways, the extracts from Ellmann, Nabokov and Booth featured in this chapter exemplify this tendency, whether by reading *A Portrait* on Stephen's terms, or balking at Joyce's evocations of the sexual and linguistic unconscious, or, as in the latter two cases, complaining that Joyce doesn't quite fit into preset generic moulds. The extracts wouldn't be included if they weren't well done, and their liberal urge to evaluation deserves better than the dismissive polemic accorded it by MacCabe in the next chapter, but they nevertheless show that much of Joyce's revolutionary achievement was still waiting for a form of criticism that would do it justice, that could speak its tongues.

The great exception to this is Hugh Kenner, who is the finest of Joyce critics as Ellmann is the greatest Joyce scholar. Tenacious, subtle and adroit, Kenner is the reader Joyce was waiting for, and both his understanding of the significance of modernism generally and his unmatched sensitivity to the inflections of tone and point of view in the novels mean that he both set the terms of debate and kept up with his contributions to it well into the age of post-structuralism. He has his blind spots, notably around issues of gender, but it is his example and insistence on the closest of reading that moved Joyce studies where they belonged, into the study of language and textuality. I make no apology for having the long extract from *Dublin's Joyce* predominate in this chapter. 'The Portrait in Perspective' was first published in 1948, but I will begin by quoting a passage from Ellmann published 11 years later in order to give an idea of how the sort of orthodoxy which prompted Kenner's reading could also remain untouched by it. Ellmann's account of *A Portrait* would be as plausible as it's shapely, if there weren't a certain problem of vocabulary.

■ To write *A Portrait of the Artist as a Young Man* Joyce plunged back into his own past, mainly to justify, but also to expose it. The book's pattern, as he explained to Stanislaus, is that we are what we were; our maturity is an extension of our childhood, and the courageous boy is father of the arrogant young man. But in searching for a way to convert the episodic *Stephen Hero* into *A Portrait of the Artist*, Joyce hit upon a principle of structure which reflected his habits of mind as extremely as he could wish. The work of art, like a mother's love, must be achieved over the greatest obstacles, and Joyce, who had been dissatisfied with his earlier work as too easily done, now found the obstacles in the form of a most complicated pattern.

This is hinted at in his image of the creative process. As far back as his paper on Mangan, Joyce said that the poet takes into the vital centre of his life 'the life that surrounds it', flinging it abroad again amid planetary music. He repeated this image in *Stephen Hero* then in *A Portrait of the Artist* developed it more fully. Stephen refers to the making of literature as 'the phenomenon of artistic conception, artistic gestation and artistic reproduction,' and then describes the progession from lyrical to epical and to dramatic art:

> The simplest epical form is seen emerging out of lyrical literature when the artist prolongs and broods upon himself as the centre of an epical event and this form progresses till the centre of emotional gravity is equidistant from the artist himself and from others. The narrative is no longer purely personal. The personality of the artist passes into the narratio itself, flowing round and round the persons and the action like a vital sea ... The dramatic form is reached when the vitality which has flowed and eddied around each person fills each person with such vital force that he or she assumes a proper and intangible aesthetic life ... The mystery of aesthetic like that of material creation is accomplished. (232–233)

This creator is not only male but female; Joyce goes on to borrow an image of Flaubert by calling him a 'god,' but he is also a goddess. Within his womb creatures come to life. Gabriel the seraph comes to the virgin's chamber and, as Stephen says, 'In the virgin womb of the imagination the word is made flesh'.

Joyce did not take up such metaphors lightly. His brother records that in the first draft of *A Portrait*, Joyce thought of a man's character as developing 'from an embryo' with constant traits. Joyce acted upon this theory with his characteristic thoroughness, and his subsequent interest in the theory of gestation, as conveyed to Stanislaus during Nora's first pregnancy, expressed a concern that was literary as well as anatomical. His decision to rewrite *Stephen Hero* as *A Portrait* in five chapters occurred appropriately just after Lucia's birth. For *A Portrait of the Artist as a Young Man* is in fact the gestation of a soul, and in the metaphor Joyce found his new principle of order. The book begins with Stephen's father and, just before the ending, it depicts the hero's severance from his mother. From the start the soul is surrounded by liquids, urine, slime, seawater, amniotic tides, 'drops of water' (as Joyce says at the end of the first chapter) 'falling softly in the brimming bowl'. The atmosphere of biological struggle is necessarily dark and melancholy until the light of life is glimpsed. In the first chapter the foetal soul is for a few pages only slightly individualised, the organism responds only to the most primitive sensory impressions, then the heart forms and musters its affections, the being struggles towards some unspecified, uncomprehended culmination, it is flooded in ways it cannot understand and control, it gropes wordlessly toward sexual differentiation. In the third chapter shame floods Stephen's whole body as conscience develops; the lower bestial nature is put by. Then at the end of the fourth chapter the soul discovers the goal towards which it has been mysteriously proceeding – the goal of life. It must swim no more but emerge into air, the new metaphor being flight. The final chapter shows the soul, already fully developed, fattening itself for its journey until at last it is ready to leave. In the last few pages of the book, Stephen's diary, the soul is released from its confinement, its individuality is complete, and the style shifts with savage abruptness.[1] □

This, particularly in the last sentences, is criticism of *A Portrait* as if it were written by Stephen Dedalus; repetitive, luridly transcendentalist, ashamed of the physical ('lower bestial nature'), and guiltily indulgent in duff rhymes (soul/goal). The passage demonstrates and presumes an act of identification (Ellmann-Joyce-Stephen-soul) which the text of *A Portrait* questions, then refuses. In Ellmann's version of the story, life is opposed to the female, and the 'soul' (the key word here) is triumphant, as is Stephen. (In the next chapter, Ellmann's daughter will write about the body as opposed to the soul.)

As Wyndham Lewis had done earlier, Kenner[2] questions whether Stephen is in fact triumphant, but he also questions the vocabulary of the soul. He reads *A Portrait* in the light of *Ulysses* and *Finnegans Wake*, and finds in the earlier book similar complexities. Where 'the two major works strive toward an inclusive mythopoeic vision embracing in an archetypal pattern of fall, struggle, and redemption every mode of human activity,' *A Portrait* does this only on the level of individual human action, suggesting 'other possible levels of analogy' by implication. By pursuing these implications, Kenner shows how the book's first two pages 'enact the entire action in microcosm'. He pursues the 'verbal leitmotif' linking whiteness, cold, and damp as a repellent complex and shows how words with their tricky meanings and associations illustrate stages in Stephen's development. Kenner argues that Stephen's 'epiphanies' that arrest and embody artistic meaning in a single moment are not Joyce's method; instead, in each chapter of the book Joyce repeats the same pattern of showing Stephen embracing a dream in contempt of reality and then seeing the dream destroyed. 'The movement of the book is dialectical; each chapter closes with a synthesis of triumph which in turn feeds the sausage-machine set up in the next chapter.' Most important, Kenner argues that 'Stephen's flight into adolescent "freedom" is not meant to be the "message" of the book'. Stephen, Kenner argues, an 'indigestibly Byronic' figure, is viewed ironically throughout. His rather Neoplatonic aesthetic is not Joyce's; his Romanticism is scorned by the more classically-minded Joyce; and instead of becoming the author of *A Portrait* and *Ulysses*, Stephen will become a 'parlour aesthete,' priggish, horrified by the sensual world, and egotistically self-involved.

■ *A Portrait of the Artist as a Young Man*, which in its definitive form initiates the second cycle, was some ten years in the writing. A 1,000-page first draft was written around 1904-1906, about the same time as the bulk of *Dubliners*. This was scrapped and a more compressed version undertaken in 1908; the third and final text was being composed in 1911, and was finished early in 1914.[3] About one-third of the first draft (the *Stephen Hero* fragment) survives to show us what was going on during the gestation of this book, the only one which it cost Joyce far more trouble to focus than to execute.

Joyce first conceived the story of Stephen Dedalus is a picaresque mode. The original title was meant to incorporate the ballad of Turpin Hero, a reference to which still survives in the final text (233). Turpin spends most of the ballad achieving gestes at the expense of a gallery of middle-class dummies, beginning with a lawyer:

> ... As they rode down by the powder mill,
> Turpin commands him to stand still;
> Said he, your cape I must cut off,
> For my mare she wants her saddle cloth.
> O rare Turpin Hero,
> O rare Turpin O.
> This caus'd the lawyer much to fret,
> To think he was so fairly bit;
> And Turpin robb'd him of his store,
> Because he knew he'd lie for more.
> O rare Turpin Hero,
> O rare Turpin O.

The lawyer's mistake was to admit the plausible stranger to his intimacy. Stephen in the same way achieves a series of dialectical triumphs over priests, parents, and schoolfellows. The typical dialogue commences amid courtesies:

Stephen raised his cap and said 'Good evening, sir'. The President answered with the smile which a pretty girl gives when she receives some compliment which puzzles her – a 'winning' smile:

– What can I do for you? he asked in a rich deep calculated voice ...

But cut-and-thrust soon follows:

– May I ask you if you have read much of [Ibsen's] writing? asked Stephen.

– Well, no ... I must say ...

– May I ask you if you have read even a single line?

– Well, no ... I must admit ...

Stephen always relieves the interlocutor of his complacence:

– I should not care for anyone to identify the ideas in your essay with the teaching in our college. We receive this college in trust ...

– If I were to publish tomorrow a very revolutionary pamphlet on the means of avoiding potato-blight would you consider yourself responsible for my theory?

– No, no, of course not ... but then this is not a school of agriculture.

– Neither is it a school of dramaturgy, answered Stephen. (S95/81).

The ballad ends with Turpin in jail condemned to the gallows; *Stephen Hero* was presumably to end, as the *Portrait* does, with Stephen Protomartyr on the brink of continental exile, acknowledged enemy of the Dublin people. This Stephen is an engaging fellow with an explosive laugh (S59/49), an image of the young Joyce whom Yeats compared to William Morris 'for the joyous vitality one felt in him', or of the student Joyce who emerges from his brother's Memoir:

Uncompromising in all that concerned his artistic integrity, Joyce was, for the rest, a sociable and amiable disposition. Around his tall, agile figure there hovered a certain air of youthful grace and, despite the squalors of his home, a sense of happiness, as of one who feels within himself a joyous courage, a resolute confidence in life and in his own powers. ... Joyce's laugh was characteristic ... of that pure hilarity which does not contort the mouth.[4]

49

When Stephen's uncompromising side occasionally becomes absurd, Joyce the recorder is always at hand to supply a distancing phrase: 'the fiery-hearted revolutionary'; 'this heaven-ascending essayist' (S80/6); 'he was foolish enough to regret having yielded to the impulse for sympathy from a friend' (S83/70). Toward the end of the existing fragment we find more and more of these excusing clauses: 'No young man can contemplate the fact of death with extreme satisfaction and no young man, specialised by fate or her stepsister chance for an organ of sensitiveness and intellectiveness, can contemplate the network of falsities and trivialities which make up the funeral of a dead burgher without extreme disgust' (S168/150). This clumsy sentence, its tone slithering between detachment, irony and anger, is typical of the bad writing which recurs in the Stephen Hero fragment to signal Joyce's periodic uncertainty of Stephen's convincingness.

The book ran down unfinished in 1906, stalled partly by its own inner contradictions, partly by the far maturer achievement of Dubliners. It had never, Joyce saw, had a theme; it was neither a novel, nor an autobiography, now a spiritual or social meditation. It contained three sorts of materials that would not fuse: documentation from the past, transcribed from the Dublin notebooks; Joyce's memories of his earlier self, transmuted by a mythopoeic process only partly controlled; and his present complex attitude to what he thought that self to have been.

Fortunately, the catalytic theme was not long in coming. In the late fall of 1906, he wrote from Rome to his brother about a new story for Dubliners, 'Ulysses'. On February 6, 1907, he admitted that it 'never got any forrarder than the title'. It coalesced, instead, with the autobiographical theme, and both subjects were returned to the smithy. A novel, Ulysses, as Joyce told a Zurich student ten years later, began to be planned as sequel to a rewritten Portrait. In 1908 Stephen Hero was discarded for good, and the job of lining up the two works began. And once the final balance of motifs for the Portrait had been at last struck and the writing of the definitive text completed, the last exorcism, Exiles, took only three spring months. Ulysses and Finnegans Wake took seven and seventeen years, but their recalcitrance was technical merely. The Portrait includes their scenario: first 'the earth that had borne him' and 'the vast indifferent dome' (Penelope, Ithaca), then sleep and a plunge into 'some new world, fantastic, dim, uncertain as under sea, traversed by cloudy shapes and beings', (187). These are lyric anticipations of the dense epic and dramatic works to come; the actual writing of those works went forward during the next quarter-century with scarcely a false step.

LINKING THEMES

In the reconceived *Portrait* Joyce abandoned the original intention of writing the account of his own escape from Dublin. One cannot escape one's Dublin. He recast Stephen Dedalus as a figure who could not even detach himself from Dublin because he had formed himself on a denial of Dublin's values. He is the egocentric rebel become an ultimate. There is no question whatever of his regeneration. 'Stephen no longer interests me to the same extent [as Bloom],' said Joyce to Frank Budgen one day. 'He has a shape that can't be changed.'[5] His shape is that of aesthete. The Stephen of the first chapter of *Ulysses* who 'walks wearily', constantly 'leans' on everything in sight, invariably sits down before he has gone three paces, speaks 'gloomily', 'quietly', 'with bitterness', and 'coldly', and 'suffers' his handkerchief to be pulled from his pocket by the exuberant Mulligan, is precisely the priggish, humourless Stephen of the last chapter of the Portrait who cannot remember what day of the week it is (192), sentimentalises like Charles Lamb over the 'human pages' of a second-hand Latin book (190), conducts the inhumanly pedantic dialogue with Cranly on mother-love (263), writes Frenchified verses in bed in an erotic swoon, and is epiphanised at full length, like Shem the Penman beneath the bedclothes (F176), shrinking from the 'common noises' of daylight:

> Shrinking from that life he turned towards the wall, making a cowl [!] of the blanket and staring at the great overblown scarlet flowers of the tattered wall-paper. He tried to warm his perishing joy in their scarlet glow, imaging a roseway from where he lay upwards to heaven all strewn with scarlet flowers. Weary! Weary! He too was weary of ardent ways. (240/241)

This new primrose path is a private Jacob's ladder let down to his bed now that he is too weary to do anything but go to heaven.

To make epic and drama emerge naturally from the intrinsic stresses and distortions of the lyric material meant completely new lyric techniques for a constatation exact beyond irony. The *Portrait* concentrates on stating themes, arranging apparently transparent words into configurations of the utmost symbolic density. Here is the director proposing that Stephen enter the priesthood:

> The director stood in the embrasure of the window, his back to the light, leaning an elbow on the brown crossblind, and, as he spoke and smiled, slowly dangling and looping the cord of the other blind, Stephen stood before him, following for a moment with his eyes the waning of the long summer daylight above the roofs or the

slow deft movements of the priestly fingers. The priest's face was in total shadow, but the waning daylight from behind him touched the deeply grooved temples and the curves of the skull. (166).

The looped cord, the shadow, the skull, none of these is accidental. The 'waning daylight', twice emphasised, conveys that denial of nature which the priest's office represented for Stephen; 'his back to the light' co-operates toward a similar effect. So 'crossblind': 'blind to the cross';[6] 'blinded by the cross'. 'The curves of the skull' introduces another death-image; the 'deathbone' from Lévy-Bruhl's Australia, pointed by Shaun in *Finnegans Wake*, (F193), is the dramatic version of an identical symbol. But the central image, the epiphany of the interview, is contained in the movement of the priest's fingers: 'slowly dangling and looping the cord of the other blind'. That is to say, coolly proffering a noose. This is the lyric mode of Ulysses' epical hangman, 'The lord of things as they are whom the most Roman of Catholics call dio boia, hangman god', (*U*201).

THE CONTRAPUNTAL OPENING

According to the practice inaugurated by Joyce when he rewrote 'The Sisters' in 1906, the *Portrait*, like the two books to follow, opens amid elaborate counterpoint. The first two pages, terminating in a row of asterisks, enact the entire action in microcosm. An Aristotelian catalogue of sense, faculties, and mental activities is played against the unfolding of the infant conscience.

Once upon a time and a very good time it was there was a moocow coming down along the road and this moocow that was down along the road met a nicens little boy named baby tuckoo. . . .

His father told him that story: his father looked at him through a glass: he had a hairy face.

He was baby tuckoo. The moocow came down along the road where Betty Byrne lived: she sold lemon platt.

> *O, the wild rose blossoms*
> *On the little green place.*
> *He sang that song. That was his song.*
>
> *O, the green wothe botheth.*

When you wet the bed, first it is warm then it gets cold. His mother put on the oilsheet. That had the queer smell.

This evocation of holes in oblivion is conducted in the mode of each of the five senses in turn; hearing (the story of the moocow), sight (his father's face), taste (lemon platt), touch (warm and cold), smell (the oil-sheet). The audible soothes: the visible disturbs. Throughout Joyce's work, the senses are symbolically disposed. Smell is the means of discriminating empirical realities ('His mother had a nicer smell than his father,' is the next sentence), sight corresponds to the phantasms of oppression, hearing to the imaginative life. Touch and taste together are the modes of sex. Hearing, here, comes first, via a piece of imaginative literature. But as we can see from the vantage-point of *Finnegans Wake*, the whole book is about the encounter of baby tuckoo with the moocow: the Gripes with the mookse.[7] The father with the hairy face is the first Mookse-avatar, the Freudian infantile analogue of God the Father.

In the *Wake*

Derzherr, live wire, fired Benjermine Funkling outa th'Empyre, sin right hand son. (*F*289).

Der Erzherr (arch-lord), here a Teutonic Junker, is the God who visited his wrath on Lucifer; the hairy attribute comes through via the music-hall refrain, 'There's hair, like wire, coming out of the Empire'.

Dawning consciousness of his own identity ('He was baby tuckoo') leads to artistic performance ('He sang that song. That was his song.') This is hugely expanded in chapter IV:

Now, as never before, his strange name seemed to him a prophecy ... of the end he had been born to serve and had been following through the mists of childhood and boyhood, a symbol of the artist forging anew in his workshop out of the sluggish matter of the earth a new soaring impalpable imperishable being. (183).

By changing the red rose to a green and dislocating the spelling, he makes the song his own ('But you could not have a green rose. But perhaps somewhere in the world you could.' (9))

His mother had a nicer smell than his father. She played on the piano the sailor's hornpipe for him to dance. He danced:

> *Tralala lala,*
> *Tralala tralaladdy,*
> *Tralala lala,*
> *Tralala lala.*

Between this innocence and its Rimbaudian recapture through the purgation of the Wake there is to intervene the hallucination in Circe's sty:

THE MOTHER
(With the subtle smile of death's madness.) I was once the beautiful May Goulding. I am dead ...

STEPHEN
(Eagerly.) Tell me the word, mother, if you know it now. The word known to all men ...

THE MOTHER
(With smouldering eyes.) Repent! O, the fire of hell! (*U*547).

This is foreshadowed as the overture to the *Portrait* closes:

He hid under the table. His mother said:

– O, Stephen will apologise.

Dante said:

– O, if not, the eagles will come and pull out his eyes. –

> *Pull out his eyes,*
> *Apologise,*
> *Apologise,*
> *Pull out his eyes.*
> *Apologise,*
> *Pull out his eyes,*
> *Pull out his eyes,*
> *Apologise.*

The eagles, eagles of Rome, are emissaries of the God with the hairy face: the punisher. They evoke Prometheus and gnawing guilt: againbite. So the overture ends with Stephen hiding under the table awaiting the eagles. He is hiding under something most of the time: bedclothes, 'the enigma of a manner', an indurated rhetoric, or some other carapace of his private world.

THEME WORDS

It is through their names that things have power over Stephen.

– The language in which we are speaking is his before it is mine. How different are the words home, Christ, ale, master, on his lips and on mine! I cannot speak or write these words without unrest of spirit. His language, so familiar and so foreign, will always be for me an acquired speech. I have not made or accepted its words. My voice holds them at bay. My soul frets in the shadow of his language. (205).

Not only is the Dean's English a conqueror's tongue; since the loss of Adam's words which perfectly mirrored things, all language has conquered the mind and imposed its own order, askew from the order of creation. Words, like the physical world, are imposed on Stephen from without, and it is in their canted mirrors that he glimpses a physical and moral world already dyed the colour of his own mind since absorbed, with language, into his personality.

Words which he did not understand he said over and over to himself till he had learnt them by heart; and through them he had glimpses of the real world about him. (74).

Language is a Trojan horse by which the universe gets into the mind. The first sentence in the book isn't something Stephen sees but a story he is told, and the overture climaxes in an insistent brainless rhyme, its jingle corrosively fascinating to the will. It has power to terrify a child who knows nothing of eagles, or of Prometheus, or of how his own grown-up failure to apologise will blend with gathering blindness.

It typifies the peculiar achievement of the *Portrait* that Joyce can cause patterns of words to make up the very moral texture of Stephen's mind:

Suck was a queer word. The fellow called Simon Moonan that name because Simon Moonan used to tie the prefect's false sleeves behind his back and the prefect used to let on to be angry. But the sound was ugly. Once he had washed his hands in the lavatory of the Wicklow hotel and his father pulled the stopper up by the chain after and the dirty water went down through the hole in the basin. And when it had all gone down slowly the hole in the basin had made a sound like that: suck. Only louder.

To remember that and the white look of the lavatory made him feel cold and then hot. There were two cocks that you turned and the water came out: cold and hot. He felt cold and then a little hot: and he could see the names printed on the cocks. That was a very queer thing. (8).

'Suck' joins two contexts in Stephen's mind: a playful sinner toying with his indulgent superior, and the disappearance of dirty water. The force of the conjunction is felt only after Stephen has lost his sense of the reality of the forgiveness of sins in the confessional. The habitually orthodox penitent tangles with a God who pretends to be angry; after a reconciliation the process is repeated. And the mark of that kind of play is disgraceful servility. Each time the sin disappears, the sinner is mocked by an impersonal voice out of nature: 'Suck!'

This attitude to unreal good and evil furnishes a context for the next conjunction: whiteness and coldness. Stephen finds himself, like Simon Moonan,[8] engaged in the rhythm of obedience to irrational authority, bending his mind to a meaningless act, the arithmetic contest. He is being obediently 'good'. And the appropriate colour is adduced: 'He thought his face must be white because it felt so cool.'

The pallor of lunar obedient goodness is next associated with damp repulsiveness: the limpness of a wet blanket and of a servant's apron:

> He sat looking at the two prints of butter on his plate but could not eat the damp bread. The table-cloth was damp and limp. But he drank off the hot weak tea which the clumsy scullion, girt with a white apron, poured into his cup. He wondered whether the scullion's apron was damp too or whether all white things were cold and damp. (9).

Throughout the first chapter an intrinsic linkage, white-cold-damp-obedient, insinuates itself repeatedly. Stephen after saying his prayers, 'his shoulders shaking', 'so that he might not go to hell when he died', curled himself together under the cold white sheets, shaking and trembling. But he would not go to hell when he died, and the shaking would stop.' (16). The sea, mysterious as the terrible power of God, 'was cold day and night, but it was colder at night', (17); we are reminded of Anna Livia's gesture of submission: 'my cold father, my cold mad father, my cold mad fiery father', (F628). 'There was a cold night smell in the chapel. But it was a holy smell'. Stephen is puzzled by the phrase in the Litany of the Blessed Virgin: Tower of Ivory. 'How could a woman be a tower of ivory or a house of gold?' He ponders until the revelation comes:

> Eileen had long white hands. One evening when playing tag she had put her hands over his eyes: long and white and thin and cold and soft. That was ivory: a cold white thing. That was the meaning of Tower of Ivory. (43).

This instant of insight depends on a sudden reshuffling of associations, a sudden conviction that the Mother of God, and the symbols appropriate to her, belong with the cold, the white, and the unpleasant in a blindfold morality of obedience. Contemplation focused on language is repaid:

Tower of Ivory. House of Gold. By thinking of things you could understand them. (43).

The white-damp-obedient association reappears when Stephen is about to make his confession after the celebrated retreat; its patterns provide the language in which he thinks. Sin has been associated with fire, while the prayers of the penitents are epiphanised as 'soft whispering cloudlets, soft whispering vapour, whispering and vanishing.' (P164/163). And having been absolved:

White puddings and eggs and sausages and cups of tea. How simple and beautiful was life after all! And life lay all before him ...

The boys were all there, kneeling in their places. He knelt among them, happy and shy. The altar was heaped with fragrant masses of white flowers: and in the morning light the pale flames of the candles among the white flowers were clear and silent as his own soul. (158).

We cannot read *Finnegans Wake* until we have realised the significance of the way the mind of Stephen Dedalus is bound in by language. He is not only an artist: he is a Dubliner.

THE PORTRAIT AS LYRIC

The 'instant of emotion', (232), of which the 300-page lyric is the 'simplest verbal vesture' is the exalted instant, emerging at the end of the book, of freedom, of vocation, of Stephen's destiny, winging his way above the waters at the side of the hawklike man: the instant of promise on which the crushing ironies of *Ulysses* are to fall. The epic of the sea of matter is preceded by the lyric image of a growing dream: a dream that like Richard Rowan's in *Exiles* disregards the fall of man; a dream nourished by a sensitive youth of flying above the sea into an uncreated heaven:

The spell of arms and voices: the white arms of roads, their promise of close embraces and the black arms of tall ships that stand against the moon, their tale of distant nations. They are held out to say: We are alone – come. And the voices say with them: We are your kinsmen. And the air is thick with their company as they call to me, their kinsmen, making ready to go, shaking the wings of their exultant and terrible youth. (275).

The emotional quality of this is continuous with that of the Count of Monte Cristo, that fantasy of the exile returned for vengeance (the plot of the *Odyssey*) which kindled so many of Stephen's boyhood dreams:

The figure of that dark avenger stood forth in his mind for whatever he had heard or divined in childhood of the strange and terrible. At night he built up on the parlour table an image of the wonderful island cave out of transfers and paper flowers and strips of the silver and golden paper in which chocolate is wrapped. When he had broken up this scenery, weary of its tinsel, there would come to his mind the bright picture of Marseilles, of sunny trellises and of Mercedes. (64/65).

The prose surrounding Stephen's flight is empurpled with transfers and paper flowers too. It is not immature prose, as we might suppose by comparison with *Ulysses*. The prose of 'The Dead' is mature prose, and 'The Dead' was written in 1908. Rather, it is a meticulous pastiche of immaturity. Joyce has his eye constantly on the epic sequel.

He wanted to meet in the real world the unsubstantial image which his soul so constantly beheld. He did not know where to seek it or how, but a premonition which led him on told him that this image would, without any overt act of his, encounter him. They would meet quietly as if they had known each other and had made their tryst, perhaps at one of the gates or in some more secret place. They would be alone, surrounded by darkness and silence: and in that moment of supreme tenderness he would be transfigured. (67).

As the vaginal imagery of gates, secret places, and darkness implies, this is the dream that reaches temporary fulfilment in the plunge into profane love, (107/8). But the ultimate 'secret place' is to be Mabbot Street, outside Bella Cohen's brothel; the unsubstantial image of his quest, that of Leopold Bloom, advertisement canvasser – Monte Cristo, returned avenger, Ulysses; and the transfiguration, into the phantasmal dead son of a sentimental Jew:

Against the dark wall a figure appears slowly, a fair boy of eleven, a changeling, kidnapped, dressed in an Eton suit with glass shoes and a little bronze helmet, holding a book in his hand. He reads from right to left inaudibly, smiling, kissing the page. (U574).

That Dedalus the artificer did violence to nature is the point of the epigraph from Ovid, *Et ignotas dimittit in artes*; the Icarian fall is inevitable.

In tedious exile now too long detain'd
Dedalus languish'd for his native land.
The sea foreclos'd his flight; yet thus he said,
Though earth and water in subjection laid,
O cruel Minos, thy dominion be,
We'll go through air; for sure the air is free.
Then to new arts his cunning thought applies,
And to improve the work of nature tries.

Stephen does not, as the careless reader may suppose, become an artist by rejecting church and country. Stephen does not become an artist at all. Country, church, and mission are an inextricable unity, and in rejecting the two that seem to hamper him, he rejects also the one on which he has set his heart. Improving the work of nature is his obvious ambition ('But you could not have a green rose. But perhaps somewhere in the world you could'), and it logically follows from the aesthetic he expounds to Lynch. It is a neo-platonic aesthetic; the crucial principle of epiphanisation has been withdrawn. He imagines that 'the loveliness that has not yet come into the world', (273), is to be found in his own soul. The earth is gross, and what it brings forth is cowdung; sound and shape and colour are 'the prison gates of our soul'; and beauty is something mysteriously gestated within. The genuine artist reads signatures, the fake artist forges them, a process adumbrated in the obsession of Shem the Penman (from Jim the Penman, a forgotten drama about a forger) with 'Macfearsome's Ossean', the most famous of literary forgeries, studying 'how cutely to copy all their various styles of signature so as one day to utter an epical forged cheque on the public for his own private profit.' (F181).

One can sense all this in the first four chapters of the *Portrait*, and *Ulysses* is unequivocal:

Fabulous artificer, the hawklike man. You flew. Whereto? Newhaven-Dieppe, steerage passenger. Paris and back. (U199).

The Stephen of the end of the fourth chapter, however, is still unstable; he had to be brought into a final balance, and shown at some length as a being whose development was virtually ended.

59

Unfortunately, the last chapter makes the book a peculiarly difficult one for the reader to focus, because Joyce had to close it on a suspended chord. As a lyric, it is finished in its own terms; but the themes of the last forty pages, though they give the illusion of focusing, don't really focus until we have read well into Ulysses. The final chapter, which is respect to the juggernaut of Ulysses must be a vulnerable flank, in respect to what has gone before must be a conclusion. This problem Joyce didn't wholly solve; there remains a moral ambiguity (how seriously are we to take Stephen?) which makes the last forty pages painful reading.

Not that Stephen would stand indefinitely if Ulysses didn't topple him over; his equilibrium in Chapter V, though good enough to give him a sense of unusual integrity in University College, is precarious unless he can manage, in the manner of so many permanent undergraduates, to prolong the college context for the rest of his life. Each of the preceding chapters, in fact, works towards an equilibrium which is dashed when in the next chapter Stephen's world becomes larger and the frame of reference more complex. The terms of equilibrium are always stated with disquieting accuracy; at the end of Chapter I we find:

> He was not alone. He was happy and free; But he would not be anyway proud with Father Dolan. He would be very quiet and obedient: and he wished that he could do something kind for him to show him that he was not proud. (60/61).

And at the end of Chapter III:

> He sat by the fire in the kitchen, not daring to speak for happiness. Till that moment he had not known how beautiful and peaceful life could be. The green square of paper pinned round the lamp cast down a tender shade. On the dresser was a plate of sausages and white pudding and on the shelf there were eggs. They would be for the breakfast in the morning after the communion in the college chapel. White pudding and eggs and sausages and cups of tea. How simple and beautiful was life after all! And life lay all before him. (158/9).

Not 'irony' but simply the truth: the good life conceived in terms of white pudding and sausages is unstable enough to need no underlining.

The even-numbered chapters make a sequence of different sort. The ending of IV, Stephen's panting submission to an artistic vocation:

Evening had fallen when he woke and the sand and arid grasses of his bed glowed no longer. He rose slowly and, recalling the rapture of his sleep, sighed at its joy.... (187),

– hasn't quite the finality often read into it when the explicit parallel with the ending of II is perceived:

... He closed his eyes, surrendering himself to her, body and mind, conscious of nothing in the world but the dark pressure of her softly parting lips. They pressed upon his brain as upon his lips as though they were the vehicle of a vague speech; and between them he felt an unknown and timid pressure, darker than the swoon of sin, softer than sound or odour. (108).

When we link these passages with the fact that the one piece of literary composition Stephen actually achieves in the book comes out of a wet dream ('Toward dawn he awoke. O what sweet music! His soul was all dewy wet', 254) we are in a position to see that the concluding 'Welcome, O life!' has an air of finality and balance only because the diary-form of the last seven pages disarms us with an illusion of auctorial impartiality.

CONTROLLING IMAGES: CLONGOWES AND BELVEDERE

Ego vs. authority is the theme of the three odd-numbered chapters, Dublin vs. the dream that of the two even-numbered ones. The generic Joyce plot, the encounter with the alter ego, is consummated when Stephen at the end of the book identifies himself with the sanctified Stephen who was stoned by the Jews after reporting a vision (Acts VII, 56) and claims sonship with the classical Daedalus who evaded the ruler of land and sea by turning his soul to obscure arts. The episodes are built about adumbrations of this encounter: with Father Conmee, with Monte Cristo, with the whores, with the broad-shouldered moustached student who cut the word 'Foetus' in a desk, with the weary mild confessor, with the bird-girl. Through this repeated plot intertwine controlling emotions and controlling images that mount in complexity as the book proceeds.

In Chapter I the controlling emotion is fear, and the dominant image Father Dolan and his pandybat; this, associated with the hangman-god and the priestly denial of senses, was to become one of Joyce's standard images for Irish clericalism – hence the jack-in-the-box appearance of Father Dolan in Circe's nightmare imbroglio, his pandybat cracking twice like thunder, (U531). Stephen's comment, in the mode of Blake's repudiation of the God who slaughtered Jesus, emphasises the inclusiveness of the image: 'I never could read His handwriting except His criminal thumbprint on the haddock.'

Chapter II opens with a triple image of Dublin's prepossessions: music, sport, religion. The first is exhibited via Uncle Charles singing sentimental ballads in the outhouse; the second via Stephen's ritual run around the park under the eye of a superannuated trainer, which his uncle enjoins on him as the whole duty of a Dubliner; the third via the clumsy piety of Uncle Charles, kneeling on a red handkerchief and reading above his breath 'from a thumb-blackened prayerbook wherein catchwords were printed at the foot of every page.' (64). This trinity of themes is unwound and entwined throughout the chapter, like a net woven round Stephen; it underlies the central incident, the Whitsuntide play in the Belvedere chapel (religion), which opens with a display by the dumb-bell team (sport) preluded by sentimental waltzes from the soldier's band (music).

While he is waiting to play his part, Stephen is taunted by fellow-students, who rally him on a fancied love-affair and smiting his calf with a cane bid him recite the Confiteor. His mind goes back to an analogous incident, when a similar punishment had been visited on his refusal to 'admit that Byron was good'. The further analogy with Father Dolan is obvious; love, art, and personal independence are thus united in an ideogram of the prepossessions Stephen is determined to cultivate in the teeth of persecution.

The dream-world Stephen nourishes within himself is played against manifestations of music, sport, and religion throughout the chapter. The constant ironic clash of Dublin vs. the Dream animates Chapter II, as the clash of the ego vs. authority did Chapter I. All these themes come to focus during Stephen's visit with his father to Cork. The dream of rebellion he has silently cultivated is externalised by the discovery of the word *Foetus* carved in a desk by a forgotten medical student:

It shocked him to find in the outer world a trace of what he had deemed till then a brutish and individual malady of his own mind. His monstrous reveries came thronging into his memory. They too had sprung up before him, suddenly and furiously, out of mere words... (95).

The possibility of shame gaining the upper hand is dashed, however, by the sudden banal intrusion of his father's conversation ('When you kick out for yourself, Stephen, as I daresay you will one of these days, remember, whatever you do, to mix with gentlemen ... '). Against the standards of Dublin his monstrous reveries acquire a Satanic glamour, and the trauma is slowly diverted into a resolution to rebel. After his father has expressed a resolve to 'leave him to his Maker' (religion), and offered to 'sing a tenor song against him' (music) or 'vault a fivebarred gate against him' (sport), Stephen muses, watching his father and two cronies drinking to the memory of their past:

> An abyss of fortune or of temperament sundered him from them. His mind seemed older than theirs: it shone coldly on their strifes and happiness and regrets like a moon upon a younger earth. No life or youth stirred in him as it had stirred in them. He had known neither the pleasure of companionship with others now the vigour of rude male health nor filial piety. Nothing stirred within his soul but a cold and cruel and loveless lust. (101/2).

After one final effort to compromise with Dublin on Dublin's terms has collapsed into futility ('The pot of pink enamel paint gave out and the wainscot of his bedroom remained with its unfinished and illplastered coat', (104)), he fiercely cultivates his rebellious thoughts, and moving by day and night 'among distorted images of the outer world', (105), plunges at last into the arms of whores. 'The holy encounter he had then imagined at which weakness and timidity and inexperience were to fall from him' (112/113), finally arrives in inversion of Father Dolan's and Uncle Charles' religion: his descent into night-town is accompanied by lurid evocations of a Black Mass (Cf. *Ulysses*, 565):

> The yellow gasflames arose before his troubled vision against the vapoury sky, burning as if before an altar. Before the doors and in the lighted halls groups were gathered arrayed as for some rite. He was in another world: he had awakened from a slumber of centuries. (107).

CONTROLLING IMAGES: SIN AND REPENTANCE

Each chapter in the *Portrait* gathers up the thematic material of the preceding ones and entwines with them a dominant theme of its own. In Chapter III the fear-pandybat motif is present in Father Arnall's crudely materialistic hell, of which even the thickness of the walls is specified; and the Dublin-vs.-dream motif has ironic inflections in Stephen's terror-stricken broodings, when the dream has been twisted into a dream of holiness, and even Dublin appears transfigured:

> How beautiful must be a soul in the state of grace when God looked upon it with love!

> Frowsy girls sat along the curbstones before their baskets. Their dank hair trailed over their brows. They were not beautiful to see as they crouched in the mire. But their souls were seen by God; and if their souls were in a state of grace they were radiant to see; and God loved them, seeing them. (152).

A rapprochement in these terms between the outer world and Stephen's desires is too inadequate to need commentary; and it makes vivid as nothing else could the hopeless inversion of his attempted self-sufficiency. It underlines, in yet another way, his persistent sin: and the dominant theme of Chapter III is Sin. A fugue-like opening plays upon the Seven Deadly Sins in turn; gluttony is in the first paragraph ('Stuff it into you, his belly counselled him'), followed by lust, then sloth ('A cold lucid indifference reigned in his soul'), pride ('His pride in his own sin, his loveless awe of God, told him that his offence was too grievous to be atoned for'), anger ('The blundering answer stirred the embers of his contempt for his fellows'); finally, a recapitulation fixes each term of the mortal catalogue in a phrase, enumerating how 'from the evil seed of lust all the other deadly sins had sprung forth', (107).

Priest and punisher inhabit Stephen himself as well as Dublin: when he is deepest in sin he is most thoroughly a theologian. A paragraph of gloomy introspection is juxtaposed with a list of theological questions that puzzle Stephen's mind as he awaits the preacher:

> ... Is baptism with mineral water valid? How comes it that while the first beatitude promises the kingdom of heaven to the poor of heart, the second beatitude also to the meek that they shall possess the land? ... If the wine change into vinegar and the host crumble into corruption after they have been consecrated, is Jesus Christ still present under their species as God and as man?
>
> – Here he is! Here he is!
>
> A boy from his post at the window had seen the rector come from the house. All the catechisms were opened and all heads bent upon them silently. (114).

Wine changed into vinegar and the host crumbled into corruption fits exactly the Irish clergy of 'a church which was the scullery-maid of Chistendom'. The excited 'Here he is! Here he is!' following hard on the mention of Jesus Christ and signalling nothing more portentous than the rector makes the point as dramatically as anything in the book, and the clinching sentence, with the students suddenly bending over their catechisms, places the rector as the vehicle of pandybat morality.

The last of the theological questions is the telling question. Stephen never expresses doubt of the existence of God nor of the essential validity of the priestly office – his *Non serviam* is not a *non credo*, and he talks of a 'malevolent reality' behind these appearances – but the wine and the bread that were offered for his veneration were changed into vinegar and crumbled into corruption. And it was the knowledge of that underlying validity clashing with his refusal to do homage to vinegar and rot that evoked his ambivalent poise of egocentric despair. The hell of Father Arnall's sermon, so emotionally overwhelming, so picayune beside the horrors that Stephen's imagination can generate, had no more ontological content for Stephen than had 'an eternity of bliss in the company of the dean of studies'. (261)

The conflict of this central chapter is again between the phantasmal and the real. What is real—psychologically real, because realised – is Stephen's anguish and remorse, and its context in the life of the flesh. What is phantasmal is the 'heaven' of the Church and the 'good life' of the priest. It is only fear that makes him clutch after the latter at all; his reaching out after orthodox salvation is, as we have come to expect, presented in terms that judge it:

> The wind blew over him and passed on to the myriads and myriads of other souls, on whom God's favour shone now more and now less, stars now brighter and now dimmer, sustained and failing. And the glimmering souls passed away, sustained and failing, merged in a moving breath. One soul was lost; a tiny soul; his. It flickered once and went out, forgotten, lost. The end: black cold void waste.
>
> Consciousness of place came ebbing back to him slowly over a vast tract of time unlit, unfelt, unlived. The squalid scene composed itself around him; the common accents, the burning gasjets in the shops, odours of fish and spirits and wet sawdust, moving men and women. An old woman was about to cross the street, an oilcan in her hand. He bent down and asked her was there a chapel near. (152).

That wan waste world of flickering stars is the best Stephen has been able to do towards an imaginative grasp of the communion of Saints sustained by God; 'unlit, unfelt, unlived' explains succinctly why it had so little hold on him, once fear had relaxed. Equally pertinent is the vision of human temporal occupations the sermon evokes:

What did it profit to gain the whole world if he lost his soul? At last he had understood: and human life lay around him, a plain of peace whereon antlike men laboured in brotherhood, their dead sleeping under quiet mounds. (135).

To maintain the life of grace in the midst of nature, sustained by so cramped a vision of the life of nature, would mean maintaining an intolerable tension. Stephen's unrelenting philosophic bias, his determination to understand what he is about, precludes his adopting the double standard of the *Dubliners*; to live both the life of nature and the life of grace he must enjoy an imaginative grasp of their relationship which stunts neither. 'No one doth well against his will,' writes Saint Augustine, 'even though what he doth, be well;' and Stephen's will is firmly harnessed to his understanding. And there is no one in Dublin to help him achieve understanding. Father Arnall's sermon precludes rather than secures a desirable outcome, for it follows the modes of pandybat morality and Dublin materiality. Its only possible effect on Stephen is to lash his dormant conscience into a frenzy. The description of Hell as 'a strait and dark and foul smelling prison, an abode of demons and lost souls, filled with fire and smoke', with walls four thousand miles thick, its damned packed in so tightly that 'they are not even able to remove from the eye the worm that gnaws it', is childishly grotesque beneath its sweeping eloquence; and the hair-splitting catalogues of pains – pain of loss, pain of conscience (divided into three heads), pain of extension, pain of intensity, pain of eternity – is cast in a brainlessly analytic mode that effectively prevents any corresponding Heaven from possessing any reality at all.

Stephen's unstable pact with the Church, and its dissolution, follows the pattern of composition and dissipation established by his other dreams: the dream for example of the tryst with 'Mercedes', which found ironic reality among harlots. It parallels exactly his earlier attempt to 'build a breakwater of order and elegance against the sordid tide of life without him' (104), whose failure, with the exhaustion of his money, was epiphanised in the running-dry of a pot of pink enamel paint. His regimen at that time:

He bought presents for everyone, overhauled his rooms, wrote out resolutions, marshalled his books up and down their shelves, pored over all kinds of price lists ...

is mirrored by his searching after spiritual improvement:

His daily life was laid out in devotional areas. By means of ejaculations and prayers he stored up ungrudgingly for the souls in purgatory centuries of days and quarantines and years... . He offered up each of his three daily chaplets that his soul might grow strong in each of the three theological virtues... . On each of the seven days of the week he further prayed that one of the seven gifts of the Holy Ghost might descend upon his soul. (159).

The 'loan bank' he had opened for the family, out of which he had pressed loans on willing borrowers 'that he might have the pleasure of making out receipts and reckoning the interests on sums lent' finds its counterpart in the benefits he stored up for souls in purgatory that he might enjoy the spiritual triumph of 'achieving with ease so many fabulous ages of canonical penances'. Both projects are parodies on the doctrine of economy of grace; both are attempts, corrupted by motivating self-interest, to make peace with Dublin on Dublin's own terms; and both are short-lived.

As this precise analogical structure suggests, the action of each of the five chapters is really the same action. Each chapter closes with a synthesis of triumph which the next destroys. The triumph of the appeal to Father Conmee from lower authority, of the appeal to the harlots from Dublin, of the appeal to the Church from sin, of the appeal to art from the priesthood (the bird-girl instead of the Virgin) is always the same triumph raised to a more comprehensive level. It is an attempt to find new parents; new fathers in the odd chapters, new objects of love in the even. The last version of Father Conmee is the 'priest of the eternal imagination'; the last version of Mercedes is the 'lure of the fallen seraphim'. But the last version of the mother who said, 'O, Stephen will apologise' is the mother who prays on the last page 'that I may learn in my own life and away from home and friends what the heart is and what it feels'. The mother remains.

THE DOUBLE FEMALE

As in *Dubliners* and *Exiles*, the female role in the *Portrait* is less to arouse than to elucidate masculine desires. Hence the complex function in the book of physical love: the physical is the analogue of the spiritual, as St. Augustine insisted in his Confessions (which, with Ibsen's, is the chief archetype of Joyce's book). The poles between which this affection moves are those of St. Augustine and St. John: the Whore of Babylon and the Bride of Christ. The relation between the two is far from simple, and Stephen moves in a constant tension between them.

His desire, figured in the visions of Monte Cristo's Mercedes, 'to meet in the real world the unsubstantial image which his soul so constantly beheld' draws him toward the prostitute ('In her arms he felt that he had suddenly become strong and fearless and sure of himself', (107)) and simultaneously towards the vaguely spiritual satisfaction represented with equal vagueness by the wraithlike E–C–, to whom he twice writes verses. The Emma Clery of *Stephen Hero*, with her loud forced manners and her body compact of pleasure, (S66/56), was refined into a wraith with a pair of initials to parallel an intangible Church. She is continually assimilated to the image of the Blessed Virgin and of the heavenly Bride. The torture she costs him is the torture his apostasy costs him. His flirtation with her is his flirtation with Christ. His profane villanelle draws its imagery from religion – the incense, the eucharistic hymn, the chalice – and her heart, following Dante's image, is a rose, and in her praise 'the earth was like swinging swaying censer, a ball of incense', (236).

The woman is the Church. His vision of greeting Mercedes with 'a sadly proud gesture of refusal':

– Madam, I never eat muscatel grapes. (65).

is fulfilled when he refuses his Easter communion. Emma's eyes, in their one explicit encounter, speak to him from beneath a cowl (72). 'The glories of Mary held his soul captive' (112), and a temporary reconciliation of his lust and his spiritual thirst is achieved as he reads the Lesson out of the Song of Solomon. In the midst of his repentance she functions as imagined mediator: 'The image of Emma appeared before him,' and, repenting, 'he imagined that he stood near Emma in a wide land, and, humbly and in tears, bent and kissed the elbow of her sleeve', (124/5). Like Dante's Beatrice, she manifests in his earthly experience the Church Triumphant of his spiritual dream. And when he rejects her because she seems to be flirting with Father Moran, his anger is couched in the anti-clerical terms of his apostasy: 'He had done well to leave her to flirt with her priest, to toy with a church which was the scullery-maid of Christendom', (239).

That Kathleen ni Houlihan can flirt with priests is the unforgivable sin underlying Stephen's rejection of Ireland. But he makes a clear distinction between the stupid clericalism which makes intellectual and communal life impossible, and his long-nourished vision of an artist's Church Triumphant upon earth. He rejects the actual for daring to fall short of his vision.

THE FINAL BALANCE

The climax of the book is of course Stephen's ecstatic discovery of his vocation at the end of Chapter IV. The prose rises in nervous excitement to beat again and again the tambours of a fin-de-siècle ecstasy:

> His heart trembled; his breath came faster and a wild spirit passed over his limbs as though he were soaring sunward. His heart trembled in an ecstasy of fear and his soul was in flight. His soul was soaring in an air beyond the world and the body he knew was purified in a breath and delivered of incertitude and made radiant and commingled with the element of the spirit. An ecstasy of flight made radiant his eyes and wild his breath and tremulous and wild and radiant his windswept limbs.
>
> – One! Two! ... Look out! –
>
> – O, Cripes, I'm drowned! – (183).

The interjecting voices of course are those of bathers, but their ironic appropriateness to Stephen's Icarian 'soaring sunward' is not meant to escape us: divers have their own 'ecstasy of flight', and Icarus was 'drowned'. The imagery of Stephen's ecstasy is fetched from many sources; we recognise Shelley's skylark, Icarus, the glorified body of the Resurrection (cf. 'His soul had arisen from the grave of boyhood, spurning her graveclothes', (184)) and a tremulousness from which it is difficult to dissociate adolescent sexual dreams (which the Freudians tell us are frequently dreams of flying). The entire eight-page passage is cunningly organised with great variety of rhetoric and incident; but we cannot help noticing the limits set on vocabulary and figures in thought. The empurpled triteness of such a cadence as 'radiant his eyes and wild his breath and tremulous and wild and radiant his windswept face' is enforced by recurrence: 'But her long fair hair was girlish: and girlish, and touched with the wonder of mortal beauty, her face', (186). 'Ecstasy' is the keyword, indeed. This riot of feelings corresponds to no vocation definable in mature terms; the paragraphs come to rest on images of irresponsible motion:

> He turned away from her suddenly and set off across the strand. His cheeks were aflame; his body was aglow; his limbs were trembling. On and on and on and on he strode, far out over the sands, singing wildly to the sea, crying to greet the advent of the life that had cried to him. (186).

What 'life' connotes it skills not to ask; the word recurs and recurs. So does the motion onward and onward and onward:

> A wild angel had appeared to him, the angel of mortal youth and

beauty, an envoy from the fair courts of life, to throw open before him in an instant of ecstasy the gates of all the ways of error and glory. On and on and on and on! (186).

It may be well to recall Joyce's account of the romantic temper:

… an insecure, unsatisfied, impatient temper which sees no fit abode here for its ideals and chooses therefore to behold them under insensible figures. As a result of this choice it comes to disregard certain limitations. Its figures are blown to wild adventures, lacking the gravity of solid bodies … (S78/66).

Joyce also called *Prometheus Unbound* 'the Schwärmerei of a young jew'.

And it is quite plain from the final chapter of the *Portrait* that we are not to accept the mode of Stephen's 'freedom' as the 'message' of the book. The 'priest of the eternal imagination' turns out to be indigestibly Byronic. Nothing is more obvious than his total lack of humour. The dark intensity of the first four chapters is moving enough, but our impulse on being confronted with the final edition of Stephen Dedalus is to laugh; and laugh at this moment we dare not; he is after all a victim being prepared for a sacrifice. His shape, as Joyce said, can no longer change. The art he has elected is not 'the slow elaborative patience of the art of satisfaction'. 'On and on and on and on' will be its inescapable mode. He does not see the girl who symbolises the full revelation; 'she seemed like one whom magic had changed into the likeness of a strange and beautiful seabird', (185), and he confusedly apprehends a sequence of downy and feathery incantations. What, in the last chapter, he does see he sees only to reject, in favour of an incantatory 'loveliness which has not yet come into the world', (273).

The only creative attitude to language exemplified in the book is that of Stephen's father:

– Is it Christy? he said. There's more cunning in one of those warts on his bald head than in a pack of jack foxes.

His vitality is established before the book is thirty pages under way. Stephen, however, isn't enchanted at any time by the proximity of such talk. He isn't, as a matter of fact, even interested in it. Without a backward glance, he exchanges this father for a myth. □

Although Kenner qualified his argument in later books and articles, his essay set the terms for the arguments of other critics. The question is that of Joyce's ironic distance from his protagonist, and since the narrative voice itself changes greatly in the course of *Portrait*, this is not easy to determine. In his critical edition of *Portrait* (1968), Chester G. Anderson summarises the debate and includes relevant essays by Wayne Booth and Robert Scholes. The Booth essay originally appeared in his *The Rhetoric of Fiction*, and contends that the degree of Joyce's irony – his 'authorial distance' – cannot be established with any certainty because Joyce at times clearly admires Stephen and at times clearly satirises him. As Booth points out, the problem is epitomised by Stephen's poem, the 'Villanelle of the Temptress': it is unclear to many readers whether we are to take the poem as a success or as a failure. For Booth the problem is that Joyce was never certain of his own attitude toward his protagonist – although when Stephen appears in *Ulysses* with his wings clipped, it seems likely that we are to assume the boy was self-deluded in his more grandiose moments. The problem, according to Booth, is a flaw in *A Portrait* itself. This argument is by no means settled, and echoes down to the present day in the debate over whether Stephen's misogyny is also Joyce's or is being ironically displayed by a Joyce sympathetic to feminism.

The Rhetoric of Fiction, from which the following extract is taken, is one of the primary pre-structuralist studies of narrative technique, and in its examination of the relation between authorial values, and point of view in the manipulation of the reader's sympathies it laid a stress on moral and emotional dimensions of fiction which much of the criticism of the time, devoted as it was to purity of form, irony and ambiguity, was inclined to neglect. As Booth says, 'no work, not even the shortest lyric, can be written in complete moral, intellectual and aesthetic neutrality'. As such he was unlikely to adopt Kenner's ironic line, and demanded to know just which side Joyce was on. Booth might appear somewhat crabbed in his refusal of double perspective, but the questions he asks of *A Portrait* are interesting and necessary ones. It is also pertinent that this and the two subsequent extracts in this chapter were written by non-Joyceans who were perhaps in a better position to ask difficult questions of the work and how it related to other literature and our sense of literature generally. Booth asserts that the skeleton keys and guides are of little help critically, and as such reinforces a distinction between reading, or criticism, on the one hand, and explication on the other, which the narrative of this guide has been determined to point up.

■ ... Jane Austen's implicit apology for Emma said, in effect, 'Emma's vision is your vision; therefore forgive her'. But modern authors have learned how to provide this apology in much more insistent form. The deep plunges of modern inside views, the various streams-of-consciousness that attempt to give the reader an effect of living thought and sensation, are capable of blinding us to the possibility of our making judgements not shared by the narrator or reflector himself.

If a master puzzle maker had set out to give us the greatest possible difficulty, he could not have done more than has been done in some modern works in which this effect of deep involvement is combined with the implicit demand that we maintain our capacity for ironic judgement. The trouble with *Moll Flanders*, such a genius of confusion might be imagined as saying to himself, is that the obvious differences between the female heroine and the author provide too many clues. Let us then write a book that will look like the author's autobiography, using many details from his own life and opinions. But we cannot be satisfied with moral problems, which are after all much less subject to dispute than intellectual and aesthetic matters. Let us then call for the reader's precise judgement on a very elaborate set of opinions and actions in which the hero is sometimes right, sometimes slightly wrong, and sometimes absurdly astray. Just to make sure that things are not too obvious, let us finally bind the reader so tightly to the consciousness of the ambiguously misguided protagonist that nothing will interfere with his delight in inferring the precise though varying degrees of distance that operate from point to point throughout the book. We can be sure that some readers will take the book as strictly autobiographical; others will go sadly astray in overlooking ironies that are intended and in discovering ironies that are not there. But for the rare reader who can make his way through this jungle, the delight will be great indeed.

The giant whom we all must wrestle with in this regard is clearly Joyce. Except for occasional outbursts of bravado nobody has ever claimed that Joyce is clear. In all the skeleton keys and classroom guides there is open assumption that his later works, *Ulysses* and *Finnegans Wake*, cannot be read; they can only be studied. Joyce himself was always explicating his works, and it is clear that he saw nothing wrong with the fact that they could not be thought of as standing entirely on their own feet. The reader's problems are handled, if they are to be handled at all, by rhetoric provided outside the work.

But the difficulties with distance that are pertinent here cannot be removed by simple study. Obscure allusions can be looked up, patterns of imagery and theme can be traced; gradually over the years a good deal of lore has accumulated, and about some of it by now there is even a certain amount of agreement. But about the more fundamental matters the skeleton keys and guides are of little help, because unfortunately they do not agree, they do not agree at all. It is fine to know that in *Ulysses* Stephen stands in some way for Telemachus and Bloom for his wandering father, Ulysses. But it would also be useful to know whether the work is comic or pathetic or tragic, or, if it is a combination, where the elements fall. Can two readers be said to have read the same book if one thinks it ends affirmatively and the other sees the ending as pessimistic? It is really no explanation to say that Joyce has succeeded in imitating life so well that like life itself his books seem totally ambiguous, totally open to whatever interpretation the reader wants to place on them. Even William Empson, that perceptive and somewhat overly ingenious prophet of ambiguity, finds himself unable to be completely permissive toward conflicting interpretations. In a long, curious essay arguing that the basic movement of *Ulysses* is toward a favourable ending, with the Blooms and Stephen united, he admits that there are difficulties, and that they spring from the kind of book it is: it 'not only refuses to tell you the end of the story, it also refuses to tell you what the author thinks would have been a good end to the story'. And yet almost in the same breath he can write as if he thought previous critics somehow at fault for not having come to his inferences about the book. 'By the way, I have no patience with critics who say it is impossible ever to tell whether Joyce means a literary effect to be ironical or not; if they don't know this isn't funny, they ought to.'[9] Well, but why should they know? Who is to mediate between Empson and those he attacks, or between Lawrance Thompson, in his interpretation of the book as comedy, and those critics with whom he is 'decidedly at odds', Stuart Gilbert, Edmund Wilson, Harry Levin, David Daiches, and T. S. Eliot, each of whom assumes, he says, that 'Joyce's artistic mode is essentially a non-comic mode, or that comedy in *Ulysses* is an effect rather than a cause'?[10]

Can it possibly make no difference whether we laugh or do not laugh? Can we defend the book even as a realistic mixture, like life itself, unless we state with some precision what the ingredients are that have been mixed together?

Rather than pursue such general questions about Joyce's admittedly difficult later works, it will be more useful to look closely at that earlier work for which no skeleton key has been thought necessary, *A Portrait of The Artist as a Young Man* (1916). Everyone seems by now agreed that it is a masterpiece in the modern mode. Perhaps we can accept it as that – indeed accept it as an unquestionably great work from any viewpoint – and still feel free to ask a few irreverent questions.

The structure of this 'authorless' work is based on the growth of a sensitive boy to young manhood. The steps in his growth are obviously constructed with great care. Each of the first four sections ends a period of Stephen's life with what Joyce, in an earlier draft, calls an epiphany: a peculiar revelation of the inner reality of an experience, accompanied with great elation, as in a mystical religious experience. Each is followed by the opening of a new chapter on a very prosaic, even depressed level. Now here is clearly a careful structural preparation – for what? For a transformation, or for a merely cyclical return? Is the final exaltation a release from the depressing features of Irish life which have tainted the earlier experience? Or is it the fifth turn in an endless cycle? And in either case, is Stephen always to be viewed with the same deadly seriousness with which he views himself? Is it to artistic maturity that he grows? As the young man goes into exile from Ireland, goes 'to encounter for the millionth time the reality of experience and to forge in the smithy' of his soul 'the uncreated conscience' of his race, are we to take this, with Harry Levin, as a fully serious portrait of the artist Dedalus, praying to his namesake Daedalus, to stand him 'now and ever in good stead'?[11] Or is the inflated style, as Mark Schorer tells us, Joyce's clue that the young Icarus is flying too close to the sun, with the 'excessive lyric relaxation' of Stephen's final style punctuating 'the illusory nature of the whole ambition'?[12] The young man views himself and his flight with unrelieved solemnity. Should we?

To see the difficulties clearly, let us consider three crucial episodes, all from the final section: his rejection of the priesthood, his exposition of what he takes to be Thomistic aesthetics, and his composition of a poem.

Is his rejection of the priesthood a triumph, a tragedy, or merely a comedy of errors? Most readers, even those who follow the new trend of reading Stephen ironically, seem to have read it as a triumph: the artist has rid himself of one of the chains that bound him. To Caroline Gordon, this is a serious misreading. 'I suspect that Joyce's *Portrait* has been misread by a whole generation.' She sees the rejection as 'the picture of a soul that is being damned for time and eternity caught in the act of foreseeing and foreknowing its damnation', and she cites in evidence the fall of Icarus and Stephen's own statement to Cranly that he is not afraid to make a mistake, 'even a great mistake, a lifelong mistake and perhaps for eternity, too'.[13] Well, which *Portrait* do we choose, that of the artistic soul battling through successfully to his necessary freedom, or that of the child of God, choosing, like Lucifer, his own damnation? No two books could be further from each other than the two we envision here. There may be a sufficient core of what is simply interesting to salvage the book as a great work of the sensibility, but unless we are willing to retreat into babbling and incommunicable relativism, we cannot believe that it is both a portrait of the prisoner freed and a portrait of the soul placing itself in chains.

Critics have had even more difficulty with Stephen's aesthetic theory, ostensibly developed from Aquinas. Is the book itself, as Grant

Redford tells us,[14] an 'objectification of an artistic proposition and a method announced by the central character', achieving for Joyce the 'wholeness, harmony, and radiance' that Stephen celebrates in his theory? Or is it, as Father Noon says, an ironic portrait of Stephen's immature aesthetics? Joyce wanted to qualify Stephen' utterances, Father Noon tells us, 'by inviting attention to his own more sophisticated literary concerns', and he stands apart from the Thomistic aesthetics, watching Stephen miss the clue in his drive for an impersonal, dramatic narration. 'The comparison of the artist with the God of the creation', taken 'straight' by many critics, is for Father Noon 'the climax of Joyce's ironic development of the Dedalus aesthetic'.[15]

Finally, what of the precious villanelle? Does Joyce intend it to be taken as a serious sign of Stephen's artistry, as a sign of his genuine but amusingly pretentious precocity, or as something else entirely?

> *Are you not weary of ardent ways,*
> *Lure of the fallen seraphim?*
> *Tell no more of enchanted days.*
>
> *Your eyes have set man's heart ablaze*
> *And you have had your will of him.*
> *Are you not weary of ardent ways? ...*

Hardly anyone has committed himself in public about the quality of this poem. Are we to smile at Stephen or pity him in his tortured longing? Are we to marvel at his artistry, or scoff at his conceit? Or are we merely to say, 'How remarkable an insight into the kind of poem that would be written by an adolescent in love, if he were artistically inclined'? The poem, we are told, 'enfolded him like a shining cloud, enfolded him like water with a liquid life: and like a cloud of vapour or like waters circumfluent in space the liquid letters of speech, symbols of the element of mystery, flowed forth over his brain.' As we recall Jean Paul's formula for 'romantic irony', 'hot baths of sentiment followed by cold showers of irony', we can only ask here which tap has been turned on. Are we to swoon – or laugh?

Some critics will no doubt answer that all these questions are irrelevant. The villanelle is not to be judged but simply experienced; the aesthetic theory is, within the art work, neither true nor false but simply 'true' to the art work – that is, true to Stephen's character at this point. To read modern literature properly we must refuse to ask irrelevant questions about it; we must accept the 'portrait' and no more ask whether the character portrayed is good or bad, right or wrong than we ask whether a woman painted by Picasso is moral or immoral. 'All facts of any kind', as Gilbert puts it, 'mental or material, sublime or ludicrous, have an equivalence of value for the artist.'[16]

This answer, which can be liberating at one stage of our development in appreciating not only modern but all art, becomes less and less satisfactory the longer we look at it. It certainly does not seem to have been Joyce's basic attitude, though he was often misleading about it.[17] The creation and the enjoyment of art can never be a completely neutral activity. Though different works of art require different kinds of judgement for their enjoyment, the position taken ... [elsewhere in *The Rhetoric of Fiction*] must stand: no work, not even the shortest lyric, can be written in complete moral, intellectual and aesthetic neutrality. We may judge falsely, we may judge unconsciously, but we cannot even bring the book to mind without judging its elements, seeing them as shaped into a given kind of thing. Even if we denied that the sequence of events has meaning in the sense of being truly sequential, that denial would itself be a judgement on the rightness of Stephen's actions and opinions at each stage: to decide that he is not growing is as much a judgement on his actions as to decide that he is becoming more and more mature. Actually everyone reads the book as some kind of progressive sequence, and to do so we judge succeeding actions and opinions to be more or less moral, sensitive, intellectually mature, than those they follow.[18] If we felt that the question of Joyce's precise attitude toward Stephen's vocation, his aesthetics, and his villanelle were irrelevant, we would hardly dispute with each other about them. Yet I count in a recent check list at least fifteen articles and one full book disputing Joyce's attitude about the aesthetics alone.[19]

Like most modern critics, I would prefer to settle such disputes by using internal rather than external evidence. But the experts themselves give me little hope of finding answers to my three problems by re-reading *Portrait* one more time. They all clutch happily at any wisp of comment or fragmentary document that might illuminate Joyce's intentions.[20] And who can blame them?

The truth seems to be that Joyce was always a bit uncertain about his attitude toward Stephen. Anyone who reads Ellmann's masterful biography with this problem in mind cannot help being struck by the many shifts and turns Joyce took as he worked through the various versions. There is nothing especially strange in that, of course. Most 'autobiographical' novelists probably encounter difficulty in trying to decide just how heroic their heroes are to be. But Joyce's explorations came just at a time when the traditional devices for control of distance were being repudiated, when doctrines of objectivity were in the air, and when people were taking seriously the idea that to evoke 'reality' was a sufficient aim in art; the artist need not concern himself with judging or with specifying whether the reader should approve or disapprove, laugh or cry.

Now the traditional forms had specified in their very conceptions a certain degree of clarity about distance. If an author chose to write comedy, for example, he knew that his characters must at least to some degree be 'placed' at a distance from the spectator's norms. His predetermination did not, of course, settle all of his problems. To balance sympathy and antipathy, admiration and contempt, was still a fundamental challenge, but it was a challenge for which there was considerable guidance in the practice of previous writers of comedy. If, on the other hand, he chose to write tragedy, or satire, or elegy, or celebration odes, or whatever, he could rely to some extent on conventions to guide him and his audience to a common attitude toward his characters.

The young Joyce had none of this to rely on, but he seems never to have sensed the full danger of his position. When, in his earliest years, he recorded his brief epiphanies – those bits of dialogue or description that were supposed to reveal the inner reality of things – there was always an implied identification of the recorder's norms and the reader's; both were spectators at the revealing moment, both shared in the vision of one moment of truth. Though some of the epiphanies are funny, some sad, and some mixed, the basic effect is always the same: an overwhelming sense – when they succeed – of what Joyce liked to call the 'incarnation': Artistic Meaning has come to live in the world's body. The Poet has done his work.

Even in these early epiphanies there is difficulty with distance; the author inevitably expects the reader to share in his own preconceptions and interests sufficiently to catch, from each word or gesture, the precise mood or tone that they evoke for the author himself. But since complete identification with the author is a silent precondition for the success of such moments, the basic problem of distance is never a serious one. Even if the author and reader should differ in interpretation, they can share the sense of evoked reality.

It is only when Joyce places at the centre of a long work a figure who experiences epiphanies, an epiphany-producing device, as it were, who is himself used by the real author as an object ambiguously distant from the norms of the work, that the complications of distance become incalculable. If he treats the author-figure satirically, as he does in much of *Stephen Hero*, that earlier, windier version of *Portrait*,[21] then what happens to the quality of the epiphanies that he describes? Are they still genuine epiphanies or only what the misguided, callow youth thinks are epiphanies? If, as Joyce's brother Stanislaus has revealed, the word 'hero' is satiric, can we take seriously that anti-hero's vision? Yet if the satirical mode is dropped, if the hero is made into a real hero, and if the reader is made to see things entirely as he sees them, what then happens to objectivity? The portrait is no longer as objective rendering of reality, looked at from a respectable aesthetic distance, but rather a mere subjective indulgence.

Joyce can be seen, in Ellmann's account, struggling with this problem throughout the revisions. Unlike writers before Flaubert, he had no guidance from convention or tradition or fellow artists. Neither Flaubert nor James had established any sure ground to stand on. Both of them had, in fact, stumbled on the same hurdles, and though each had on occasion surmounted the difficulties, Joyce was in no frame of mind to look behind their claims as realists to the actual problems and lessons that lay beneath their evocative surfaces. A supreme egoist struggling to deal artistically with his own ego, a humorist who could not escape the comic consequences of his portrait of that inflated ego, he faced, in the completed *Stephen Hero*, what he had to recognise as a hodgepodge of irreconcilables. Is Stephen a pompous ass or not? Is his name deliberately ridiculous, as Stanislaus, who invented it, says? Or is it a serious act of symbolism? The way out seems inevitable, but it seems a retreat nonetheless: simply present the 'reality' and let the reader judge. Cut all of the author's judgements, cut all of the adjectives, produce one long, ambiguous epiphany.[22]

Purged of the author's explicit judgement, the resulting work was so brilliant and compelling, its hero's vision so scintillating, that almost all readers overlooked the satiric and ironic content – except, of course, as the satire operated against other characters. So far as I know no one said anything about irony against Stephen until after *Ulysses* was published in 1922, with its opening in which Icarus-Stephen is shown with his wings clipped. Ironic readings did not become popular, in fact, until after the fragment of *Stephen Hero* was published in 1944. Readers of that work found, it is true, many authoritative confirmations of their exaltation of Stephen – for the most part in a form that might confirm anyone's prejudice against commentary.' ... When he [Stephen] wrote it was always a mature and reasoned emotion which urged him' (p. 155). 'This mood of indignation which was not guiltless of a certain superficiality was undoubtedly due to the excitement of release ... He acknowledged to himself in honest egoism that he could not take to heart the distress of a nation, the soul of which was antipathetic to his own, so bitterly as the indignity of a bad line of verse: but at the same time he was nothing in the world so little as an amateur artist' (p. 130). 'Stephen did not attach himself to art in any spirit of youthful dilettantism but strove to pierce to the significant heart of everything' (p. 25). But readers were also faced with a good many denigrations of the hero. We can agree that *Portrait* is a better work because the immature author has been effaced; Joyce may indeed have found that effacing the commentary was the only way he could obtain an air of maturity. But the fact remains that it is primarily to this immature commentary that we must go for evidence in deciphering the ironies of the later, purer work.

What we find in *Stephen Hero* is not a simple confirmation of any reading that we might have achieved on the basis of *Portrait* alone. Rather we find an extremely complicated view, combining irony and admiration in unpredictable mixtures. Thus the Thomist aesthetics 'was in the main applied Aquinas and he set it forth plainly with a naïf air of discovering novelties. This he did partly to satisfy his own taste for enigmatic roles and partly from a genuine predisposition in favour of all but the premises of scholasticism' (p. 64). No one ever inferred, before this passage was available, anything like this precise and complex judgement on Stephen. The combination of blame and approval, we may be sure, is different in the finished *Portrait*; the implied author no doubt often repudiates the explicit judgements of the younger narrator who intruded into *Stephen Hero*. But we can also be sure that his judgement has not become less complex. Where do we find, in any criticism of *Portrait* based entirely on internal evidence, the following kind of juxtaposition of Stephen's views with the author's superior insight? 'Having by this *simple process* established the literary form of art as the most excellent he *proceeded to examine it in favour of his theory*, or, *as he rendered it*, to establish the relations which must subsist between the literary image, the work of art itself, and that energy which had imagined and fashioned it, the centre of conscious, re-acting, particular life, the artist' (p. 65, italics mine). Can we infer, from *Portrait*, that Joyce sees Stephen as simply rationalising in favour of his theory? Did we guess that Joyce could refer to him mockingly as a 'fiery-hearted revolutionary' and a 'heaven-ascending essayist'?[23]

In *Stephen Hero*, the author's final evaluation of the aesthetics is favourable but qualified: 'Except for the eloquent and arrogant peroration Stephen's essay was a careful exposition of a carefully meditated theory of aesthetics' (p. 68). Though it might be argued that in the finished book he has cut out some of the negative elements, such as the 'eloquent and arrogant peroration', and has presented the pure theory in conversational form, it is clear that Joyce himself judged his hero's theory in greater detail than we could possibly infer from the final version alone.

Similar clarifications can be found in *Stephen Hero* of our other two crucial problems, his rejection of the priesthood and his poetic ability. For example, 'He had swept the moment into his memory ... and ... had brought forth some pages of sorry verse' (p. 57). Can the hero of *Portrait* be thought of as writing 'sorry verse'? One would not think so, to read much of the commentary by Joyce's critics.

79

But who is to blame them? Whatever intelligence Joyce postulates in his reader – let us assume the unlikely case of its being comparable to his own – will not be sufficient for precise inference of a pattern of judgements which is, after all, private to Joyce. And this will be true regardless of how much distance from his own hero we believe him to have achieved by the time he concluded his final version. We simply cannot avoid the conclusion that to some extent the book itself is at fault, regardless of its great virtues. Unless we make the absurd assumption that Joyce had in reality purged himself of all judgement by the time he completed his final draft, unless we see him as having really come to look upon all of Stephen's actions as equally wise or equally foolish, equally sensitive or equally meaningless, we much conclude that many of the refinements he intended in his finished *Portrait* are, for most of us, permanently lost. Even if we were now to do our homework like dutiful students, even if we were to study all of Joyce's work, even if we were to spend the lifetime that Joyce playfully said his novels demand, presumably we should never come to as rich, as refined, and as varied a conception of the quality of Stephen's last days in Ireland as Joyce had in mind. For some of us the air of detachment and objectivity may still be worth the price, but we must never pretend that a price was not paid.[24] □

Although Booth ascribes to others the opinion that *Ulysses* and *Finnegans Wake* cannot be read, only studied, his insistence on reading *A Portrait* in isolation from might explain his perplexity and eventual rejection of the novel, and it is surely significant that Kenner's more supple and suggestive reading draws on a thorough knowledge of the later works.

The next short extract is from Vladimir Nabokov's series of undergraduate lectures on European fiction at Cornell in the early 1950s, sign in itself that by this time *Ulysses* had escaped its banned status and was becoming absorbed into the official curriculum. Nabokov offers a typically haughty and elegant introduction to the novel and its difficulties, warning the students off reading for human interest, mocking the efforts of those (including Gilbert) he calls pedants and bores, who insist on tracing minutely the Homeric parallels, and himself insisting on the centrality and the pathos of Bloom as well as on the importance, indeed the necessity of the novel's shifts in style. Nabokov's own *Lolita* was to inherit *Ulysses'* erstwhile notoriety, and it is remarkable how, just as with Eliot, his description of Joyce's text could be read equally as a justification of his own: when he remarks that, 'at any moment, in switching his styles, or within a given category, Joyce may intensify a mood by introducing a musical lyrical strain, with alliterations and lilting devices, generally to render wistful emotions,' he is also describing the manner of *Lolita*, with its swooping transitions between the parodic and the hopelessly nostalgic, and his identification of the main theme of *Ulysses* also offers a pre-echo of his own novel. Even the sententious, pseudo-clinical admonition of Bloom as 'if not on the verge of insanity, at least a good clinical example of extreme sexual preoccupation and perversity with all kinds of curious complications' anticipates the one-eyed dismissal of Humbert Humbert by Nabokov's parodic creation 'John Ray Jnr. Ph.D.'.[25]

■ James Joyce was born in 1882 in Ireland, left Ireland in the first decade of the twentieth century, lived most of his life as an expatriate in continental Europe and died in 1941 in Switzerland. *Ulysses* was composed between 1914 and 1921 in Trieste, Zurich, and Paris, In 1918 parts began to appear in the so-called Little Review. *Ulysses* is a fat book of more than two hundred sixty thousand words; it is a rich book with a vocabulary of about thirty thousand words. The Dublin setting is built partly on data supplied by an exile's memory, but mainly on data from Thom's Dublin Directory, whither professors of literature, before discussing *Ulysses*, secretly wing their way in order to astound their students with the knowledge Joyce himself stored up with the aid of that very directory. He also used, throughout the book, a copy of the Dublin newspaper the *Evening Telegraph* of Thursday, 16 June 1904, price one halfpenny, which among other things featured that day the Ascot Gold Cup race (with Throwaway, an outsider, winning), an appalling American disaster (the excursion steamer General Slocum on fire), and a motorcar race for the Gordon Bennett Cup in Homburg, Germany.

Ulysses is the description of a single day, the sixteenth of June 1904, a Thursday, a day in the mingled and separate lives of a number of characters walking, riding, sitting, talking, dreaming, drinking, and going through a number of minor and major physiological and philosophical actions during this one day in Dublin and the early morning hours of the next day. Why did Joyce choose that particular day, 16 June 1904? In an otherwise rather poor though well-meaning book, *Fabulous Voyager: James Joyce's Ulysses* (1947), Mr. Richard Kain informs me that this was the day on which Joyce met his future wife, Nora Barnacle. So much for human interest.

Ulysses consists of a number of scenes built around three major characters; of these major characters the dominant one is Leopold Bloom, a small businessman in the advertising business, an advertising canvasser to be exact. At one time he was with the firm of Wisdom Hely, stationer, in the capacity of a traveller for blotting paper, but now he is on his own, soliciting ads and not doing too well. For reasons that I shall mention presently Joyce endowed him with a Hungarian-Jewish origin. The two other major characters are Stephen

Dedalus, whom Joyce had already depicted in *Portrait of the Artist as a Young Man* (1916), and Marion Bloom, Molly Bloom, Bloom's wife. If Bloom is the central figure, Stephen and Marion are the lateral ones in this triptych: the book begins with Stephen and ends with Marion. Stephen Dedalus, whose surname is that of the mythical maker of the labyrinth at Knossos, the royal city of ancient Crete; other fabulous gadgets; wings for himself and Icarus, his son – Stephen Dedalus, aged twenty-two, is a young Dublin schoolteacher, scholar, and poet, who in his days of schooling had been subjected to the discipline of a Jesuit education and now violently reacts against it but remains of an essentially metaphysical nature. He is a rather abstract young man, a dogmatist even when drunk, a freethinker imprisoned in his own self, a brilliant pronouncer of abrupt aphoristic sayings, physically fragile, and as unwashed as a saint (his last bath took place in October, and this is June), a bitter and brittle young fellow – never quite clearly visualised by the reader, a projection of the author's mind rather than a warm new being created by an artist's imagination. Critics tend to identify Stephen with young Joyce himself, but that is neither here nor there. As Harry Levin has put it, 'Joyce lost his religion, but kept his categories,' which is also true of Stephen.

Marion (Molly) Bloom, Bloom's wife, is Irish on her father's side and Spanish-Jewish on her mother's side. She is a concert singer. If Stephen is a highbrow and Bloom a middlebrow, Molly Bloom is definitely a lowbrow and a very vulgar one at that. But all three characters have their artistic sides. In Stephen's case the artistic is almost too good to be true – one never meets anybody in 'real life' who has anything approaching such a perfect artistic control over his casual everyday speech as Stephen is supposed to have. Bloom the middlebrow is less of an artist than Stephen but is much more of an artist than critics have discerned: in fact, his mental stream flows now and then very close to Stephen's mental stream, as I will explain later. Finally, Molly Bloom, despite her triteness, despite the conventional quality of her ideas, despite her vulgarity, is capable of rich emotional response to the superficially lovely things of life, as we shall see in the last part of her extraordinary soliloquy on which the book ends.

Before discussing the matter and manner of the book, I have still a few words to say about the main character Leopold Bloom. When Proust portrayed Swann, he made Swann an individual, with individual, unique characteristics. Swann is neither a literary type nor a racial type, though he happens to be the son of a Jewish stockbroker. In composing the figure of Bloom, Joyce's intention was to place among endemic Irishmen in his native Dublin someone who was as Irish as he, Joyce, was, but also who was an exile, a black sheep in the fold, as he, Joyce, was. Joyce evolved the rational plan, therefore, of selecting for the type of an outsider, the type of the Wandering Jew, the type of the exile. However, I shall explain later that Joyce is sometimes crude in the way he accumulates and stresses so-called racial traits. Another consideration in relation to Bloom: those so many who have written so much about *Ulysses* are either very pure men or very depraved men. They are inclined to regard Bloom as a very ordinary nature, and apparently Joyce himself intended to portray an ordinary person. It is obvious, however, that in the sexual department Bloom is, if not on the verge of insanity, at least a good clinical example of extreme sexual preoccupation and perversity with all kinds of curious complications. His case is strictly heterosexual, of course – not homosexual as most of the ladies and gentlemen are in Proust (*homo* is Greek for same, not Latin for man as some students think) – but within the wide limits of Bloom's love for the opposite sex he indulges in acts and dreams that are definitely subnormal in the zoological, evolutional sense. I shall not bore you with a list of his curious desires, but this I will say: In Bloom's mind and in Joyce's book the theme of sex is continually mixed and intertwined with the theme of the latrine. God knows I have no objection whatsoever to so-called frankness in novels. On the contrary, we have too little of it, and what there is has become in its turn conventional and trite, as used by so-called tough writers, the darlings of the book clubs, the pets of clubwomen. But I do object to the following: Bloom is supposed to be a rather ordinary citizen. Now it is not true that the mind of an ordinary citizen continuously dwells on physiological things. I object to the continuously, not to the disgusting. All this very special pathological stuff seems artificial and unnecessary in this particular context. I suggest that the squeamish among you regard the special preoccupation of Joyce with perfect detachment.

Ulysses is a splendid and permanent structure, but it has been slightly overrated by the kind of critic who is more interested in ideas and generalities and human aspects than in the work of art itself. I must especially warn against seeing in Leopold Bloom's humdrum wanderings and minor adventures on a summer day in Dublin a close parody of the *Odyssey*, with the adman Bloom acting the part of Odysseus, otherwise Ulysses, man of many devices, and Bloom's adulterous wife representing chaste Penelope while Stephen Dedalus is given the part of Telemachus. That there is a very vague and very general Homeric echo of the theme of wanderings in Bloom's case is obvious, as the title of the novel suggests, and there are a number of classical allusions among the many other allusions in the course of the book; but it would be a complete waste of time to look for close parallels in every character and every scene of the book. There is nothing more tedious than a protracted and sustained allegory based on a well-worn myth; and after the work had appeared in parts, Joyce promptly deleted the pseudo-Homeric titles of his chapters when he saw what scholarly and pseudoscholarly bores were up to. Another thing. One bore, a man called Stuart Gilbert, misled by a tongue-in-cheek list compiled by Joyce himself, found in every chapter the domination of one particular organ – the ear, the eye, the stomach, etc. – but we shall ignore that dull nonsense too. All art is in a sense symbolic; but we shall say 'stop, thief' to the critic who deliberately transforms an artist's subtle symbol into a pedant's stale allegory – a thousand and one nights into a convention of Shriners.

What then is the main theme of the book? It is very simple.

1. The hopeless past. Bloom's infant son has died long ago, but the vision remains in his blood and brain.

2. The ridiculous and tragic present. Bloom still loves his wife Molly, but he lets Fate have its way. He knows that in the afternoon at 4:30 of this mid-June day Boylan, her dashing impresario, concert agent, will visit Molly – and Bloom does nothing to prevent it. He tries fastidiously to keep out of Fate's way, but actually throughout the day is continuously on the point of running into Boylan.

3. The pathetic future. Bloom also keeps running into another young man – Stephen Dedalus. Bloom gradually realises that this may be another little attention on the part of Fate. If his wife must have lovers then sensitive, artistic Stephen would be a better one than vulgar Boylan. In fact, Stephen could give Molly lessons, could help her with her Italian pronunciations in her profession as a singer, could be in short a refining influence, as Bloom pathetically thinks.

This is the main theme: Bloom and Fate.

Each chapter is written in a different style, or rather with a different style predomination. There is no special reason why this should be – why one chapter should be told straight, another a stream-of-consciousness gurgle, a third through the prism of a parody. There is no special reason, but it may be argued that this constant shift of the viewpoint conveys a more varied knowledge, fresh vivid glimpses from this or that side. If you have ever tried to stand and bend your head so as to look back between your knees, with your face turned upside down, you will see the world in a totally different light. Try it on the beach: it is very funny to see people walking when you look at them upside down. They seem to be, with each step, disengaging their feet from the glue of gravitation, without losing their dignity. Well, this trick of changing the vista, of changing the prism and the viewpoint, can be compared to Joyce's new literary technique, to the kind of new twist through which you see a greener grass, a fresher world.

The characters are constantly brought together during their peregrinations through a Dublin day. Joyce never loses control over them. Indeed, they come and go and meet and separate, and meet again as the live parts of a careful composition in a kind of slow dance of fate. The recurrence of a number of themes is one of the most striking features of the book. These themes are much more clear-cut, much more deliberately followed, than the themes we pick up in Tolstoy or in Kafka. The whole of *Ulysses*, as we shall gradually realise, is a deliberate pattern of recurrent themes and synchronisation of trivial events.

Joyce writes in three main styles:

1. The original Joyce: straightforward, lucid and logical and leisurely. This is the backbone of Chapter 1 of the first part and of Chapters 1 and 3 of the second part; and lucid, logical, and leisurely parts occur in other chapters.

2. Incomplete, rapid, broken wording rendering the so-called stream of consciousness, or better say the stepping stones of consciousness. Samples may be found in most chapters, though ordinarily associated only with major characters. A discussion of this device will be found in connection with its most famous example, Molly's final soliloquy, part three, Chapter 3; but one can comment here that it exaggerates the verbal side of thought. Man thinks not always in words but also in images, whereas the stream of consciousness presupposes a flow of words that can be notated: it is difficult, however, to believe that Bloom was continuously talking to himself.

3. Parodies of various non-novelistic forms: newspaper headlines (part two, Chapter 4), music (part two, Chapter 8), mystical and slapstick drama (part two, Chapter 12), examination questions and answers in a catechistic pattern (part three, Chapter 2). Also, parodies of literary styles and authors: the burlesque narrator of part two, Chapter 9, the lady's magazine type of author in part two, Chapter 10, a series of specific authors and literary periods in part two, Chapter 11, and elegant journalese in part three, Chapter 1.

At any moment, in switching his styles, or within a given category, Joyce may intensify a mood by introducing a musical lyrical strain, with alliterations and lilting devices, generally to render wistful emotions. A poetic style is often associated with Stephen, but an example from Bloom occurs, for instance, when he disposes of the envelope of the letter from Martha Clifford: 'Going under the railway arch he took out the envelope, tore it swiftly to shreds and scattered them towards the road. The shreds fluttered away, sank in the dank air: a white flutter then all sank.' Or, a few sentences later, the end of the vision of a huge flood of spilled beer 'winding through mudflats all over the level land, a lazy pooling swirl of liquor bearing along wide-leaved flowers of its froth'. At any other moment, however, Joyce can turn to all sorts of verbal tricks, to puns, transpositions of words, verbal echoes, monstrous twinning of verbs, or the imitation of sounds. In these, as in the overweight of local allusions and foreign expressions, a needless obscurity can be produced by details not brought out with sufficient clarity but only suggested for the knowledgeable. □

The final extract in this chapter comes from Cleanth Brooks' essay 'Joyce's *Ulysses*: Symbolic Poem, Biography or Novel?',[26] the title of which bespeaks a continuing indecision over how to place the work, and again, as with Booth, the issue of categorisation is implicated with that of evaluation.

■ One has to concede the fact that *Ulysses* is a kind of private logbook and spiritual diary containing Joyce's own personal revenges on particular people, his private jokes, and allusions to incidents and happenings that had some particular meaning for him. The fabric of the book is intricate. The tone is of an equivalent complexity. Commentators, in their anxiety to find a happy ending, have insisted on the book's compassion and on its final optimism, have over-simplified and probably distorted its meaning. In any case, whatever conclusions about the meaning of this novel we are to draw will require testing against the fictional structure – will have to be matched with what can actually be found in the novel. Too often the commentator has argued in effect that the meaning of *Ulysses* is the development of James Joyce, and if we venture to ask why it is so important to learn about the artistic development of James Joyce, we are told that this is important because James Joyce was able to write *Ulysses*. The hopelessly circular nature of this argument needs no comment. □

CHAPTER FOUR

Post-structuralist Joyce

The end of the last chapter saw criticism of Joyce reaching some kind of an impasse, unable to answer the questions it had set, wondering how it was possible that a novel's importance could be determined only with reference to the importance of its author, and vice versa, while also half-regretting, half-resenting the fact that Joyce's work could never quite fit into prevailing categories of the literary. One way out of this impasse might be to suggest that it was up to literary criticism to accommodate itself to the achievement and consequences of Joyce's work, rather than the other way round, so that rather than simply introduce another set of readings of Joyce – this time under the heading of post-structuralism – it might be better to think of Joyce as the ideal introduction to post-structuralism.

A clue to this assertion is to be found in Samuel Beckett's remark in his 1929 essay on *Finnegans Wake*: 'Here form is content, content is form ... His writing is not about something; it is that thing itself.' In other words, Joyce's texts are to be thought of less in terms of a representation of some reality out there than as a construction of reality. The problems troubling Booth in the last chapter presume a consistent division between signifier and signified, between what is written and what is written about, which is impossible to sustain in language. Although Beckett was writing specifically of *Finnegans Wake*, his remark can be seen to apply retrospectively to the rest of Joyce's work, in the way that all of his work must be read retrospectively. The preceding chapters have charted a heroic effort of accommodation by critics. Whether following on from Eliot in tracing mythic patterns, or Pound's celebration of Joyce as superrealist, or Budgen's celebration of Bloom's (and Joyce's) humanity, critics were largely engaged in the attempt to 'recuperate Joyce' – to make his works more accessible in traditional terms and according to traditional justifications of literature. But that which was seen as problematic by the previous generation of critics, that is to say the excess of Joyce's language to the represented world, was taken as cause for celebration by the proponents of post-structuralism. Joyce's work answered (or predicted) what might in shorthand be called the three main tenets of post-structuralism: first, the insistence on the primacy of language with its attendant assault on the conventions of mimesis; second, the dethronement of the individual controlling Subject, and with it the death of the Author; and finally the replacement of ideals of formal unity with a celebration of signifiers at play. The title of Colin MacCabe's study, *James Joyce and the Revolution of the Word*,[1] reflects as much on the contemporary revolution in English studies as it does on Joyce's achievement, associated with the struggle around modernism, but this time with readers and critics rather than authors as protagonists. Chris Baldick, himself a veteran of the campaign, recently characterised the revolution in English Studies as follows:

■ **The pious jargon of formal harmony employed by the old schools (integration, poise, organic wholeness) was abruptly abandoned in favour of a grimly violent new set of metaphors suited more to the military hospital than to the library. Literary form was now to be spoken of in terms of deformity and internal breakage, and poems were to be 'interrogated' so as to reveal their wounds, mutilations, amputations, scars, lesions, sutures, punctures, fissures, fractures and ruptures. And as the figurative 'body' of the text was cut up, so was its 'voice', which now became a pandemonium of contending cries: as the new vocabularies had it, the text was to be seen as polyvalent, multivocal, polyphonic, dialogic, multi-accentual, and preferably convulsed in schizophrenic babble.** □

Signs and symptoms of the above will be seen in the following extracts, which is no reason at all to reject them. This, if anything, is the lesson of Joyce; that any discourse, with all its faults and blind spots, can be useful to the moment, however silly it looks in retrospect, and that, above all, no discourse is ever final or definitive. Readers of Joyce would be the first to recognise the point of Roland Barthes' assertion that 'a text is not a line of words releasing a single "theological" meaning (the "message" of the Author/God) but a multi-dimensional space in which a variety of writings, none of them original, blend or clash.'[2] One of the central tenets of MacCabe's work, extracts from which follow, is that there is no final metalanguage; that is to say no language that can regard other languages as material while holding itself to be transparent. By refusing metalanguage, Joyce's texts throw criticism into disarray; the critical discourse, suggests MacCabe, is unable to obtain any purchase on the text.

■ **None of the discourses which circulate in *Finnegans Wake* or *Ulysses* can master or make sense of the others and there is, therefore, no possibility of the critic articulating his reading as an elaboration of a dominant position within the text. In Joyce's writing, all positions are constantly threatened with dissolution into the play of language. The critic cannot grasp the content of Joyce's texts, for the texts investigate the very processes which produce both content and form, object-languages and meta-language.** □

Derek Attridge offers a further commentary on Joyce and metalanguage in the introduction to *Post-structuralist Joyce*, insisting that the point is not to apply a particular theory to a text: for the text reads the theory at the same time as it is read by it.

■ This is particularly true of Joyce: any reader cannot but feel that the text constantly overreaches the landmarks established by the best critical constructions. It is impossible to exert any mastery over it, its *shifts* are such that you can never pin it down in any definite place – it always turns up again, laughing, behind your back. In fact, the aim is not to produce a *reading* of this intractable text, to make it more familiar and exorcise its strangeness, but on the contrary to confront its unreadability; not to produce an indefinite accumulation of its meanings (or search for the one authentic meaning), but to look at the mechanisms of its infinite productivity; not to explore the psychological depths of the author or characters, but to record the perpetual flight of the Subject and its ultimate disappearance; not to reconstruct the world presented by the text, but to follow up within it the strategies that attempt a deconstruction of representation ... [Joyce's text] acts from within the great tradition of narrative fiction, violently dragging that tradition out of itself. It is as the culmination of Western culture that it leads that culture irretrievably astray, far towards the limits of madness. □

Joyce's refusal to place different discourses in a hierarchy, as is the case with what MacCabe calls classic realist texts such as those of George Eliot, is marked by his rejection of the inverted comma as a sign of demarcation between a dominant, quasi-authorial discourse and subordinate ones.[3] Given that the trajectory of Joyce's work, from *Dubliners* to *Finnegans Wake*, was one of relentless linguistic invention and reinvention, it is indeed surprising that, as MacCabe says, there had been a general failure by linguists and literary critics to deal seriously with Joyce's use of language, one sign of this being a reluctance to discuss or come to terms with the later chapters of *Ulysses*, where style is increasingly in excess of the demands of realist representation. Accordingly MacCabe, after his theoretical preamble on the state and limitations of literary criticism, provides an analysis of one of the more difficult, least 'realistic' chapters of *Ulysses*, 'The Sirens', showing how the text operates as a montage of discourses in which the materiality of sound and writing is stressed, without at any time offering the reader a final metalanguage (an author's impersonal voice) that could control the riot of language that composes the text. Also excerpted here is a short assessment of *A Portrait* that places the author not as a transparently discursive extra-textual authority, but rather as the play of possibilities produced by the various discourses of the text. Throughout MacCabe's study there is an emphasis on play and performance, in which the reader plays a full and active part, since as Margaret Schlauch pointed out as early as 1939, 'Joyce demands more active participation from his public than any writer I can recall.'[4]

■ Before undertaking the analysis of Joyce's practices of writing it is necessary to consider briefly the inadequacies of the discourse of literary criticism. It would be comforting to pretend, as most literary critics do, that literary criticism is unimportant, a transient epiphenomenon which can be ignored in favour of the original literary text. It is true that particular works of literary criticism appear and disappear with startling rapidity and no obvious effectivity. But the discourses and institutions of literary criticism, which support and make possible individual critical works, permit and condition our reading. To pretend we can go direct to the text is to take literary criticism at its word and believe that the text is a simple and definable object. But every text is already articulated with other texts which determine its possible meaning and no text can escape the discourses of literary criticism in which it is referred to, named and identified.

The theoretical inadequacy of literary criticism, demonstrable for any work, is compounded by its practical failure with Joyce. To write about Joyce is to write about an author who is universally acknowledged as great but who is little read except by those who make his work their major preoccupation. The charge is doubly damning if one considers, as I do, that he is the major writer in English since Shakespeare. If many have read *A Portrait of the Artist as a Young Man*, few have read *Ulysses* with the necessary attention and fewer still have done more than open *Finnegans Wake*. Literary criticism – and there is no shortage of books devoted to Joyce – preserves him as unread. In part this lack of readers relates to features of the text but the situation has been aggravated by the persistent refusal of commentators to come to terms with the radical novelty of Joyce's work. Instead Joyce's texts are transformed into complicated crossword puzzles whose solution is the banal liberal humanism of the critic. The reason for the failure of the critics to give an account of Joyce's texts is not some congenital inability on their part but that literary criticism itself cannot cope with Joyce's texts because those texts refuse to reproduce the relation between reader and text on which literary criticism is predicated. The literary critic labours under the same delusion as Professor Jones in *Finnegans Wake*. He is unable to decipher the letter because he mistakes its very constitution; his error is not that he cannot find the right interpretation but that he tries to interpret at all. The aim of this work is not to provide the meaning of Joyce's work but to allow it to be read. Hence, problems concerning the discourse of literary criticism (more colloquially, the habits of reading that have developed over the last 150 years) will be a constant focus of attention.

Central to the discourse of literary criticism is the philosophical category of the subject. This category, under a variety of names (of which 'author' is the most common), is indispensable to the very activity of literary criticism. Traditionally the function of the category was to provide a unity for the field of experience such that one could give an account of judgement between possibilities within that experience. The subject provided both the limit and the unity of experience. In constituting its own limits it gave itself a position of dominance from which to judge items within the field of experience. But in providing this unity and homogeneity it also provided something else: it allowed for the possibility of a representational theory of language.

It is only given the essential homogeneity of experience and a position from which the elements within it can be judged that it is possible to talk of a representational theory of language. If experience is heterogeneous then there can be no simple one-to-one relation between it and language, and even if it is homogeneous there can be no possibility of its representation in language unless there is a position from which word can be aligned against thing. Literary criticism depends on a theory of the subject in order to carry out its task of interpretation. Interpretation is the search for meaning and meaning is dependent on a divorce between language and the world which is both made possible and guaranteed by the subject.

Joyce's texts, however, refuse the subject any dominant position from which language could be tallied with experience. *Ulysses* and *Finnegans Wake* are concerned not with representing experience through language but with experiencing language through a destruction of representation. Instead of constructing a meaning, Joyce's texts concern themselves with the position of the subject in language. If the literary critic is interested in meaning, Joyce's texts are concerned with the various positions from which meaning becomes possible. In order to grasp the activities of Joyce's texts it becomes necessary to understand the construction of the position of the subject and what is always buried in that construction. Joyce's texts disrupt the normal position assigned to a reader in a text and thus alter the reader's relation to his or her discourses.

...

In order to carry out its task of interpretation, the discourse of literary criticism must always be able to identify what is represented, independently of the form of the representation. This identification is only possible if the discourse of the critic is in a position to transform the text into content, and, to undertake this transformation, the relation between the language of the text and the language of the critic must be that which obtains between an object- and a meta-language. A meta-language 'talks about' an object-language and transforms it into content by naming the object-language (accomplished through the use of inverted commas) and thus being able to identify both the object-language and its area of application[5] it is from the position of the meta-language that correspondence between word and world can be established.

A text is made up of many languages, or discourses, and the critic's ability to homogenise these articulations is related to their prior organisation within the text. Joyce's texts refuse the very category of meta-language and a critical discourse is thus unable to obtain any purchase on the text. None of the discourses which circulate on *Finnegans Wake* or *Ulysses* can master or make sense of the others and there is, therefore, no possibility of the critic articulating his or her reading as an elaboration of a dominant position within the text. In Joyce's writing, indeed, all positions are constantly threatened with dissolution into the play of language. The critic cannot grasp the content of Joyce's texts, for the texts investigate the very processes which produce both content and form, object-languages and meta-language.

The absence of a meta-language in Joyce's work is evident in his refusal, a refusal which dates from his earliest writings, to use what he called 'perverted commas'.[6] While those sections in a work which are contained in inverted commas may offer different ways of regarding and analysing the world, they are negated as real alternatives by the unspoken prose that surrounds and controls them. The narrative prose is the meta-language that can state all the truths in the object-language(s) (the marks held in inverted commas) and can also explain the relation of the object-language to the world. This relation of dominance allows the meta-language to understand how the object discourses obscurely figure truths which find clear expression in the meta-language. A meta-language regards its object discourses as material but itself as transparent. And this transparency allows the identity of things to shine through the window of words in the unspoken narrative whereas the spoken discourses which clothe meaning with material are necessarily obscure. At all costs the meta-language must refuse to admit its own materiality, for insofar as the meta-language is itself treated as material, it, too, can be re-interpreted; new meanings can be found for it in a further meta-language.[7]

...

The possibility of a meta-language is inscribed in the distance

92

between the language of the text and the language of the reader. Joyce's writing involves ever greater efforts to abolish this distance.

What is essential to grasp in the articulation of Joyce's texts is that there is no position within them where the reading subject can insert itself to consume some paralysed reality. The writing subject, confronted by the ever-present demand of this reality to declare its identity and repress desire, institutes desire through splitting itself within the processes of signification. The reading subject must follow the positions taken up by the writing subject and in the split thus instituted can begin to read its own discourses – not as some transparent window onto an evident reality but as a set of significant oppositions in which the subject's world is constituted and in which, if the subject begins to listen attentively to them, it can hear its desire speak. It is this attention to the forms of discourse which characterises Joyce's practice of writing, its displacement from classic realism:

> This shift is not to be understood in the traditional terms of a change from 'social realism' to 'psychological realism' or whatever, but in terms of the deconstruction of the very 'innocence' of realism. Its foundation is a profound experience of language and form and the demonstration of that experience in the writing of the novel which, transgressed, is no longer repetition and self-effacement but work and self-presentation as text. Its realism is not the mirroring of some 'Reality' but an attention to the forms of intelligibility in which the real is produced, a dramatisation of possibilities in language, forms of articulation, limitations, of its own horizon.[8]

There are endless discussions of *A Portrait* which turn around the attempts to find the position of the author in this 'authorless work'.[9] All such attempts ignore the fact that the structure of the work allows for no such authorial stance and that the reader, too, is displaced from any such position. The reader is constantly at work as discourse after discourse must be taken up without any fixed hierarchy to ensure the control and distance necessary to a position. We can locate Joyce's position in the arrangement of discourses, in the montage. This, however, is not a position but an articulation, the articulation which is the 'I' at the end of the text. The 'I' of the closing diary is not a transparent position which can be reduced to a set of third person statements but a set of effects of language, the result of a montage of discourses. The end of the text is the guarantee of its beginning as the artist is produced who will write it. This guarantee is not that the enunciation of the text is possible from the end of the time of the enounced. It is that the enounced has been displayed as enunciation and at that point it is possible to compose a montage of the articulations that produce a body in language. In this montage there is no moment of dominance from which the reader's discourses are invited to a complacent and suppressed entry. It is this lack of dominance which enables us to locate the author – not as a simple source who, outside the text, can identify himself and then communicate this identity through a transparent discourse but rather as the play of possibilities within the different discourses of the text. The discourses in question are those of Catholicism and nationalism, of aesthetics and the artist, discourses which produce the 'I' that ends the text and immediately starts it again.[10] ...

Writing menaces any simple notion of origin – any simple notion of an author – and with it the complementary notions of correspondence and coherence. In the Sirens episode in *Ulysses* the opposition between writing and the voice becomes the focus of the text's attention. As the material of language becomes the concern of the text, the reader can no longer pass through signifier to signified, can no longer bathe in the imaginary unity of a full self but must experience him or herself as divided, distanced, as *other*. The Sirens interrogates the distinction between the spoken and the written and this interrogation involves the deconstruction of any possible moment of origin offered by the figure of the father (or, indeed of the author). This deconstruction has definite political effects as it demonstrates a contradiction between writing and nationalism.

The Sirens commences with 58 phrases of unequal length varying from the single word 'Listen' (329) to the seven short sentences of 'Decoy. Soft word. But look! The bright stars fade. O rose! Notes chirruping answer. Castille. The morn is breaking.' (329) and the eleven phrases of 'Avowal. *Sonnez*. I could. Rebound of garter. Not leave thee. Smack. *La cloche*! Thigh smack. Avowal. Warm. Sweetheart, goodbye! (329). Of these 58 phrases, 57 of them occur within the body of the text although they are often transformed and altered in their appearance. Thus the very first phrase 'Bronze by gold, heard the hoofirons, steelyringing Imperthnthn thnthnthn' (328) gets distributed through the first two pages of the continuous text. We find the 'Bronze by gold, Miss Douce's head by Miss Kennedy's head, over the crossblind of the Ormond bar heard the viceregal hoofs go by, ringing steel.' (331) but 'Imperthnthn thnthnthn' recurs a page later in 'Imperthnthn thnthnthn, bootsnout sniffed rudely, as he retreated as she threatened to as he had come'(332), while the exact phrase 'heard the hoofiron, steelyringing' does not recur at all. Or, to take another example, the phrase 'A moonlight nightcall: far: far.' (329) recurs on pages 259–260 as 'Sour pipe removed he held a shield of hand beside his lips that cooed a moonlight nightcall, clear from anear, a call from

94

afar, replying'. The 57th phrase of the opening sequence 'Done'(330) is the same word that closes the whole section.

What we can read from this passage is the interplay of letters and words as material. Far from attempting to efface the process by which meaning is produced, Joyce is concerned to show how the mechanism of writing works. The first two pages, in which phrases without a context litter the text, refuse all possible meaning. Deprived of a context which would allow us to read them (that is to say ignore them as signifiers in order to consume the signifieds that they communicate), the words become material objects which rest on the page and resist our attempts to subject them to meaning. Words without context cannot be read in terms of meaning because words derive their meaning, not from the fact that each word is charged with a definite thought, but from their position in regard to other words. It is the flow of whole sentences and paragraphs that allows us to pass over the word and ignore it in favour of meaning. A word is defined in terms of difference: the different letters that go to make it up, the different words that surround it, and this difference is a difference which is activated across time and space through reading.

The Sirens force our attention on the activity of reading, which we can no longer claim is the consumption of a unity but must recognise as the constant movement of division. This section undertakes an investigation of writing as an activity in both time and space, for difference can only be produced *across* the page and *through* time. The spatial organisation of letters is what determines meaning but this spatial organisation is grasped in its particularity, as difference, through time and it is always in a deferred moment that the reader grasps the meaning of various signs. This deferred moment is at work throughout *Ulysses* as we constantly find phrases or words in new contexts which cause us to re-read their earlier occurrences. But The Sirens is that section in which the deferred moment is the major productive principle at work. After the 57 opening phrases we have the command 'Begin!' which institutes the process of writing, and this process will be exaggerated throughout The Sirens. The repetition (our second reading) provides a large enough space of difference for the original phrases, and thus through time we can read their meaning. We cannot ignore the materiality of the letter because the words, no longer caught in a normal set of differences (which accord with our expectations and are thus ignored) are strange to us. This strangeness of the words is a strangeness of ourselves; they/we are no longer an evident source of meaning.

In this emphasis on the materiality of writing, Joyce's text breaks with a notion of internal thought or external reality outside a materially existent socially formed language. Thus the use of the

Greek 'e', the difference of material inscription, marks the distinction between the text of Bloom and the text created by Bloom which is signed by Henry Flower. And as Bloom creates the character of Henry Flower so Joyce creates the character of Bloom, not in terms of creation and consciousness but in terms of production and language. Meaning is produced through a practice of writing, a process of differentiation of material signs. And as the Greek 'e' marks the different articulation of space so, in the text, this spatial organisation is grasped through time in a deferred moment.

'On, Know what I mean. No, change that ee.' (360)

'You know now. In haste. Henry. Greek ee.'(361)

There are many other instances where at macro-levels within the text the significance engendered by the material of words becomes a focus of attention. Two examples: on page 334 we read: 'Bloom whose dark eye to read Aaron Figather's name. Why do I always think Figather? Gathering figs I think', and on page 346:

– You did, averred Ben Dollard. I remember those tight trousers too. That was a brilliant idea, Bob.

Father Cowley blushed to his brilliant purply lobes. He saved the situa. Tight trou. Brilliant ide.

In this second example, the words 'situation', 'trousers', and 'idea' are de-composed into material letters, but, in addition, the meaning of the word 'brilliant' is defined by what follows, by the difference that comes afterwards in a deferred moment. In Homer's Odyssey, the Sirens represent a pure voice which cannot be described by the text, for the text is implicated in the differential production of writing.[11] Within Joyce's text, however, the Sirens episode does not function as an example of the power of the voice and the spoken word but undertakes the decomposition (in the musical sense of compose) of the voice and sound into the same play of material difference (play here considered in its mechanical sense, as the space in or through which a piece of mechanism can and does move) which constitutes writing. We have discussed the way in which the voice offers an experiential effacement of the material signifiers but it must be remembered that it is an effacement and not an abolition of this material. Marx was one of the first to emphasise the materiality of the spoken word when he wrote: 'From the start the "spirit" is afflicted with the curse of being "burdened" with matter, which here makes its appearance in the form of agitated layers of air, sounds, in short, of language.'[12] The Sirens can be read as the dramatisation of the materiality of language and it is Bloom as the writer of the drama who acts for the reader as the de-composer of the voice and music into material sounds. The voice is involved in the same play of difference through time and space that the text enacts in the practice of writing. Bloom, indeed, is identified as aiding the reading of this section when, in order to gain a pre-text for writing, he looks at the pages of the *Freeman*: 'Down the edge of his *Freeman* baton ranged Bloom's *your other eye*, scanning for where did I see that' (360; my emphasis). It is Bloom who is the reader's other eye and is, at the same time, his other I. By introducing writing, Bloom reads the voice for us but this reading introduces difference – introduces otherness – to the reader. Bloom locates the voice and music in material terms for the reader: 'The human voice, two tiny silky chords. Wonderful, more than all the others. That voice was a lamentation. Calmer now. It's in the silence you feel you hear. Vibrations. Now silent air.' (357). Bloom decomposes the voice into the difference set up by the vibrations and their absence, the fundamental opposition on which the voice is dependent. Similarly it is Bloom who recognises the importance of time (the deferred moment) in understanding sound:

> Numbers it is. All music when you come to think. Two multiplied by two divided by half is twice one. Vibrations: chords those are. One plus two plus six is seven. Do anything you like with figures juggling. Always find out this equal to that, symmetry under a cemetery wall. He doesn't see my mourning. Callous: all for his own gut. Musemathematics. And you think you're listening to the ethereal. But suppose you said it like: Martha, seven times nine minus x is thirty-five thousand. Fall quite flat. It's on account of the sounds it is.

> Instance he's playing now. Improvising. Might be what you like till you hear the words. Want to listen sharp. Hard. Begin all right: then hear chords a bit off: feel lost a bit. In and out of sacks over barrels, through wirefences, obstacle race. Time makes the tune. (359)

Bloom insists that music is a production of significance and not the magical result of a moment of creation. It is 'time that makes the tune' and Bloom repeats this insight later in the chapter when he thinks: 'Beauty of music you must hear twice.' (367)

Bloom, however, is not the only indicator of the materiality of sound. Pat, the deaf waiter, stands as an example of a figure deprived of the experience of the effacement of the signifier in the voice. He 'seehears lipspeech' (365) and this dependence on vision entails an awareness of the voice as a production of a set of differences. (One might remark that it is exactly this 'seehearing' that is required for the 'soundscript' (219.29) of *Finnegans Wake*.) Symmetrically the blind piano-tuner depends on the different vibrations caused by his ubiquitous tapping stick and he must thus experience sound as material. But perhaps the most powerful image of the materiality of sound is the tuning-fork which rests in the centre of the Ormond Bar as a reminder to the reader of the vibrations that produce sound. It is interesting to note within this perspective that Joyce appears to have told Gilbert that the tuning-fork could be identified with Bloom.

Writing in The Sirens subverts any notion of a full presence in the act of reading through an attention to, and a dramatisation of, the exteriority and the materiality of writing. In the same movement it dramatises the voice and sound (it is in this sense that we can understand the sequence as an 'imitation' of music) as the play of difference through time and space. This subversion destroys the possibility of the text representing some exterior reality and, equally, it refuses the text any origin in such a reality. The author does not create the meanings which are then conveyed by the text. For, as the meanings of the text are demonstrably produced by the distribution of words through space and time, it is impossible to isolate the words of the text from the contemporary words surrounding it: the words of the reader. Despite appearances there is no definite limit to a book. The fact that we can read it involves a play of discourses which runs beyond the covers of the book and beyond any individual reader in the same moment. We cannot make the move to an author *outside* the text who produces meanings *inside* the text because we cannot locate the outside of the text; although we can distinguish its physical limits, we cannot 'close' the book. For if meanings are produced through the interplay of discourses then there is no outside to the text, there are no words which are not implicated in the play of the text. Thus is the text caught up in time and the movement of history. The attempt to move outside language and to find (found) the author as the creator of meanings is the attempt to fix meanings in an origin 'outside' the text. This attempt may often be desperate for if we cannot close the endless distance and difference opened up by the text then there is no longer any possibility of 'closing' ourselves. As the covers of the book dissolve, so we, too, lose our definite limits and the bodies of discourse which we are, become evidently open to a continuous re-articulation.

The image with which we can elaborate this radical concept of text is the shell which Miss Douce has brought back from the beach at Rostrevor and which adorns the shelf below the bar mirror 'where hock and claret glasses shimmered and in their midst a shell' (332). Those in the bar who listen to the shell and who are caught up in the experience of speech, locate the sound as present in the shell and originating in the sea. For us, however, guided by our *writer* Bloom, the sound is produced by the process of listening: 'The sea they think they hear. Singing. A roar. The blood is it. Souse in the ear sometimes. Well, it's a sea. Corpuscle islands' (363). Our ideas about what happens when we read a text are similar to the ideas of the drinkers about the shell. As we read a text we are convinced that the meanings we consume are present in the text and originate in the author. But just as the interaction of the shell and ear produce the roar that the drinkers hear, so it is the interaction between the discourses of the reader and the discourses of the text which produces the meanings that we extract. The sound is not present for the ear in the shell as the meanings are not present for the eye in the text. The sound is produced between the shell and the ear but this 'between' does not indicate a specific place 'between' the shell and the ear but rather the whole process produced 'between' (in the sense of together) the shell and the ear.

The sea which the hearers wish to locate outside the act of hearing is, in fact, within it; indeed, it is constituted by it. It is not the sea of Rostrevor they hear but the sea of their own blood. There is no beginning, no origin outside the act of representation and therefore the representational field is not constituted by a set of identities which are re-presented but by a play of differences in which each presence is defined metonymically by the absences that surround it. The lack of a simple beginning can be read in the text in the place of the command 'Begin'. This is the 58th phrase of the opening sequence and constitutes the beginning of the text we are reading, but the command is already caught up within the flow of signifiers and cannot be situated outside it. There is no outside to the text where meaning originates before language, rather the text's meanings are constantly being produced in the act of reading: in, that is, the juxtaposition of the discourses of the reader and the text.

The separation of the elements that Brecht demanded as the condition of an epic and political theatre was, above all, directed against any 'fusion'. It is, of course, at that moment in the text when Bloom submits to the singing – to the effacement of the signifier – that such a moment of fusion occurs. Caught up in the signified everyone merges into a single identity:

> The voice of Lionel returned, weaker but unwearied. It sang again to Richie Poldy Lydia Lidwell also sang to Pat open mouth ear waiting, to wait. How first he saw that form endearing, how

sorrow seemed to part, how look, form, word charmed him Gould Lidwell, won Pat Bloom's heart. (354)

It is this general fusion that provides the particular case of 'Siopold' (356). As everybody in the bar forgets difference to become a fictional unity (they are all Lionel), Leopold and Simon join together. It is with such a moment of identity that the interchangeability of pronouns is established: 'Come. Well sung. All clapped. She ought to. Come. To me, to him, to her, to you, me, us.' (356)

It is also, of course, famously the moment of the illusion of fatherhood, the moment when the text finds an origin for itself as issued from the double loins of Leopold Bloom and Simon Dedalus. But, as with all such moments which are the products of the effacement of the signifier, the result is not simply unity but also, and necessarily, paralysis. This paralysis is produced in the Circe episode when the mirror (emblem of the effacement of the signifier) is the cause of a fusion between Stephen and Bloom This imaginary union of the two is a paralysed Shakespeare and it is this same paralysis which grips those drinking and talking in the bar but which Bloom can escape through writing. It is as Bloom begins to write to Martha that he emphasises that every signifier produced threatens to reveal a different message from that entrusted to it. The world of writing will demonstrate our subjectivity as constituted by division and difference (each new meaning subverts the unitary position of the subject) unlike the world of spoken communication where the apparent reception of our meaning by another ensures our own identity as we successfully identify with that other in the position of hearer. It is to the world of writing that the Sirens introduces the reader; we read the text as a 'letter selfpenned to one's other' (489.33/34). It is this world that Lacan indicates in his often repeated pronouncement that the speaking subject receives his or her own message from the other (the hearing subject) who returns it in inverted form.

The political effects of the recognition of this divided and distanced subject are manifold – for Joyce, most specifically, it meant the refusal of the full unified identity offered by ultra-nationalism. As the drinkers listen in sentimental unity to the song of the Croppy boy, Bloom considers Emmett's last words from the dock, those words which deny any possibility of writing until the achievement of nationhood: 'When my country takes her place among Nations of the earth. Then and not till then let my epitaph be written. I have done.' Emmett's words spell out the paralysis of nationalism in its demand that writing must be stopped until the achievement of nationhood. But such a demand represses the only activity that can furnish a lasting liberation from the dominance of priest and king (priest and king being so many names for the signified). Bloom's response to Emmett's injunction is to fart. Bloom's anality introduces a *process of separation* which denies to the subject the *position of separated* from the world. In order to accede to the world of absence, the world of the sign, there must be instituted a division between the subject and the world. Such a division both relies on and represses the anal drive. Relies on, insofar as it is with anality that a distinction between inside and outside is established, represses, insofar as the anal drive constantly ruins that very distinction. The re-introduction of a process of separation corrodes both the identity of the subject and the transparency of the sign. As the subject dissolves so we leave the world of the sign and are confronted with the materiality of the signifier ... the barrage of letters that are sprinkled through the closing lines of the section.

Emmett, and nationalism, wish to fix meanings and abolish writing. The last word of The Sirens is 'Done'. As part of the Emmett quote, the word has only one meaning, but within the text of The Sirens it gains the further meanings that the sequence has finished and that Bloom has farted. This fissuration of 'I have done' ensures that there is no final end to the text from which a one-to-one relation between signifier and signified can be imposed and this refusal of an ending is further emphasised by the fact that the 'Done' refers back to the command 'Begin'.

It was a common conceit at the end of the nineteenth century that music could be understood as the supreme expressive medium, as a perfect voice.[13] Underlying this idea was an ideology of the work of art as a vehicle for communicating a meaning from an origin (the artist) to a similarly discrete and unitary recipient (the aesthetic reader or listener). By insisting on the materiality of the vehicle (words or sounds), *Ulysses* transforms its relation both of the author and readers. An interesting parallel can be found in the contemporary efforts of the revolutionary composer Eisler and the revolutionary writer Brecht to alter the relation between art and audience. Walter Benjamin comments on their efforts as follows:

In other words, the task consisted in the 'functional trans-formation' of the concert-hall form of music in a manner which had to meet two conditions: that of removing, first, the dichotomy of performer and audience and, secondly, that of technical method and content. On this point Eisler makes the following interesting observation: 'we should beware of over-estimating orchestral music and thinking of it as the only high art-form. Music without words acquired its great importance and its full development only under capitalism.' This suggests that the task of transforming concert music requires help from the word. Only such help can, as Eisler puts it, transform a concert into a political meeting. The fact that such a transformation may really represent a peak achievement of both musical and literary technique – this Brecht and Eisler have proved with their didactic play *The Measures Taken*.[14]

This passage of Benjamin's is perhaps the best introduction we can have to reading The Sirens. For The Sirens makes of the reader a Brechtian crowd, a crowd which is not a unity but a set of divisions which constitute opposing forces.

The Sirens dramatises the lack of a simple origin for a text – it deconstructs any possible author – and this dramatisation, deconstruction has immediate results. Deprived of the necessary interchangeability of pronouns, no dominant discourse can regulate and homogenise the heterogeneous discourses that are grouped under any one name in the text. With the end of an agreed 'it' of narration, there can be no more of those endless characters that the psychological novel is condemned to repeat and instead we can enjoy the contradictory interplay of language. □

Maud Ellmann's 'Disremembering Dedalus' featured in one of the first and most influential collections of post-structuralist criticism, Robert Young's *Untying the Text*, and Young's introduction to the essay restates usefully the post-structuralist position on Joyce, reflecting back on the debates and dead-ends exemplified in this guide by Kenner, Booth and others.

■ Anglo-American criticism has largely been engaged in the attempt to recuperate Joyce – so that Bloom in *'Ulysses'* becomes the 'realest' everyman of all, while, paradoxically, he is surrounded by ever-more erudite systems and texts of allusion, reference and influence. Criticism of *A Portrait* has largely been preoccupied with the 'problem' of aesthetic distance in the novel, as if *A Portrait* were about the tension between sympathy and judgement, as in the conventional reading of Browning's dramatic monologues. Yet what such approaches do not take into account is the materiality of writing in the novels: at all points, Joyce's texts resist their appropriation back into the discourse of realism, of representation, because of the oddness and opacity of their language. What is perhaps most remarkable, in view of the challenge which Joyce's novels present, has been the tenacity with which they have been read as windows on to the world or into the mind. □

Ellmann shares with MacCabe the conviction that Joyce's language does not seek to express, represent, reconstitute or describe 'experience' or 'reality', but to construct it. She also, like MacCabe, employs Lacanian theory to deconstruct the idea of the unified, authentic subject, seeing instead movements of fragmentation, dispersal, exchange and substitution, involved in the constitution of the subject through and in discourse. Discussions as to whether Stephen is sympathetic or not, or about which is the real Stephen, become irrelevant as Ellmann engages in an exhilaratingly inventive and visceral reading of the text. MacCabe's concern with the materiality of language is here complemented with an awareness of the complexity of psycho-physical drives and engagements – in her words, the convergence of lust and language – which is in sharp contrast with the coyness or moralising of previous critics and shows a significant advance on her father Richard Ellmann's transcendentalist reading. The name of the father and the mother's namelessness are here contrasted, as the submerged significances of *A Portrait*, of women, bad taste and dirty words, are brought out into the open.

■ A stranger once came up to Joyce in a café and cried, 'Let me kiss the hand that wrote *Ulysses*!' Joyce promptly replied, 'It's done a lot of other things too.' In *A Portrait of the Artist as a Young Man*, a thought occurs to Stephen which seems, curiously, to anticipate this joke without – for the thinker – being jokey:

> If ever his soul, re-entering her dwelling shyly after the frenzy of his body's lust had spent itself, was turned towards her whose emblem is the morning star, *bright and musical, telling of heaven and infusing peace*, it was when her names were murmured softly by lips whereon there still lingered foul and shameful words, the savour itself of a lewd kiss.[15] (112)

What appals Stephen – as it amuses Joyce – is the way lust and language may converge in a single bodily member. The hand, in the one case, and the lips, in the other, are stained by their intimacy. These organs are puns in bad taste. They betray, between the text and sexuality, an intercourse more cunning than a rhyme.

How, then, can these members remember? Among the things the hand that wrote *Ulysses* did was to write *A Portrait of the Artist*. In fact, it wrote three portraits of him: a first draft, whose rejection gave rise to *Stephen Hero* and to what we regard, teleologically, as the final text. As for this last version, the indefinite article of its title suggests that it, too, may represent yet another Wordsworthian preparation to write. It is *a* portrait, not 'The Portrait'. At first, a repetition of the author's life, Joyce autobiography seems henceforth destined to repeat itself. What can it be about self-portraiture, for Joyce as for Wordsworth, that makes them so reluctant to conclude?

To account, in the case of 'The Prelude', for the growth of a poet's mind, Wordsworth must read his own life backwards. Through memory, he must retrieve the seeds from which – organically speaking – the poem and the mind that wrote it grew. If memory is constructed in the present, the past, as such, can never be recovered. So we behold, in autobiography, a paradoxical procedure by which memory writes the past to discover how the past wrote and determined memory. In this sense, the autobiographer decomposes the present that the past composed: unwrites the hand that writes. Remembering becomes dismembering: or more precisely, 'disremembering' – to borrow Davin's Irishism from *A Portrait* (p. 181). It is to forget oneself – in the most indiscreet ways.

If *A Portrait* borrows from 'The Prelude' any model of the poet's mind, it is not the metaphor of growth. Rather it is Wordsworth's notion of 'spot of time' that fascinates the text. 'Islands in the unnavigable depth of our departed time': the spot of time, which Wordsworth seems to use to mean a space, or place, or interlude, includes, among a plethora of definitions, the idea of a blemish, stain, spot, or scar. And indeed, it is a scar which hollows out the 'spot' in the Gibbet-Mast episode of Wordsworth's autobiography: the scar that remains of an identity.[16] This scar is the name of a murderer. Neither the name, nor the hand that carved it, is disclosed: all that the passage intimates is the act of cutting it and its indelibility. Naming is maiming. 'To this hour,' the text insists, the letters, 'carved by some unknown hand' are 'all still fresh and visible'. *A Portrait*, too, as I shall try to show, conceives identity as a scar without an author, without an origin, and at last, without even a name. And this identity is a wound that constantly re-opens, so that its letters may remain 'all fresh and visible'.

It is important, however, to stress that *A Portrait* is not 'about' a scar. To say that the text is 'about' something reinstitutes the polarity of content and form which Joyce's writing constantly stretches and transgresses. Daedalus's labyrinth lurks in *A Portrait*'s imagery as if to halt us in our hermeneutics. For the secret of a labyrinth is only the way out, whereas I, for one, am looking for a way in. The scar is not a secret, but a principle of structure: a punctuation. Because it is a living scar, it constantly resurges and reiterates itself. And the signification of the text is lodged in the very blanks and repetitions that mark and mask its cicatrix. For the scar belongs not only to the subject but to the text itself, which both suffers and enacts the mutilation by which identity reconstitutes itself. Purloined letters, the lacunae of the narrative – its scars – are only hidden in that they are too blatant to be seen. Rather than the secret of *A Portrait*, the scar insinuates itself as a secretion: a word which describes at once the operations of hoarding, fission, and emission which undo the fixity of identity and hyphenate autobiography.

In this essay I shall pursue the notion of identity as process: in fact, as a series of processes, which *A Portrait* joins in a 'brisure'. 'Brisure', which I borrow from Derrida, encompasses the ambiguities of 'cleaving' in the sense of splitting, and 'cleaving' in the sense of joining or embracing. So in translation let's enflesh brisure by calling it a cleavage.

One process that proceeds from the cleavage of identity consists of scarrification. This has two sides, which could be described as nomination and punctuation. In the act of nomination, word is stained with flesh and flesh with word, for the name, like the name of Wordsworth's 'murderer', emerges in this text as a cicatrix. Once named and maimed, the subject, rather than a plenitude, erupts henceforth as punctuation, as a gap or wound that rips the fabric of the text at irregular intervals.

Punctuation	)		(	repeats
	)		(	
	)	SCAR	(	
Nomination	)		(	secretes

Both aspects of scarrification make themselves felt in the fourth section of Chapter 2 (91–102), the trip to Cork, which I shall take as a point of departure.

But we only know the scar by its secretion: by that which issues from and enters into it. What proceeds from scarrification is circulation: and *A Portrait* sets in motion a complex circulation of sexual and textual economies. The diagram will suggest, inevitably, a schematic rigidity: but if we keep in mind that each overlaps and overleaps the other, to abstract them in this way may help us to discern their furious rhythm.

Circulation occurs in three forms, each of which involves the linguistic and corporeal equivalents that I have listed, respectively, under WORD and FLESH. Each also corresponds to the strategies of disremembering that constitute the subject of autobiography [see next page].

SEXUAL/TEXTUAL ECONOMIES

	ECONOMY	FLESH	WORD
MARKET PLACE	1 Flows	dismembering emission	synecdoche
	2 Influence	remembering incorporation	metaphor or tautology
LITERATURE	3 'Detaining' Hoarding	retention chastity	lacunae and the 'literal'

The first is an economy of flows, whereby the subject purges or evacuates himself, and issues forth in all kinds of secretions.

> His sins trickled from his lips, one by one, trickled in shameful drops from his soul, festering and oozing like a sore, a squalid stream of vice. The last sins oozed forth, sluggish, filthy. (156)

Semen, blood, urine, breath, money, saliva, speech and excrement provide the currencies for this economy. Menstruation also figures among these flows, for the text at this level (though not at others) is as indifferent to gender as to the formal separation of excrement and sexuality. Not to mention vomit, which is a perpetual danger in this text – not only for Stephen but for his reader. Rhetorically, the economy of flows corresponds to the trope of synecdoche – the part for the whole – for through these flows, any notion of totality disintegrates, and the subject is dispersed into the fragments and the waste that stand for him.

What passes out of Stephen must, however, first pass into him. So, working in tandem with the rhythm of his flows is an economy of influence. Food, particularly the bread and wine of the eucharist, figures in this economy, but on the whole it is Stephen's nose, rather than his mouth, that opens him to influence.

The odours that so besiege our hero's nose are more frequently noxious than sweet. In fact, they are the odours of mortality: of dead flesh, and, as I shall show, dead speech. The worst stench of all is that of writing – dead speech stored in literature – which passes into Stephen through his nose and passes through his mouth as speech again. So, influence retains its literary implications: Stephen inhales the literary tradition and re-members it in his secretions.

This transaction with the past resembles the Eucharist which changes spirit into wine, until at last – as Mulligan mischievously adds – the wine becomes water again. It compares also to the other conversions which enthral the text: of money into goods, lust into language, peristalsis into metre, or the gross earth into art. And vice versa. Trans-substantiation and digestion meet as the loci of metaphor. But Stephen's own transactions with influence tend to conclude, as we shall see, not in metaphor, but in repetition and tautology.

'Literature' is the name that Stephen gives to the third economy, the economy of hoarding. This baptism occurs in the context of a conversation with the English dean:

> – One difficulty, said Stephen, in aesthetic discussion is to know whether words are being used according to the literary tradition or according to the tradition of the marketplace. I remember a sentence of Newman's in which he says of the Blessed Virgin that she was detained in the full company of the saints. The use of the word in the marketplace is quite different. *I hope I am not detaining you.*
>
> – Not in the least, said the dean politely.
>
> – No, no, said Stephen, smiling, I mean ...
>
> – Yes, yes: I see, said the dean quickly, I quite catch the point: detain. (203)

In this conversation, the word 'detain' itself becomes 'literature' when it elicits no response. 'Detain', of course, is not unlike 'retain' except, importantly, that its implications are less absolute. 'Literature' consists of words and flesh detained, held back, withdrawn for a time from circulation. In opposition to the marketplace of flow and influence, literature detains language as the miser hoards his money and the petulant infant withholds what Lacan calls his 'gift of shit'. Nor is it by accident that it is Mary, in this passage, who is detained: for her chastity also represents a form of hoarding. Speech in storage, 'literature' functions as hiatus, blocking the exchange of word for flesh and flesh for words. Literature – to borrow a word from *Dubliners*, is the paralysis of language.

Stephen's proclaimed aesthetic of 'silence, exile and cunning' seems, like 'scrupulous meanness', to bespeak the linguistic avarice of 'literature'. His *Portrait* too practises a politics of 'detaining', hoarding words in the transcendentalised retentions of epiphany. These occulted episodes erupt as blank spots in the narrative. In their very literality they refuse to flow, to undergo the exchange and transformation of synecdoche or metaphor.

But withdrawing words from circulation can only bring about a temporary pause, before the text embezzles them in new transactions. In the passage I shall presently discuss, the word 'Foetus', paralysed as 'literature', surreptitiously, and with explosive implications, reinfiltrates the text's economies. But before we embark on these semantics, let's survey the text's whole economic policy.

A capitalist economy operates by withdrawing funds from circulation in order, paradoxically, for money and commodities to circulate at all. All these economies depend upon the hoarding of the bank vault and the interest racket. Thus, in *A Portrait*, words and flesh take the place of money and commodities, and 'literature' of hoarding mischievously completes the cycle of a capitalist economy in miniature.

I now turn to the further section of Chapter 2 (91–102), which will provide a paradigm for the procedures of disremembering. Nomination, punctuation, and all the sexual and textual economies work their commerce here. What is more, the section represents an autobiography within an autobiography: for it describes Simon Dedalus's sentimental journey to his origins in Cork, and his struggle to remember his fugitive history. His nostalgia reaches its climax in the search for his own initials, carved as indelibly as the name of Wordsworth's 'murderer' in the dark stained wood of a school desk.

But another scar precedes these initials, and in a sense pre-empts them: the word 'Foetus', which I alluded to before, whose carved letters move Stephen to a horror as extreme as it is unexplained. While the father's rehearsals of his past, and his excavation of his name, seem to represent a repossession of identity, the brute material motive of the journey belies his sentiment. For he returns to his origins only to sell them away. He is to auction his belongings, and to dispossess himself and his resentful son. Remembering reverts to disremembering.

Duplicity, indeed, begins with the opening sentence of the section.

Stephen was once again seated beside his father in the corner of a railway carriage at Kingsbridge. (91)

'Once again' is a curious sleight of hand: Stephen has never shared a railway carriage with his father in the text before. This is a first time masquerading as a repetition. It recalls the first sentence of the whole autobiography: 'Once upon a time and a very good time it was', where the first time turns out not to be the beginning of Stephen's story, but of a story told to Stephen by his father. The trip to Cork is also an episode in which Stephen's story grafts itself upon his father's story, and they compete for autobiographies. We begin to suspect some relation between the father and false starts; and to suspect, perhaps, the very notion of beginning.

But some form of recollection is taking place here, which prevents the 'once again' from startling us. In the second half of the paragraph, the reader undergoes a repetition:

> He saw the darkening lands slipping away past him, the silent telegraph poles passing his window swiftly every four seconds, the little glimmering stations, manned by a few silent sentries, flung by the mail behind her and twinkling in a moment in the darkness like fiery grains thrust backwards by a runner. (92)

This passage does not repeat a real event, but a dream that Stephen had at Clongowes:

> The train was full of fellows: a long long chocolate train with cream facings. The guards went to and fro opening, closing, locking, unlocking the doors. They were men in dark blue and silver; they had silvery whistles and their keys made a quick music: click, click: click, click.

> And the train raced on over the flat lands and past the hill of Allen. The telegraph poles were passing, passing. The train went on and on. It knew. (18)

Just as the beginning of Stephen's story is another story, so here the real train evolves out of the dream. This order makes a fiction of experience.

What the reader undergoes, through the repetition of the dream-sequence, is the constitution of his own memory. The logic of repetition works backward in this text: the second episode reverts upon the first, and modifies its structure and its sense. In other words, it takes the second episode to activate the scar left by the first. This, perhaps, is why the text cannot begin. By the same strategy of repetition, text and reader are deprived of their originality. Like the autobiographer himself, we as readers are forced to read backwards: we, too, are disremembering.

We recall that the autobiographer must unwrite the present in order to write the past. These two passages capture the moment when remembering reverses into disremembering: when the present 'passes' into memory and the past 'presents' itself as desire. They enact the very process of 'passing', a word invested in *A Portrait* with multiple reverberations, and which repeats itself insistently in these two homecomings:

> The telegraph poles were passing, passing. (18)

> He saw the darkening lands slipping away past him, the silent telegraph poles passing his window swiftly every four seconds. (92)

The two journeys themselves do not precisely represent events, but passages between events: interstices between the present and the past. They have no content: none, that is, but the passing and missing of a content: the landscape that slips past, and the stations and the sentries flung behind. This train not only passes by content but passes it out, evacuates and disremembers it. All that remains is a wake: the trail of fiery flakes thrust backwards as if by a runner.

Another wake occurs a little further on: the wake of Stephen's words, which falls into the rhythm of the train's evacuation:

> At Maryborough he fell asleep. When he awoke the train had passed out of Mallow and his father was stretched asleep on the other seat. The cold light of the dawn lay over the country, over the unpeopled fields and the closed cottages. The terror of sleep fascinated his mind as he watched the silent country or heard from time to time his father's deep breath or sudden sleepy movement. The neighbourhood of unseen sleepers filled him with strange dread as though they could harm him; and he prayed that the day might come quickly. His prayer, addressed neither to God nor saint, began with a shiver, as the chilly morning breeze crept through the chink of the carriage door to his feet, and ended in a trail of foolish words which he made to fit the insistent rhythm of the train; and silently, at intervals of four seconds, the telegraph poles held the galloping notes of the music between punctual bars. This furious music allayed his dread and, leaning against the windowledge, he let his eyelids close again. (92–93)

Twice Stephen falls asleep, and twice he wakes; but while he wakes, his father, instead, dozes with the neighbourhood of unseen sleepers. Merging with the intermittency of the telegraph poles, this alternation makes consciousness the music of its interruptions: the rhythm of its own repeated exile. It suggests, also, that Stephen's being will involve the eclipse of his father's, and that his consciousness achieves itself by means of the annihilation of his father and the world. And while the punctual bars of the telegraph poles puncture and punctuate, rupture and redistribute, the galloping music of the train, a trail of foolish words gushes from Stephen's lips to complete the cycle of evacuation. These words, too, have no content: none, at least, that the text conceded to circulate. They only mark the fading of consciousness and the gaps between the poles.

What's left, then, of the subject after all this 'passing', all this evacuation? In the course of disremembering, a different kind of subject emerges from the text: different, and radically opposed to the tradition of the human subject and to the orthodox conception of the subject matter of a text. The subject erupts as punctuation. As the silence woven into music, the absence woven into vision: as the pulsation of the unconscious. Like Philippe in a dream that Laplanche and Leclaire have analysed, the subject here dissolves from a positive substance into a scar in the shape of a comma.[17] We behold the repetition of a Mallarméan genesis, where 'les blancs' – the whites, the scars of punctuation – hollow out a universe of space and time.

This punctuation establishes itself even prior to the dream at Clongowes, in a series of what we might call ontological experiments:

> He leaned his elbows on the table and shut and opened the flaps of his ears. Then he heard the noise of the refectory every time he opened the flaps of his ears. It made a roar like a train at night. And when he closed the flaps the roar was shut off like a train going into a tunnel. That night at Dalkey the train had roared like that and then, when it went into the tunnel, the roar stopped. He closed his eyes and the train went on, roaring and then stopping; roaring again, stopping. It was nice to hear it roar and stop and then roar out of the tunnel again and then stop. (14)

Is Stephen shutting the world out of himself, or himself out of the world? This game reverts upon the player. While he seems to be mastering the world, controlling its presence and its absence, the child is establishing his own intermittency, his own punctuation. This fiction uncreates the fabricator.

The punctuation of the earflap game gradually accrues to itself a number of semantic oppositions which invest it with a form of representability.

> First came the vacation and then the next term and then vacation again and then another term and then again the vacation. It was like a train going in and out of tunnels and what was like the noise of boys eating in the refectory when you opened and closed the flaps of your ears. Term, vacation; tunnel, out; noise, stop. How far away it was! (14)

Each time the scar recurs, it amalgamates another binarism. Now its punctuation leans upon the oppositions of in and out, home and school, vacation and term, and the train that enters and emerges from the tunnel, with its sudden roar. These alternatives articulate the scar, and constitute a bank of representatives to be embezzled by the dream.

Later in the book, the sermon seems to parody this process of accretion, when the priest gathers compound interest on the words 'ever never'.

111

A holy saint (one of our own fathers I believe it was) was once vouchsafed a vision of hell. It seemed to him that he stood in the midst of a great hall, dark and silent save for the ticking of a great clock. The ticking went on unceasingly; and it seemed to this saint that the sound of the ticking was the ceaseless repetition of the words: ever, never; ever, never. Ever to be in hell, never to be in heaven; ever to be shut off from the presence of God, never to enjoy the beatific vision; ever to be eaten with flames, gnawed by vermin, goaded with burning spikes, never to be free from these pains; ever to have the conscience upbraid one, the memory enrage, the mind filled with darkness and despair, never to escape; ever to curse and revile the foul demons who gloat fiendishly over the misery of their dupes, never to behold the shining raiment of the blessed spirits. (143)

Et cetera. This is the rhythm of exile from the sight of God; the music of mortality. Reading backwards – as the text demands – we can see that the former alternations also involve an ostracism: the punctuation and its representatives all bespeak Stephen's exile from home, and his desire to return to his origins. Confounding the journey home with the ticking of eternity, this rhythm links the end to the beginning, staining with mortality the search for origins. And we too, reading backwards in pursuit of a first time, are caught in its furious music. As punctuation, the subject is never fully present, but is always either coming into, or dying out of, being. 'Coming' and 'dying': both are orgasmic: and the rhythm of exile also resembles a 'frottage'. The furious music of the train passes through Stephen to die in an 'ejaculation'. Most of Stephen's verses 'come' in this way. He vacillates between two states described habitually as 'unrest' and 'weariness' (67, 81, 82, 110), broken by ejaculations. This brings us to the first of the textual economies: the economy of flows.

Like the landscape that passes by Stephen on the train, passing out of him in foolish words, verses, throughout the book, associate themselves consistently with the circuitous itinerary of the verb 'to pass'.

Such moments passed and the wasting fires of lust sprang up again. The verses passed from his lips and the inarticulate cries and the unspoken brutal words rushed forth from his brain to force a passage. (106)

Lust, for the hand that wrote *Ulysses*, passes incessantly through language, staining flesh with words and words with flesh. The two can scarcely be distinguished. No more can they detach themselves from any other form of passing or evacuation. The streams and floods which pass from Stephen's lips could be urethral, or menstrual, as well as seminal: breath, blood, vomit and saliva also issue from this orifice in the form of speech:

He stretched forth his arms in the street to hold fast the frail swooning form that eluded him and incited him: and the cry that he had strangled for so long in his throat issued from his lips. It broke from him like a wail of despair from a hell of sufferers and died in a wail of furious entreaty, a cry for an iniquitous abandonment, a cry which was but the echo of an obscene scrawl which he had read to the oozing wall of a urinal. (106)

This cry is in the strictest sense a dirty word. It is a matter of indifference to the metaphor whether it 'passes' or it 'comes' from Stephen's lips. A movement – orgasmic, bowel or urethral – releases it to die into a wail: to ooze into an echo of a scar on the wall of a urinal. The subject's body is a mint which issues him in wakes, trails, fragments and secretions. 'Issue', a word the text relishes as much as 'passing', may be applied to publication, currency or generation: and all the flows which 'issue' from the subject constitute the means by which he duplicates, or publishes, or coins himself. These secretions – verbal or corporeal – invisibly depart, and enter henceforth into circulation.

Everything that 'passes' through Stephen's consciousness 'issues' forth emptied or dismembered. In one of his attempts at poetry:

It seemed as if he would fall again, but, by dint of brooding on the incident, he thought himself into confidence. During this process all those elements which he deemed common or insignificant fell out of the scene. There remained no trace of the tram itself nor of the tram men nor of the horses: nor did he and she appear vividly. The verses told only of the night and the balmy breeze and of the maiden lustre of the moon. Some undefined sorrow was hidden in the hearts of the protagonists as they stood in silence between the leafless trees ... After this the letters L.D.S. were written at the foot of the page. (74)

Only the initials at the end of this verse receive direct quotation, as Stephen, earlier, had halted, blocked, at the initials of its dedication (73). Apart from these detailed letters ('literature') the passage offers a paralyptical account of the content of the verses: or rather, of the voiding of their content. Also without content are the letters of a different kind – epistles – which emerge as frequently from Stephen's failures in verse:

> He saw himself sitting at his table in Bray the morning after the discussion at the Christmas dinner table, trying to write a poem about Parnell on the back of one of his father's second moiety notices. But his brain had then refused to grapple with the theme and, desisting, he had covered the page with the names and addresses of his classmates. (73)

These are letters that are never sent.

Both forms of reduction to the letter occur in the following passage:

> He could scarcely interpret the letters of the signboards of the shops. By his monstrous way of life he seemed to have put himself beyond the limits of reality. ... He could scarcely recognise as his own thoughts, and repeated slowly to himself:
>
> – I am Stephen Dedalus. I am walking beside my father whose name is Simon Dedalus. We are in Cork, in Ireland. Cork is a city. Our room is in the Victoria Hotel. (98)

As well as the words he writes, the words Stephen reads are constantly disintegrating into a debris of letters. And he responds by composing a letter to himself: his name and his address, without a message. This is the art of disremembering.

An art of living. Just as the word is shattered into letters, so the flesh decomposes into an inventory of its members and secretions. Other people Stephen apprehends as voices, faces, eyes, hands, clothes, glances or footsteps. The woman he desires, for instance, he perceives as breath, a glance, and the tapping of shoes:

> Her glance travelled to his corner, flattering, taunting, searching, exciting his heart ... sprays of her fresh warm breath flew gaily above her cowled head and her shoes tapped blithely on the glassy road. (72)

The text, however, demolishes the flesh fastidiously. Here it reduces the woman's body specifically to its exchange values. Not just any parts are itemised, but the parts that issue forth in circulation. The face, the gaze, the footstep and the voice represent the currency through which the subject enters the economies of flow and influence.

But the text does not halt at mere dismemberment. The face, the gaze, the footstep and the voice degenerate into images and echoes of themselves. This is how, for instance, its rhetoric mutilates the priest at Clongowes:

> Stephen smiled again in answer to the smile he could not see on the priest's shadowed face, its image or spectre only passing rapidly across his mind as the low discreet accent fell upon his ear. (168)

These are smiles of the order of the Cheshire cat. In this reverse apotheosis, the priest dematerialises, leaving in his wake a trace in Stephen's consciousness: an image or a spectre of an accent and a smile.

There seems to be no agency apart from consciousness that could assume responsibility for the priest's explosion. Yet Stephen's consciousness appears to be the victim of the fall-out too. His own gestures are not precisely self-determined actions, but mimetically return the images projected from the priest. Blinded by the shadows – which also are projections of the interlocutors – Stephen answers, rather than broaches, the first smile, whose image passes of its own accord across his mind, while the disembodied accent falls upon his passive ear. Both parties to this dialogue reflect, refract, and echo one another: each is the other's mirror, and the subject but the speculation of the object, in a triple sense. Dismembering reverts upon the disrememberer. It is through an ambush of synecdoche that Emma Clery and the priest disintegrate into their exchange values. But it is also by means of this dismemberment that either gains admission to Stephen's consciousness as an 'image'. So that synecdoche represents a kind of rhetorical chewing which prepares experience for ingustation. This second process takes us into the domain of metaphor, or in fleshly terms into the economy of influence. Flow and influence constantly converge, however, in that Stephen's overflows, spontaneous as they may be, are always derived from a previous source. Many of his verses are only paraphrased, but those few that the text vouchsafes directly tend to be quotations. Even the word 'weariness' which terminates his feelings of unrest is recycled from Shelley and Ben Jonson. Or else 'the 'soft speeches of Claude Melnotte' rise to his lips to 'ease his unrest', rise to his lips to 'ease his unrest' (106). Even Stephen's dirty word is the echo of the graffito in the urinal, where the wake of language – writing – is stained by urine, the wake of the flesh. Every word that 'passes' out of Stephen originates in 'literature': from whence its stench conducts it to his nose, and issues henceforth from his lips, and issues henceforth from his lips. While the dirty word reeks of excrement, the legends in shop windows which confront him later stink of mortality, diffusing in the air around him a tenuous and deadly exhalation and he found himself glancing from one casual word to another on his right or left in stolid wonder that they had been so silently emptied of instantaneous sense until every mean shop legend bound his mind like the words of a spell and his soul shrivelled up, sighing with age as he walked on in a lane among heaps of dead language. His own consciousness of language was ebbing from his brain and trickling into the very words themselves which set to band and disband themselves in wayward rhythms:

> The ivy whines upon the wall,
> And whines and twines upon the wall,
> The yellow ivy on the wall,
> Ivy, ivy up the wall.

Did anyone ever hear such drivel? Lord almighty! Whoever heard of ivy whining on a wall?

This is the smell of dead language. It is the smell of words which have been heaped up in mean shop legends: withdrawn from circulation and hoarded in writing. These words, like flesh, disintegrate in Stephen's consciousness into meaningless concatenations. He cannot help but absorb their deadly exhalations and pass them out again – in 'drivel'.

This passage, then, unfolds the interactions of all three economies: the 'flow' of drivel: the 'Influence of mortal odours'; and the dead language, the 'literature' which occasions these deferred effects. To complete the disremembering of Dedalus, we have only now to see how the letters of his name – his founding 'literature' – also constitute, with their deferred effects, a cicatrix.

So, by this commodious vicus of recirculation, we return to Cork. Stephen, now, is trying to track down the initials that stand for his father's name – and also, incidentally, his own:

They passed into the anatomy theatre where Mr Dedalus, the porter aiding him, searched the desks for his initials. Stephen remained in the background, depressed more than ever by the darkness and silence of the theatre and by the air it wore of jaded and formal study. On the desk he read the word 'Foetus' cut several times in the dark stained wood. The sudden legend startled his blood: he seemed to feel the absent students of the college about him and to shrink from their company. A vision of their life, which his father's words had been powerless to evoke, sprang up before him out of the word cut in the desk. A broad-shouldered student with a moustache was cutting in the letters with a jack-knife, seriously. Other students stood or sat near him laughing at his handiwork. One jogged his elbow. The big student turned on him, frowning. He was dressed in loose grey clothes and had tan boots.

Stephen's name was called. He hurried down the steps of the theatre so as to be as far away from the vision as he could be and, peering closely at his father's initials, hid his flushed face. (95)

Concerned as this passage is with spotting, it also functions as a blank spot in the narrative. It remains, like the legend of the desk, unalterably literal: no trope can induce it into circulation. Neither Stephen, nor the reader, nor the text, can incorporate the word 'Foetus' which erupts so inexplicably.

What the passage emphasises most about these letters is the act of cutting them. Like a scar, and like the dead letters in shop windows, this literature administers deferred effects. Clearly, it is not just a word that we are dealing with, but a wound: an old wound, indeed, that Stephen activates in reading it. He responds with an hallucination: he feels himself surrounded by the absent students who once scarred the desk with this uncanny legend. This word, unlike the father's memories, can resurrect the dead. By two strategies, then, this word usurps the father's place: it emerges where the father's name should be; and it summons up a vision of the dead which his father's words – thinks Stephen – had been 'powerless to evoke'. But the initials that the word pre-empts are also the initials of Stephen Dedalus.

That the initials of the name of the father should present themselves as a scar is thinkable within a psychoanalytic frame of reference. In 'Moses and Monotheism', Freud connects the scar of circumcision to the patronym; and Lacan uses the term 'Name of the Father' as a synonym for the Law of Castration. For the psychoanalytic critic, it is almost wearisome to find that SD has been made into a wound. But why, in this account of things, should another word achieve priority, and an earlier scar forestall the laceration of the name? And why is this word 'Foetus'?

Why, if not because this first scar is a navel, to which the Foetus is, of course, attached? Attached, not to the father's name, but to the mother's namelessness? Why the horror, if not because the phallus has surrendered to the omphalos?

In another autobiography, 'The Interpretation of Dreams', Freud's heuristics direct him to the navel as ineluctably as those of his Irish namesake:

> There is often a passage in even the most thoroughly interpreted dream which has to be left obscure; this is because we become aware during the work of interpretation that at that point there is a tangle of dream-thoughts which cannot be unravelled and which moreover adds nothing to our knowledge of the content of the dream. This is the dream's navel, the spot where it reaches down into the unknown. The dream-thoughts to which we are led by interpretation cannot from the nature of things have any definite endings; they are bound to branch out in every direction into the intricate network of our world of thought. It is at some point where this meshwork is particularly close that the dream-wish grows up, like a mushroom out of its mycelium.[18]

According to this description, the navel represents at once the origin and essence of the dream – its wish – and yet contributes 'nothing' to its content. At once a knot and a lacuna, where meaning, in its very density, dissolves, the navel is the seam of the dream. Strangely, this absence occurs where sense is most concentrated, in the closest tangle of the dream thoughts. If, as Freud suggests, the navel constitutes the dream's origin, it is, moreover, an incongruous metaphor for him to use. For even anatomically, the navel is the point at which the foetus was once fastened parasitically upon its mother: where, indeed, the body has no definite ending, nor beginning, but branches out in every direction into the intricate network of the amniotic world. The navel marks the spot where such identity dissolves.

In The Oxen of the Sun in *Ulysses*, Stephen repudiates the notion that our first parents' bellies lacked a blemish. Similarly, in Michelangelo's 'Creation' in the Sistine Chapel, Adam's navel, in mute blasphemy, forswears the fatherhood of God. The umbilicus, that Stephen calls the 'strandentwining cable of all flesh', belies the firstness of the father, and the originality of His creation. For rather than an origin, this blemish is the footnote of the flesh.

To award this footnote the status of an origin offers as a model of artistic evolution only the alternatives of foetal theft or natal fragmentation. *Finnegans Wake* and *A Portrait* are both, in their different ways, omphalocentric. 'The last word in stolentelling', the *Wake* adopts the first alternative of foetal theft, and circumnavigates the navel. It restores to the currencies of word and flesh a seamless amniotic fluency. Narrative itself becomes umbiliform. If, in *A Portrait*, to remember is to dismember, in the *Wake*, memory is mammary.

A Portrait, on the other hand, incessantly short-circuits. In its repeated births, its repeated exiles, it compulsively returns to the moment of fracture and the scar. After the phallus, then, and Derrida's corrective technics of the hymen, I proffer the navel as the prototype of

Dedalus's scars. A prototype, but not an origin: for already we have seen, in the knotting and entanglement of Freud's own metaphor, that the navel necessarily resists the very structures of priority, centrality, originality. Omphalocentrism is that movement which deflects, supplants, transverses and attenuates the notion of a first, or a last, instance. In *A Portrait*, the word 'foetus' does not 'mean' navel, but rather carves the spot where word and flesh meet in a single scar. These scars, or letters, or 'scarletters' – to contract Hawthorne's pertinent title – are littered through the *Wake*, and weave also through *Ulysses* like an invisible cord. 'Gaze in your omphalos', Stephen counsels to himself in Proteus: and his 'Portrait' is a contemplation of the navel, with all its narcissistic implications. As onanistic as the *Wake* is incestuous, the rhythms of *A Portrait* are not those of fluid interchange, but the rhythms of 'ejaculation' in the loneliness of exile, those of a hundred wet and navelled dreams. □

The final short extract in this chapter, from David Lodge's *After Bakhtin*,[19] is much less adventurous in tone and ambition than MacCabe or Ellmann. (His generous but dogged caution is best exemplified in the pastiche of Penelope with which he ends one of his novels, replacing Joyce's 'Yes' with his own 'Perhaps'.)[20] Lodge is in tune with the post-structuralist insistence on the primacy of language and textuality, having throughout his career stressed the linguistic and rhetorical nature of fiction, and he has performed a worthwhile role in adapting continental theory to more traditional criticism, but he appears to be observing his own duty-free quotas in the importation of ideas, always maintaining a strict embargo on the banned substances of Freud and Marx. Lodge's typically succinct and approachable contribution here uses Joyce to explain Bakhtin's dialogic theory as much as it uses Bakhtin to explain Joyce's practice. Bakhtin's work itself offers a singular example of belatedness in the relation of criticism to literature in this century, since his work, originally written in the 1920s, was only translated into English in the 1960s. One can well understand Lodge's wistfulness when he comments of the following observation of Bakhtin's –

■ Parodic-travestying literature introduces the permanent corrective of laughter, of a critique of on the one side seriousness of the lofty direct word, the corrective of reality that is always richer, more fundamental and most importantly *too contradictory and heteroglot* to be fitted into a high and straightforward genre. □

– that he might have been writing about *Ulysses* in such a passage, and had the insights of Bakhtin been available to Anglophone readers, the history of Joyce criticism might have been quite different. Lodge also

119

values Bakhtin for offering the intellectual stringency of post-structuralism without what he deplores as its strident anti-humanism, with the Bakhtinian concepts of heteroglossia and *skaz* being particularly suited to an understanding of even the most recalcitrant of the later chapters of *Ulysses*, such as Eumaeus.

■ At this point it is useful to switch to Bakhtin's typology of literary discourse. There are three main categories:

The direct speech of the author. This corresponds to Plato's diegesis.

Represented speech. This includes Plato's mimesis – i.e. the quoted direct speech of the characters; but also reported speech in the pictorial style.

Doubly-oriented speech, that is, speech which not only refers to something in the world but refers to another speech act by another addresser.

Bakhtin subdivides this third type of discourse into four categories, stylisation, parody, *skaz* (the Russian term for oral narration) and what he calls 'dialogue'. Dialogue means here, not the quoted direct speech of the characters, but discourse which alludes to an *absent* speech act. In stylisation, parody and *skaz*, the other speech act is 'reproduced with a new intention'; in 'dialogue' it 'shapes the author's speech while remaining outside its boundaries'. An important type of dialogic discourse in this sense is 'hidden polemic', in which a speaker not only refers to an object in the world but simultaneously replies to, contests, or makes concessions to some other real or anticipated or hypothetical statement about the same object.

These categories all have their subcategories which can be combined and shifted around in the system in a somewhat bewildering way, but the basic distinctions are clear, and I think useful. Let me try and illustrate them with reference to *Ulysses*, a text as encyclopaedic in this respect as in all others.

The direct speech of the author. This is the narrator who speaks in, for instance, the first lines of the book:

> Stately, plump Buck Mulligan came from the stairhead, bearing a bowl of lather on which a mirror and razor lay crossed.[21]

This is the purely diegetic plane of the text. The sentence describes Mulligan emerging on to the roof of the Martello tower not as Stephen Dedalus sees him (Stephen is below), nor as Mulligan sees himself, but as seen by an objective narrator. Since most narration in *Ulysses* is focalised, and stylistically coloured, by a character's consciousness, or permeated by doubly-oriented speech, such examples are comparatively rare. The author's speech as a distinct medium of communication is scarcely perceptible, in accordance with Joyce's aesthetic of impersonality: 'The artist, like the God of the creation, remains within or behind or beyond or above his handiwork, invisible, refined out of existence, indifferent, paring his fingernails.'

Represented speech. This includes all the dialogue in the usual sense of that word – the quoted direct speech of the characters, which Joyce preferred to mark with an introductory dash, rather than the usual inverted commas. This category also includes all the passages of interior monologue – mimesis in Plato's terms, but representing thought instead of uttered speech. Molly Bloom's reverie in the last episode, 'Penelope', is perhaps the purest example:

> Yes because he never did a thing like that before as ask to get his breakfast in bed with a couple of eggs since the City Arms hotel when he used to be pretending to be laid up with a sick voice doing his highness to make himself interesting for that old faggot Mrs Riordan that he thought he had a great leg of ... (871)

... and so on, for twenty thousand uninterrupted words.

The presentation of the thought of Stephen and Leopold Bloom is more varied and complex, combining interior monologue with free indirect speech and focalised narration – in short, a mixture of mimesis and diegesis, in which mimesis dominates. Here, for example, is Bloom in the porkbutcher's shop in 'Calypso':

> A kidney oozed bloodgouts on the willowpatterned dish: the last. He stood by the nextdoor girl at the counter. Would she buy it too, calling the items from a slip in her hand? Chapped: washingsoda. And a pound and a half of Denny's sausages. His eyes rested on her vigorous hips. Woods his name is. Wonder what he does. Wife is oldish. New blood. No followers allowed. Strong pair of arms. Whacking a carpet on the clothesline. She does whack it, by George. The way her crooked skirt swings at each whack. (70)

The various kinds of speech in this passage may be classified as follows:

A kidney oozed bloodgouts on the willowpatterned dish: Narrative (focalised through Bloom).

the last. Interior monologue.

He stood by the nextdoor girl at the counter. Narrative (focalised through Bloom).

Would she buy it too, calling the items from a slip in her hand? Free indirect speech.

Chapped: washingsoda. Interior monologue.

121

And a pound and a half of Denny's sausages. Free direct speech (i.e., the girl's words are quoted but not tagged or marked off typographically from Bloom's).

His eyes rested on her vigorous hips. Narrative (focalised through Bloom).

Woods his name is, etc. (to end of paragraph). Interior monologue.

Doubly-oriented speech. In the later episodes of *Ulysses*, the authorial narrator who, however self-effacing, was a stable, consistent and reliable voice in the text, disappears; and his place is taken by various manifestations of Bakhtin's doubly-oriented discourse. 'Stylisation' is well exemplified by 'Nausicaa', in which Joyce borrows the discourse of cheap women's magazines and makes it serve his own expressive purpose:

> Gerty was dressed simply but with the instinctive taste of a votary of Dame Fashion for she felt there was just a might that he might be out. A neat blouse of electric blue, self tinted by dolly dyes (because it was expected in the *Lady's Pictorial* that electric blue would be worn) with a smart vee opening down to the division and kerchief pocket (in which she always kept a piece of cottonwool scented with her favourite perfume because the handkerchief spoiled the sit) and a navy three quarter skirt cut to the stride showed off her slim graceful figure to perfection. (455)

Who speaks here? Clearly it is not the author – he would not use such debased, cliché-ridden language. But we cannot take it, either, to be the author's report of Gerty's thought in free indirect speech. Free indirect speech can always be transposed into plausible direct speech (first person, present tense) and clearly that would be impossible in this case. It is a written, not a spoken style, and a very debased one. It is neither diegesis nor mimesis, nor a blend of the two, but a kind of pseudodiegesis achieved by the mimesis not of a character's speech but of a discourse, the discourse of cheap women's magazines at the turn of the century. (In fact, the style of today's romantic fiction of the Mills & Boon type displays a remarkable consistency and continuity with Gerty's reading. Compare, for example: 'Her dress was white, made from white Indian cotton. Skimpy little shoulderstraps led to a bodice which was covered with layers of narrow, delicate lace finishing at the waist where it fitted Gina's slender figure to perfection.')[22] It is essential to the effect of 'Nausicaa' that we should be aware of the style's double reference – to Gerty's experience, and to its own original discursive context. We are not to suppose that Gerty literally thinks in sentences lifted from the *Lady's Pictorial*. But the style of the *Lady's Pictorial* subtly manipulated, heightened, 'objectified'

(Bakhtin's word) vividly communicates a sensibility pathetically limited to the concepts and values disseminated by such a medium. The author, like a ventriloquist, is a silent presence in the text, but his very silence is the background against which we appreciate his creative skill.

This is stylisation – not the same thing as parody. Parody, as Bakhtin points out, borrows a style and applies it to expressive purposes that are in some sense the reverse of the original purpose, or at least incongruous with it. For example, one of the headlines in 'Aeolus' parodies the style of American tabloid journalism by applying it to an episode in classical antiquity recalled in more appropriate language by Professor MacHugh:

SOPHIST WALLOPS HAUGHTY HELEN SQUARE ON PROBOSCIS. SPARTANS GNASH MOLARS. ITHACANS VOW PEN IS CHAMP

– You remind me of Antisthenes, the professor said, a disciple of Georgias, the sophist. It is said of him that none could tell if he were bitterer against others or against himself. He was the son of a noble and a bondwoman. And he wrote a book in which he took away the palm of beauty from Argive Helen and handed it to poor Penelope. (188)

The anonymous narrator of 'Cyclops' provides an example of Irish *skaz* – the anecdotal chat of pubs and bars:

I was just passing the time of day with old Troy of the D.M.P. at the corner of Arbour Hill there and be damned but a bloody sweep came along and he near drove his gear into my eye. I turned around to let him have the weight of my tongue when who should I see dodging along Stony Batter only Joe Hynes.

– Lo, Joe, says I. How are you blowing? Did you see that bloody chimney-sweep near shove my eye out with his brush? (376)

We never discover who this narrator is, or to whom he is talking, or in what context. But clearly it is oral narration – *skaz*. There is no perceptible difference, either in syntax or type of vocabulary, between the discourse before and after the dash that in *Ulysses* introduces direct or quoted speech.

Of all the many styles in Ulysses, perhaps the most baffling to critical analysis and evaluation has been that of 'Eumaeus', a style which Stuart Gilbert classified as 'Narrative: old'. Rambling, elliptical, cliché-ridden, it is, we are told, meant to reflect the nervous and physical exhaustion of the two protagonists. As with 'Nausicaa', we cannot read the discourse either as author's narration or as representation of Bloom's consciousness, though it does seem expressive of Bloom's character in some respects: his friendliness bordering on servility, his fear of rejection, his reliance on proverbial wisdom. Bakhtin's definition of 'hidden polemic' seems to fit it very well: 'Any speech that is servile or overblown, any speech that is determined beforehand not to be itself, any speech replete with reservations, concessions, loopholes and so on. Such speech seems to cringe in the presence, or at the presentiment of, some other person's statement, reply, objection.'[23]

> *En route* to his taciturn, and, not to put too fine a point on it, not yet perfectly sober companion, Mr Bloom who at all events, was in complete possession of his faculties, never more so, in fact, disgustingly sober, spoke a word of caution re the dangers of night-town, women of ill fame and swell mobsmen, which, barely permissible once in a while though not as a habitual practice, was of the nature of a regular deathtrap for young fellows of his age particularly if they had acquired drinking habits under the influence of liquor unless you knew a little jujitsu for every contingency as even a fellow on the broad of his back could administer a nasty kick if you didn't look out. (706) □

CHAPTER FIVE

Against Authority

The essays and extracts in Chapter 4 all resisted, in their various ways, the idea of author as authority, preferring to think of Joyce's texts as sites of contended meaning rather than sources of unitary truths. This trend is continued in this final chapter, where the cultural and political consequences of *A Portrait* and *Ulysses* are considered. Feminist and post-colonial readings of Joyce are encouraged by the dialogic nature of his texts, both in *A Portrait*'s subtle hinting that it is his relation to politics and women that are the real unacknowledged determinants of Stephen's predicament, and in *Ulysses*' gradual move towards a celebration of Bloom and Molly, outsiders by race and gender respectively.

For all that Joyce can be viewed as a champion of the subaltern, however, it remains true that his is the case *par excellence* of the modernist author as cultural authority. One of Joyce's boasts to Frank Budgen was that, if Dublin were to be destroyed, it could be rebuilt from the pages of *Ulysses*, a stunning gesture of cultural appropriation that reinvents the world as a book. Extracts in this chapter from Mahaffey, Henke and Cheng show how Joyce grants freedom of communication to women, to excluded races, to outsiders generally, but always on his terms, within his system. In this respect Joyce is the Bill Gates of literature, and in this book's final selections Jacques Derrida and Leo Bersani warn against the dangers of a Joycean monopoly of information, Bersani contending that 'far from contesting the authority of culture, *Ulysses* reinvents our relation to Western culture in terms of exegetical devotion, that is, as the exegesis of *Ulysses* itself'.

Since both of the longer excerpts in the last chapter addressed, or were aware of, the importance of feminist and other political critique, this section can exist not as a ghetto but as a supplement. It is silly, however true, to say that the politics of gender and nation are important to Joyce's work, since they are important to all work. What ought to be addressed is rather the ignoring of such aspects in an aestheticised criticism which purports to be above and beyond such matters, just as Dedalus the manicured panurge aspired to be. As women and sexuality – women because of their sexuality – were denied and displaced in the mind of *A Portrait*'s hero, so criticism of Joyce was reluctant to do anything but primly excuse Joyce's 'dirty bits'. This is a matter of politics, the other great unmentionable, and it is at first sight troubling that the voice in *A Portrait* that insists on censoring political discussion is that of a woman, Dante O'Riordan. If one accepts, on the other hand, the idea of Joyce's texts as enacting the drama of misrecognition, it is quite in keeping with the dynamic of his developing work that the word of women should not be essentialised as such any more than are the words of male characters. The last word of *Ulysses* is left to Molly, and, if *Finnegans Wake* has a narrator, she is female.

Women begin to make their presence felt in the closing chapters of *Ulysses*, but in troublingly stereotypical guises: virgin (Gerty McDowell), mother (Mina Purefoy) and whore (the prostitutes in Circe). Molly might transcend these categories, but it is as archetype, an archetype being a stereotype with her best clothes on. Critics have been even more divided over Molly than they have been over Stephen, traditionally in terms of elevation and debasement which are more germane to Stephen's misogynistic/narcissistic patterns of thinking than to any realistic engagement with women. Molly's soliloquy did, however, encourage Hélène Cixous and later critics to consider it as a model for an *écriture féminine* independent of male discursive practices,[1] even if this area is fraught with problems arising from the male author's working as much in a tradition which created Mrs Malaprop and Flora Finching as in that of Virginia Woolf or Gertrude Stein. Sandra Gilbert and Susan Gubar are not alone in 'refusing to be Mollified by feminologist re-Joyceings'.[2] The next two excerpts maintain a post-structuralist position which, while keeping gender in focus, does not regard it as the only item on the agenda.

Vicky Mahaffey's *Reauthorising Joyce* takes up the idea of Joyce's texts as sites of warring discursive forces, but her study, while equally stimulating, is less embattled in its arguments than, say, MacCabe's: 'I learned from Joyce what others were learning from contemporary theory, that a reading guided solely by the desire to uncover the author's meaning relies upon the same assumptions about authority – here authorship – that support monotheistic religions and centralised governments, those licenced by representation as well as those established by fact.' Accordingly, Mahaffey allows her study to be governed, like Joyce's texts, by shifting forms of authority, appealing eclectically to feminist, deconstructionist and Marxist approaches as well as to more traditional forms of reading, while refusing finality to any of these discourses. Although Mahaffey's enthusiasm sometimes spills over into the blithely opportunistic, her contribution is worthwhile, not least in her literalising the metaphor of text to examine the figures of weaving, textures and textiles in *Ulysses*.[3]

■ **The delusion that inspires Stephen more often than any other is the delusion that he can transcend the meanness of his environment. The euphoria that accompanies his anticipations of transcendence is** expressed in many ways – in the literal uplift that raises him above his fellows at the end of the first chapter, as he is carried along in 'a cradle of their locked hands' (60); in his expectation that he will be transfigured when he encounters his Mercedes, that 'weakness and timidity and inexperience would fall from him in that magic moment' (67); in the ascent of prayers from his purified heart (160); in the idealised flights that conclude both the fourth and the fifth chapters. The most celebrated passage in *A Portrait of the Artist* is one in which Stephen directly expresses his determination to transcend the claims of his environment:

> When the soul of a man is born in this country there are nets flung at it to hold it back from flight. You talk to me of nationality, language, religion. I shall try to fly by those nets. (203)

It is Stephen's desire for transcendence that makes him heroic in both a classical and a romantic sense, yet the continuity of life and narrative impedes any real transcendence, which would be possible only through death. Any reader of *Portrait* whose reading is impelled by a transcendent ideal, by a desire to escape the 'nets' of language, religion, and nationality and in so doing ascend into an esthetic ether, will experience the resistance the book offers to such flightiness. The only lecture Stephen attends in the last chapter is on the subject of electrical resistance, which should alert us to the importance of resistance as a paradigm for Joyce's narrative technique; yet the precise nature of the resistance the book offers, as well as the significance of that resistance, are among its least understood aspects.

In *A Portrait of the Artist*, as in *Dubliners*, *Ulysses* and *Finnegans Wake*, the last chapter recomplicates the context in which the book has been read up to that point. Chapter five makes it clear that Stephen's struggle is the struggle between an individual and his context, a struggle that also defines the process of reading. The end of the chapter, in particular, is not only a diary of a young man preparing for flight, his entries alternately callow and full of hope – dismissive of the past, contemptuous of the present, and in love with the 'wild spring' of the future – but also a compressed casebook of the problems posed by language, nationality, and religion, bringing them into shared focus as representative problems of context: the pressure of a collective, past-laden present on the future-oriented individual. Stephen's 'nets' are the nets of context (from *contextus*, woven together), nets that can and must be unwoven and rewoven, but can never be left behind, as the comic ironies of the first four chapters demonstrate.

A character can alter his or her context, but context also determines character. Like Gerty MacDowell in 'Nausicaa', who not only authors a fiction of soulful encounter but is authored in turn by fictions such as *The Lamplighter* that unconsciously determine the style and structure of her own inner narratives, Stephen is authored by religion (Christ and Lucifer), language (classicism and romanticism, with their emphases on truth versus beauty), and nationality (the native foreignness of Dublin). The last chapter focuses on Dublin as a double city in a divided country, its divisions subsuming and authorising the divisions inherent in religion, language, and in Stephen himself.

What Stephen lacks is not an awareness of his own contradictory nature, but an acceptance of it. This is apparent throughout the last chapter, where Stephen's omissions help to create the very context by which he can be evaluated. What he omits in his theoretical discussion with Lynch is consistent with what is lacking in each of the other climactic scenes of the last chapter: he tells Lynch that 'When we come to the phenomena of artistic conception, artistic gestation and artistic reproduction I require a new terminology and a new personal experience,' and Lynch replies, 'But you will tell me about the new personal experience and new terminology some other day' (227). Similarly, in the scene with Cranly, Stephen is unable to answer when Cranly asks him if he has ever loved anyone (261); during his composition of the villanelle, Stephen's onanism suggests that his artistic creations are as fruitless as is his solitary, physical ejaculation. Artistic conception, gestation, and reproduction result from a union of opposites in the act of love, a doubling that, together with Dublin, Stephen elects to escape. What he fails to understand is the double nature of authority, an awareness that would make him as 'artist' as well as a portrayed subject, an acceptance of the fact that, in the words of Jeremy Lane, there is 'no final authorisation, no simple authority, no single author; but a relative authorisation, the sanction of relation whose dual principle seeds plurality, admitting and containing its contrary.'[4]

To paraphrase Wordsworth's famous statement, an author differs from other characters in degree, but not in kind. What differentiates authors – and readers – of a fiction from the characters within a fiction is, potentially, a more disturbing awareness of the nets that no individual can elude, and that all must attempt to elude, a sensitivity to the complex interdependence of all human and verbal contexts, and an acceptance of the multiplicity and sameness of all characters participating in an interactive system. With such an awareness, an 'author' can recreate and interpret such systems through imaginative doubling, whereas without such an awareness the 'character' will re-enact prior narratives in unintentional and unproductive – repetitive – ways. However, this distinction between 'author' and 'character' is itself, like all oppositions, an heuristic one, since it is impossible to be permanently inside or outside a system so long as that system and our awareness of it are subject to change. Every author is necessarily a character, or subject, and every character an author – and authority – in a dialogical process that produces no final synthesis: Joyce is, alternately, both within and outside the book, as are other authors, such as Shelley and Byron, and all of its readers, including ourselves. In this respect, as in several others, the language of the book defines a community not unlike the community Stephen is attempting to escape at the end, as he goes 'to encounter for the millionth time the reality of experience' (*P* 252–3). Ironically, the book ends with Stephen asking his father, and author, to direct him by his precedent: 'Old father, old artificer, stand me now and ever in good stead' (*P* 253). Stephen is recording his hope that his father will continue to do what he was doing for Stephen when the book opened, authoring and authorising the story of Stephen's youth.

Molly celebrates the materialisation of dream through marriage, but she also laments that realisation, periodically seeking to recover the lost poetry of youth. As unlikely as it may initially seem, Molly, with her sensitivity to the figurative dimension of words and names, is a poetic figure, a counterpart to Stephen, Echo to his Narcissus. ... The final irony of *Ulysses* is the realisation that Molly, so frequently regarded as a 'great lust-lump' preoccupied with exclusively material concerns, uses the material world to live out a private poetry, trying to keep faith with her memory of a dream.

Molly's poetic sensibility is apparent not only in her attraction to poets, but also in her literal approach to words and names. In *Ulysses*, Bloom and Molly's unfaithfulness to one another is inextricable from their faithfulness to dream. Both chafe against the tailoring of their desires and the straitening of their potential that marriage implies; both regard their mutual 'suitability' as a kind of closing to the openness of their youth. Both express their protests against the constraints of custom through an obsession with costume: Molly once ran a used clothing business, and Bloom fetishises underclothing as a material substitute for understanding. Yet what makes their attitude toward clothes significant is not the peculiarities of their respective attitudes, but their instinctive recognition of the way that cloth lays bare the mechanisms of communication, figuring connection and isolation by turns.

The growing opacity and obscurity of Joyce's style, accompanied by an equally marked adulteration of the authorial voice, is the natural culmination of a lifetime of experimentation with the politics of style and the 'biology' of artistic reproduction. Joyce sought, not merely to redirect our attention to the 'female' dimension of language, the texture that subtly comprehends its authoritarian impulses, making it more democratic, but to restore awareness of the complicated interdependence of revealing and reveiling by emphasising the equal agency of the mother in any 'genesis'. He saw that our habits of interpretation tend to highlight sameness at the expense of difference, the general to the detriment of the particular, the author rather than the authored, the past regardless of a future. His fiction works to correct this cultural imbalance through an increasing attention to the interrelationship of language and cloth, of 'male' and 'female' styles.

Ulysses is haunted by the three greatest barriers to human understanding – difference of age, difference of gender, and difference of race or creed. Those differences can only be bridged, and preserved, by systems of mediation, such as language and clothes, but the interconnective and disconnective capabilities of these particular systems have been straitened by the way that they have been segregated from one another. By regarding language and clothes as complementary versions of a single communicative system, Joyce is able to draw attention to the opacity, as well as the transparency, of language, and to emphasise the transparency, as well as the opacity, of clothes. Stylistically, Joyce attempts to restore wholeness of perception by drawing attention to the texture of words as well as their meaning. He prompts his readers to look at individual words, and not just to peer through them; he emphasises the comic way that words thwart and misdirect our attempts to channel them toward a straightforward goal. Grammar may be linear, but language is weblike, constantly suggesting a network of connections between similar sounds and images that subvert our desire to turn language from a truly communal art form into an instrument. As Hillis Miller argues, narrative proffers a labyrinth as well as a line.[5]

Both 'text' and 'textile' come from the Latin *texere*, 'to weave'. Joyce attempted to recover the threads of connection between texts and textiles, and in so doing to restore the awareness that 'weaving', as an expression of the rhythm of fabrication and wear, interconnection and gradual isolation, is a dynamic process common to both life and art. This oscillating movement between the coherence and dissolution of disparate phenomena is the neglected partner of logocentrism, its natural spouse. It is the variegated play of impressions that Pater referred to as 'that strange, perpetual weaving and unweaving of ourselves', the movement that to Pater constituted the essence of life. And it is this pattern that Penelope translates into action by diurnally weaving and unweaving Laertes' shroud, thereby resisting the pressure to confine herself to a single suitor, or a single 'suit' – which is always, by implication, a shroud.

The process of weaving and unweaving becomes a new – or at

least a recovered – model of the way that both language and perception can and should operate. This is a view indebted to the ancient past and prophetic of the future; it is born of the symmetrical relationship between Odysseus and Penelope in *The Odyssey*, nurtured by the perceptual theories of Pater, and it anticipates some aspects of theoretical positions that postdate *Ulysses*: feminist critiques of patriarchal epistemologies; Todorov's descriptions of the critical *praxis*; Hillis Miller's analyses of the 'threads' of narrative; Derrida's play on the fluctuations of discourse, its power to deconstruct its own constructions. And it is a movement that defines the borders of *Ulysses*, its fundamentally identical margins of word and world.

Weaving and unweaving is a process of fabrication. What every text fabricates anew is human and literary history, on the one hand, and language, on the other. Moreover, as T. S. Eliot asserted in 'Tradition and the Individual Talent', the reverse is equally true: history and language, together with the history *of* language, also fabricate every text, serving as reconstructed context and pretext. There is a complex 'logic' to the interrelations between a character and his or her refabricated precursors, a logic that is always reinforced by the unexpected interconnections among sounds, images, and letters that are the 'illegitimate' offspring of the attempt to manipulate meaning.

As a pattern for thought, Penelope's cunning strategy of weaving and unweaving a shroud in order to remain 'faithful' yields several insights into the nature of physical and mental activity. It suggests that reality is neither hierarchical nor dialectical; instead, it is an alternating movement between coherence and incoherence. In the language of *Finnegans Wake*, 'The untireties of livesliving being the one substance of a streamsbecoming. Totalled in toldteld and teldtold in tittletell tattle. ... Why? It is a sot of a swigswag, systomy dystomy, which everabody you ever anywhere at all doze. Why? Such me.' (*FW* 597.7–22). Joyce's 'answer' to the challenge of human existence is not male logocentrism and identity-building alone, nor does it centre around female prescience in dismantling male structures; rather, it takes as its pattern the continuous, diurnal oscillation between coherence and destabilisation, between day and night. This emphasis on life as a process of interconnection between complex extremes also reaffirms the importance of deconstructing any proposition in order to remain 'faithful' to a reality in which the opposite of any given proposition is also true.

The Penelope model emphasises the labyrinthine interconnectedness and disconnectedness of *any* created system.

It suggests that *all* systems are, in a sense, shrouds woven to conceal the ugly and inescapable incoherence of death. Alternately, these shrouds, or systems, must be periodically unwoven or else they turn the intimation of death into a present reality, since any ossified system kills the process of life. It affirms the value of inconsistency, which has been culturally designated as a 'female' trait.

Finally, the process of weaving and unweaving serves as a paradigm for the labyrinthine interconnectedness and disconnectedness of all phenomena on the one hand, and as an image of intimate physical 'connection' in the form of dressing, undressing, and redressing, on the other. But it also serves as a model for human identity, in which each individual is, like Odysseus, both everyman and noman; this is the sense in which Pater used the metaphor. For him, the 'strange, perpetual weaving and unweaving of ourselves' was a way of defying the encroachment of death upon life; a way of admitting the contradictions of human experience as something that oscillates between community and isolation; and finally, a metaphor for the human individual, who possesses an entire world and no world within the circumference of a single flesh-case.

The implications of Joyce's affirmation of weaving and unweaving as a metaphor that can describe the process of both physical and mental life are important: the issues he raises and the metaphor he adopts to 'resolve' them, through an admission of the insufficiency of any final resolution, continue to haunt and even divide numerous schools of contemporary thought. What are 'structuralism' and 'deconstruction' but weaving and unweaving, applied not to the material world but to the linguistic one, clothed not in a 'female' metaphor but in a metaphor culturally determined as 'male'? Hillis Miller has responded to the logocentric implications of structuralism and deconstruction by restoring the female analogy for the workings of language. Feminist critics such as Mary Daly have announced their intent to restore the original dualism of traditionally female activities such as weaving and spinning. In *Gyn/Ecology*, Daly exhorts women to rediscover the interconnectedness of existence, arguing that women 'must be able to weave and unweave, discovering hidden threads of connectedness.'[6] The labyrinth, along with the thread or narrative necessary to penetrate it, has even become a dominant metaphor in the works of several post-modernist writers, including Borges, Barthelme, and Pynchon.

The fact that so many writers are preoccupied in so many ways with weaving and unweaving suggests that the issues that Joyce raised are still very much alive. Joyce suggests that the problems of gender-defined identity will never be resolved until we adopt different attitudes toward *all* the oppositions that our culture has appended to the opposition between 'male' and 'female' principles. In Joyce's view, the most fundamental of 'weighted' oppositions is the

132

supposed dominance of spiritual over physical truth. He suggests that spirituality, and language, must have a symbiotic relationship to physicality, to Aristotelian appearances; if this relationship lapses or fails to be renewed, then the spirit becomes a mere phantom (this is one of its meanings), and the body a *corpus*, or corpse. Joyce's most memorable contribution to this debate is not theoretical, however, but practical: he uses language in such a way that we are forced to explore the relationship between its texture, its rich metaphoric potential, and its textuality. We are asked to look at words, to hear them, to dissect and reassemble them, as well as to use them as windows in the always voyeuristic attempt to gain knowledge. In the language of clothes, we are asked to look again at our tendency to treat words as mere signs and not as artifacts with a wantonly sensual referentiality. With this perspective in mind, it become easier to appreciate the irony and appropriateness of Joyce's plays on 'Pen' and 'Penelope'; his pairing of 'sailors' and 'tailors' as people who deal with yarn/yarns, and as those who say and *tell*; his association of Molly with breeches as well as breaches; his insistence that Molly is both a flower and a 'flow-er'. Finally, it reawakens us to the power of literature to reach out and encompass life in its fictionally coherent yet comically unstable webs. Joyce's fictions certainly grew out to meet the coincidences of his own life: the Fates, those original spinners, gave Joyce as his most faithful and consistent benefactress, a feminist woman of letters named Weaver. □

Suzette Henke's *James Joyce and the Politics of Desire*[7] is heavily influenced by the French feminist thought of Cixous, Kristeva and Irigaray. The discussion of Chapters 4 and 5 of *A Portrait* included here comes from a section of her book subtitled 'A Portrait of the Artist as a Young Narcissist' and examines the role of women in the novel. As Henke points out, female characters are present everywhere and nowhere in *A Portrait of the Artist as a Young Man*. They pervade the novel, yet remain elusive, since they are portrayed almost exclusively from Stephen's point of view and hence coloured by his psychological fantasies. Stephen's aestheticisation of experience is then seen as an act of displacement and denial. In contrast, the closing pages of Molly's monologue in *Ulysses* is held up as a celebration of erotic jouissance, androgynous and resolutely anti-patriarchal in nature.

■ In his return to ritualistic devotion, Stephen becomes involved in an aesthetic love affair with his own soul. The anima, the feminine aspect of the psyche, has won his passion and holds him enthralled. Like Narcissus, Stephen has fallen in love with his projected self-image clothed in female garb. 'The attitude of rapture in sacred art, the raised and parted hands, the parted lips and eyes as of one about to swoon, became for him an image of the soul in prayer, humiliated and faint before her Creator' (162). In the glorified female, 'man also perceives his mysterious double; man's soul is Psyche, a woman.'[8] The feminine side of Stephen's identity, personified as the soul, swoons in erotic ecstasy before her creator, just as the young man earlier swooned in the welcoming arms of a Dublin prostitute.

The Catholic priesthood offers Stephen a chance to consummate this narcissistic love affair with his psyche. It bequeaths on the soul the magical power of transubstantiation, and it promises a rite of passage into male mysteries that successfully counteract female authority: 'No angel or archangel in heaven, no saint, not even the Blessed Virgin herself has the power of a priest of God' (171). A Jesuit vocation would guarantee Stephen ascendancy over the Catholic matriarch. By virtue of the 'secret knowledge and secret power' of an exclusively masculine fraternity, he would be admitted to the inner sanctum of male religious privilege.

The price, however, of this 'awful power of which angels and saints stood in reverence' is an irrevocable act that would 'end for ever, in time and in eternity, his freedom' and condemn him to the 'grave and ordered and passionless life' of Jesuit conformity (174). Still painting himself in the images of Lord Byron and the Count of Monte Cristo, Stephen passionately embraces a destiny triumphantly marginal and 'elusive of social or religious orders. ... He was destined to learn his own wisdom apart from others or to learn the wisdom of others himself wandering among the snares of the world' (174). He chooses 'the misrule and confusion of his father's house' (175), the messiness and chaos of sensuous experience, over a 'mirthless reflection of the sunken day' (174) evinced by the priest's spectral visage. Turning away from this symbolic death's head, Stephen rejects the 'eyeless obedience' demanded by Catholic orders and reminiscent of those eagles of authority that originally threatened him with a loss of sight and mastery. He will commit himself, instead, to the pagan priesthood of old Father Daedalus, that 'fabulous artificer, ... a symbol of the artist forging anew in his workshop out of the sluggish matter of the earth a new soaring impalpable imperishable being' (183).

Stephen's intellectual choice of an artistic vocation seems to be experimentally confirmed by a climactic encounter with a mysterious female who evokes luminous trails of earthly beauty:

A girl stood before him in midstream, alone and still, gazing out to sea. She seemed like one whom magic had changed into the likeness of a strange and beautiful seabird. Her long slender bare legs were delicate as a crane's and pure save where an emerald trail of seaweed had fashioned itself as a sign upon the flesh. Her thighs, fuller and soft-hued as ivory, were bared almost to the hips where the white fringes of her drawers were like featherings of soft white down. (185)

The young woman revealed in Stephen's epiphany amalgamates a plethora of metaphorical features from pagan, Christian, and Celtic iconography. She is at once mortal and angelic, sensuous and serene. Her soft-hued, ivory thighs recall Eileen's ivory hands as well as the Catholic Virgin, Tower of Ivory. Her avian transformation harks back to the Greek myth of Leda and the swan. And because her bosom, like 'the breast of some darkplumaged dove', suggests the Holy Ghost of Catholicism, Stephen, as purveyor of the word, imaginatively begets a surrogate Holy Spirit in his ecstatic vision of this semi-mystical muse.

Joyce's irony at this point in the novel is subtle but implicit. If Stephen feels incipient sexual arousal in the presence of exposed female thighs, he quickly sublimates erotic agitation beneath effusions of purple prose. The young man catches sight of an attractive nubile form and immediately detaches himself from emotional participation in the scene. His reaction is self-consciously static, theoretically purged of desire and loathing. Once again, his leap into aesthetic fantasy quenches an initial impulse to approach the girl, to reach out and touch her, or to risk the possibility of social intercourse. Stephen feels he must distance and depersonalise her tantalising figure through the voyeuristic displacements of oculocentric regard.

As the young woman rises out of the sea, she is reminiscent of Venus, the goddess of love born of the ocean foam. She is pure and virginal, yet 'an emerald trail of seaweed' functions as a sign of mortality (and perhaps of Irish nationality) stamped upon her flesh. She belongs to the mundane world of decay and corruption, and the vegetation clinging to her ankle suggests a fetishistic image of emotional entrapment. The woman appears as an 'angel of mortal youth and beauty, an envoy from the fair courts of life' (186). Tellingly, in his 1904 essay 'A Portrait of the Artist', Joyce uses similar phrases in masochistic invocation of a phantasmal prostitute from the red light district of Dublin: 'Beneficent one! ... thou camest timely, as a witch to the agony of self devourer, an envoy from the fair courts of life.'

Like an Irish Circe, the nymph in *Portrait* has the potential to drag Stephen down into the emerald-green nets of Dublin paralysis. In sociological terms, this attractive young woman, approached and courted, might well threaten Stephen with the kind of domestic entrapment associated with Irish Catholic marriage. The aspiring poet knows that he may look but not touch, admire but not speak. He glorifies the wading girl as an angelic messenger from the 'fair courts of life', but he never actually joins her in the teeming ocean waters. His communication is a matter entirely of narcissistic projection. 'Her image had passed into his soul for ever and no word had broken the holy silence of his ecstasy' (186). Afraid of the 'waters circumfluent in space' that symbolise the fluidity of female desire, Stephen is determined to control the world of physiological process by freezing life in the sacrament of art. His 'spiritual-heroic refrigerating apparatus' has already begun to implement this psychological flight from woman. His response to this seductive creature is exclusively specular, as he takes refuge in a masculine, visual sexual economy and sublimates tactile and olfactory drives that might move him toward sensuous contact. The mimesis of romantic passion offers Stephen a successfully mediated and comfortably mastered form of sexual satisfaction.

For Joyce's young man, an exercise in scopophilia (love of looking) masquerades as aesthetic delight. If, as Freud suggests, the specular gaze is anal and obsessive – an unconscious expression of a sadistic will to power – then Stephen's cold, pellucid regard penetrates its object through a strategy of phallocentric framing and claims it as a fetishistic trophy to grace the scene of writing. The bird-girl functions as an imaginary symbol of beauty and coherence, of a wholeness and plenitude that mimics the unity of the transcendental signifier. Celebrating the female as a fictive and mystifying centre, Stephen seizes the Lacanian *objet petit a* and replicates it as a figure of *différance* – desire playfully, masterfully, and joyously deferred through an endless dissemination of creative *jouissance*. Woman proves to be the blindspot in Stephen's poetic discourse. She is represented as a fantasised paradigm of psychic cohesion, the Other whose realistic fragmentation would threaten the poet's idealised aesthetic project. Because the girl remains a mute, fetishised, and perpetually mediated object of desire, her difference assures psychological stability to the speaking/seeing subject, the authorial I/eye who frames and appropriates her figure.

At nightfall, the exhausted poet feels his soul 'swooning into some new world, fantastic, dim, uncertain as under sea, traversed by cloudy shapes and beings. A world, a glimmer, or a flower?' (187). His spirit seems to embark on an archetypal journey toward the multifoliate rose of Dante's beatific vision. The bird-girl has imaginatively served as Stephen's profane virgin, a Beatrice who ushers him into paradisal happiness. The Dantesque underworld may symbolise the artistic unconscious, but the pre-Raphaelite rose imagery casts satirical light on Stephen's romantic reverie. As the young man attempts to 'still the riot of his blood', he swoons in languorous ecstasy. He moodily contemplates an opening flower: 'Glimmering and trembling,

trembling and unfolding, a breaking light, ... it spread in endless succession to itself, breaking in full crimson and unfolding and fading to palest rose, leaf by leaf and wave by wave of light, flooding all the heavens with its soft flushes, every flush deeper than other' (187). Sublimating the sexual component of his experience, Stephen vividly imagines a metaphorical rose engulfing the heavens, and his language of flowers suggests a psychoanalytic exercise in erotic mimesis. The boy's fantasy re-creates a repressed vision of female genitalia spreading in luxuriant rose-pink petals before his aroused phallic consciousness. Stephen's active libido summons veiled images of a woman's body revealing its vulvular mysteries and palpitating with the crimson flush of physical stimulation. Florid prose imitates the orgasmic rhythms of sexual excitement, as tension mounts 'leaf by leaf and wave of light by wave of light' until the dream suddenly climaxes in a flood of 'soft flushes'. Stephen may want to believe that he has purified his sensuous encounter by making it into a mimetic replication of spiritual transcendence, but even his Dantesque beatitude is founded on sexual passion thinly disguised by the language of Freudian displacement.[9]

FLIGHT FROM THE MOTHER

Although the gates of salvation open at the end of Chapter Four, Stephen finds himself, at the beginning of Chapter Five, exiled from the Garden of Eden. Chewing crusts of fried bread, he remembers the turf-coloured water in the bath at Clongowes – a spectral image that resonates with associations of death, drowning, and spiritual claustrophobia. As the nascent artist tries to escape the sordid reality of Dublin life by taking shelter in a world of words, he continues to struggle for liberation from the nets of a cloying family life, the demands of Irish nationality, and the stultifying authority of the Catholic religion.

Proclaiming his proud *Non Serviam*, Stephen nevertheless relies on his mother's service for physical nurturance and psychological support. Mary Dedalus washes her son's face and ears, enjoins him to receive the Eucharist, and packs his second-hand clothes in preparation for his exodus to France. Having magically transmuted the power of the female into a static object of aesthetic contemplation, Stephen is once again accosted by ubiquitous reminders of Mother Church and Mother Ireland. He feels compelled simultaneously to reject all three mothers – biological, ecclesiastical, and political. His refusal to take communion at Easter is as much a gesture of rebellion against a pleading Mary Dedalus as it is a rejection of Catholic authority. The image of woman metonymically absorbs all the paralysing nets that constrain the potential artist. Unlike his companion Cranly, who celebrates mother love, Stephen resolves to detach himself from 'the sufferings of women, the weaknesses of their bodies and souls' (266). He determines to 'discover the mode of life or of art' that will allow his spirit to 'express itself in unfettered freedom' (267). In casting off the yoke of matriarchy, Stephen asserts his manhood in fraternal collusion with his classical mentor, old Father Daedalus.

It is not enough, however, to repudiate the female: the artist must successfully usurp her procreative powers. Stephen seems to consider the aesthetic endeavour a kind of couvade – a rite of psychological compensation for the male inability to give birth. He describes the act of aesthetic postcreation in metaphors of parturition, explaining to Lynch: 'When we come to the phenomena of artistic conception, artistic gestation and artistic reproduction I require a new terminology and a new personal experience' (227). When Stephen awakens to 'a tremulous morning knowledge, a morning inspiration', his experience is oddly passive: 'A spirit filled him, pure as the purest water, sweet as dew, moving as music. But how faintly it was inbreathed, how passionlessly, as if the seraphim themselves were breathing upon him!' (235). It soon becomes clear that it is not simply angels who are breathing upon the artist, but the Holy Ghost in a drama that re-enacts the mystery of Christ's Incarnation. The poet welters in a confused haze of light and beauty, but the instant of inspiration is climactic: 'O! In the virgin womb of the imagination the word was made flesh. Gabriel the seraph had come to the virgin's chamber' (236).

Stephen, possibly awakening from a wet dream, feels inspired to compose a lyrical aubade unwinding in sensuous, liquid verses.[10] His soul climaxes in Shelley's 'enchantment of the heart', then luxuriates in the rosy afterglow of poetic ecstasy. The moment of inspiration and mental conception simulates a sexual process culminating in erotic *jouissance*. In a strange instance of mental transsexuality, Stephen's imagination is impregnated by the Holy Spirit, and he himself imitates the Virgin Mary giving birth to the Word of God. As the artist falls into a vision of rapturous enchantment, he conflates the ingenuous Emma with Mercedes and the bird-girl, then re-creates this female figure in the awesome, uncanny form of an eternal temptress – a seductive Lilith luring the seraphim from heaven. This courtly villanelle is inspired by a shudder in the loins that engenders not Leda or a burning Troy, but a handful of precious verses: 'he felt the rhythmic movement of a villanelle. ... The roselike glow sent forth its rays of rhyme' (235–6).

The enchantment of the heart that Stephen and Shelley both praised for its radiance now bursts forth into fire and flame – a conflagration strangely ominous in its association with the fires of

138

hell, as well as the more homely hearth-fire lit by the Dean of Studies. The metaphor of smoky praise issuing from a chivalric heart seems puerile at best – part of an ecclesiastical rite complete with swaying censer and ellipsoidal incense-balls. With decadent weariness, Stephen gropes for his tablets and finds, instead, an abandoned cigarette packet. The smoke from the censer of the world is recorded on the cardboard remnant of a package of smokes, all smoked but one. Stephen longs to immerse himself in a Dantesque ambience of secret roses reminiscent of the multifoliate flower of paradise, but he is forced to fashion a phantasmal rose-strewn path to heaven from the 'great overblown scarlet flowers of tattered wallpaper' that plaster his dingy room in Dublin. 'He tried to warm his perishing joy in their scarlet glow, imagining a roseway from where he lay upwards to heaven all strewn with scarlet flowers. Weary! Weary! He too was weary of ardent ways' (241).[11]

Unable to win the young and fickle heart of Emma, Stephen re-creates her in baleful aesthetic guise. His composition of the villanelle unfolds as an onanistic, as well as a dialectical exercise. The archaic verse-form has nostalgically been forged from erotic fantasy and the memory of loss. Stephen desires Emma, but he fears the domestic nets associated with a household where young men are 'called by their christian names a little too soon' (238). In his sacramental verses, Emma is present in the mode of absence as a cloudy, intangible figure. Caught in a blushing moment of 'rose and ardent light', her radiant complexion evinces an abstract portrait of a temptress bathed in pink-tinted auras that recall the prostitute at the end of Chapter Two. Stephen remembers Emma the night of the carnival ball – whiteclad, dancing, and flitting like a bird. Her eyes, about to trust him, do not. Her hand seems a soft merchandise that he refuses to purchase. He prefers to define himself as alien to Dublin domesticity, an ascetic monk devoted to secret, hermetic arts. Assuming the role of heretic Franciscan and courting Emma with a web of sophistry whispered in her ear, he plays the devil in clerical garments – a rebellious shaman antagonistic to the proletarian priest Father Moran.

'Rude brutal anger' over Emma's intimacy with the Catholic prelate momentarily shatters Stephen's idealised fantasy and scatters it in realistic mimesis throughout the Dublin landscape. 'He had done well to leave her to flirt with her priest, to toy with a church which was the scullerymaid of christendom' (239), he assures himself. Emma's figure is kaleidoscopically reflected in memories of lower-class peasant women – a flowergirl 'with damp coarse hair and a hoyden's face', a kitchengirl 'with the drawl of a country singer', a girl who mocked him, and a vamp whose 'small ripe mouth' made her good enough to eat. 'And yet he felt that, however he might revile and mock her image, his anger was also a form of homage' (239). Seeing Emma on the steps of the National Library, Stephen wonders if her life might be as 'simple and strange as a bird's life' and her heart as 'simple and wilful as a bird's' (235). But the bird, an emblem of simplicity and trust, quickly melds with the iconography of the inscrutable bat, a creature whose enigmatic flight and dark habitation makes it a symbol of mystery and cunning. 'Bat', too, is Irish slang for 'prostitute' – a suggestion implicitly evoked in the multiple bat references that pepper the final pages of *A Portrait*.

Stephen condescends to think of Emma as a younger incarnation of the pregnant woman who tried to seduce Davin in the Ballyhoura hills and who emerges as a symbol of Mother Ireland – a nurturant and guileless female ingenuously bedding the stranger. Emma, too, becomes 'a figure of the womanhood of her country, a batlike soul waking to the consciousness of itself in darkness and secrecy and loneliness, tarrying awhile, loveless and sinless' (239–40). She prostitutes herself before the priest of Catholicism and, confessing her sins in darkness and secrecy, indulges in a titillating ritual of spiritual self-revelation. Arising slowly from the primordial sludge of Dublin, this Caliban soul, blind and batlike, will be transformed into an Irish Ariel by Stephen-Prospero, 'a priest of eternal imagination, transmuting the daily bread of experience into the radiant body of everliving life' (240).

Stephen proceeds to compose his own *Pange Lingua*, a 'hymn of thanksgiving' on the model of Thomistic verse. The bread of experience assumes artistic immortality, but the wafer that houses Christ's body also suggests an analogous assimilation of the female body through the sacrament of art. By purging Emma of naturalistic dross, by abstracting her from an Irish domestic scene of horsehair and flirtation and celebrating her *sub specie aeternitatis*, Stephen meta-phorically consumes her in aesthetic communion. Erotic union gives way to a spiritual Eucharist, as the poet raises the sacred chalice of devotion before the altar of the muse. Emma, as eternal temptress, surrenders herself to the artist who symbolically – and onanistically – conquers her voluptuous form: 'Her nakedness yielded to him, radiant, warm, odorous and lavish-limbed, enfolded him like a shining cloud, enfolded him like water with a liquid life' (242).

Stephen has paradoxically composed the villanelle out of the same pornographic passion that his Thomistic theory earlier censured. The fires of lust inspire his aubade, a poetic explosion that conceals lascivious motives: 'A glow of desire kindled again his soul and fired … his body' (242). Art, once again, promises Stephen logocentric control over the realm of semiotic process. Rejected by Emma, he re-creates her as seductress and muse, uses her as an object of sexual fantasy, then refrigerates her in crystalline spheres of lyrical stasis. Weary of the ardent ways of frustrated passion, he cools his blazing heart through a masturbatory ritual that explodes in both aesthetic and physical *jouissance*. By raising Emma to heights of Circean power that pique her erotic desirability, Stephen magically defuses her flirtatious spell and reduces her to a mystified figure subordinate to and controlled by his priestly imagination.

Does Emma fade out of the novel as the temptress of Stephen's villanelle? Does she 'lure the seraphim' and have her will of man through *'languorous look and lavish limb'* (243)? This is hardly the Emma we recognise from the novel. The formal, highly wrought verses of Stephen's poem reveal his perpetual obsession with the terrifying eroticism of the female. Art enables him temporarily to subdue the archetypal seductress, whose *'eyes have set man's heart ablaze'* from the beginning of time. Against overwhelming enchantment, Stephen arrays the forces of aesthetic transformation. As poet-priest, he transubstantiates the eternal feminine into a disembodied muse that, once out of nature, ceases to threaten. Consigned to the realm of Byzantium, the Circean figure can no longer arouse animal lust or sensuous desire.

Throughout the novel, Stephen has sought the evacuation of affect from language and a re-inscription of his filial self into the symbolic order and law of the Father. By replicating himself in a discursive process of substitutability, he acquires a male aesthetic signature and triumphantly appropriates the female body/text. Inscribing himself into an august company of paternal authority figures (Daedalus, Edmond Dantes, Lord Byron, Dante Alighieri, Father Conmee, Father Arnall, Simon Dedalus, and Cranly), he fabricates an authorial persona purged of unsettling libidinal drives. The eternal temptress he celebrates is a disguised replica of the phallic mother who tantalises with nurturant pleasure, then obstinately withholds satisfaction. Incestuous attraction to the body of the mother is repressed and displaced onto a radiant icon of female beauty. Emma provides a substitute for the mother (both consubstantial and Catholic Madonna) whose image, in turn, is reproduced in the specular icon of a wading bird-girl, then lyrically transformed into an enchantress idealised out of existence and consigned to the icy realm of Platonic stasis.

The figure of woman as mother/temptress/whore is doubled in the many mirrors of art until she is apotheosised as the virgin goddess of a new artistic religion. The poet simultaneously achieves masturbatory emission and an ejaculatory outburst of *sèmes* lyrically simulating orgasmic *jouissance*. His love is symbolically cryogenic. Substituting pen for phallus, he penetrates the opaque image of woman as inaccessible Other and, through a series of seminal outpourings, gains

141

onanistic satisfaction from an archetypal figure elevated beyond the unsettling immediacy of sexual difference.

Toward the end of *A Portrait*, Stephen's Platonic reveries give way to flippant remarks and lewd jokes that consign women to the libidinal margins of pornographic amusements. In the company of Lynch, he follows a 'sizable hospital nurse' and comments on her cow-like proportions. The predatory young men resemble two 'lean hungry greyhounds walking after a heifer' (270). The 'wild spring turns Stephen's roving eye to voyeuristic gaping at girls 'demure and romping. All fair or auburn: no dark ones. They blush better' (273). The motif of shame and humiliation continues to inform his impressions of female sexuality when he imagines Emma 'humbled and saddened by the dark shame of womanhood' (242) and thinks of menstruation as a fall from childhood innocence. He remarks facetiously that, according to Lynch, statues of women 'should always be fully draped, one hand of the woman feeling regretfully her own hinder parts (273). In Stephen's mind, woman is still the veiled and mysterious Other, shame-wounded by nature, bovine and buttocks-bound, and ineluctably shackled to the scatological burdens of bodily process.

In his final meeting with Emma, Stephen stabilises her image in the guise of an idealised Beatrice by opening the 'spiritual-heroic refrigerating apparatus, invented and patented in all countries by Dante Alighieri' (275). He concedes in his diary: 'Yes, I liked her today' (275). But the seeds of friendship or affection will not be allowed to blossom. Rejecting the arms of women, Stephen chooses 'the white arms of roads, their promise of close embraces and the black arms of tall ships that stand against the moon, their tale of distant nations' (275). Nevertheless, he seems to imply that the one hope for salvation residual in the Irish race lies deeply buried in the hearts of women, who serve as repositories for a slumbering national conscience. In order to rouse his countrymen from spiritual torpor, he must learn how to 'cast his shadow over the imaginations of their daughters' and insinuate himself into the minds of a responsive female audience.

Throughout *A Portrait*, Stephen has manifested a psychological horror of woman as a figure of immanence, a symbol of unsettling sexual difference, and a perpetual reminder of bodily abjection. At the conclusion of Chapter Five, he prepares to flee from all the women who have served as catalysts in his own adolescent development. His journey into exile will release him from what he perceives as a cloying matriarchal authority. He must blot from his ears 'his mother's sobs and reproaches' and strike from his eyes the insistent 'image of his mother's face' (244). Alone and proud, isolated and free, Stephen proclaims joyful allegiance to the masculine fraternity of Daedalus, his priest and patron: 'Welcome, O life! I go to encounter for the millionth time the reality of experience and to forge in the smithy of my soul the uncreated conscience of my race. ... Old father, old artificer, stand me now and ever in good stead' (275–6). The hyperbolic resonance of Stephen's invocation leads us to suspect that his fate will prove Icarian rather than Daedalian. Insofar as women are concerned, he goes to encounter the reality of experience not for the millionth time, but for the first.

Joyce's protagonist has relentlessly attempted to achieve mastery over the outer world by adopting a male model of creation. In the very act of word-shaping, he can impose his will on a resistant environment and reduce the chaotic fluidity of life to the controlled stasis of art. Much of the irony in *A Portrait*, however, results from Joyce's satirical rendering of Stephen's logocentric paradigm. The sociopathic hero, pompous and aloof, passionately gathers phrases for his word-hoard without infusing his 'capful of light odes' with the generative spark of human sympathy.

Certainly the reader may feel baffled or uneasy about the degree of irony implicit in Joyce's portrait of the artist as a young narcissist. Stephen/Icarus has flown from one youthful illusion to another – first trusting the rectitude of his Clongowes masters and emulating the Count of Monte Cristo, then sliding into illicit sexual exultation in an initiation ritual immediately undercut by scenes of debased sensuality and emotional self-hatred. As the body, in turn, is disciplined and mortified, a devotion to the priesthood of art displaces the young man's Catholic asceticism. Embracing his new-found mission with all the exuberance of an aesthetic convert, Stephen is left exhausted and swooning before the sanctified icon of a wading girl transformed in his imagination into a mystical muse. Incapable of sustaining this romantic fantasy in the hostile urban environment of Dublin, he takes psychological refuge in vaguely erotic verses generated by the *imago* of an eternal temptress. In the end, nothing is left for the would-be poet but voluntary exile, to be undertaken in a spirit of secrecy, cunning, detachment, and indifference. Toward the conclusion of the novel, Stephen adopts a Wildean pose of triumphant perversity as he proclaims revolutionary freedom and projects a vision of liberating flight 'across the kathartic ocean' (*FW* 185.6) to the haunts of bohemian Paris. Emotionally static and incapable of meaningful connection with other human beings, Stephen is poised in a stance of Icarian impotence. The last diary entries of *A Portrait* suggest imminent emigration, but they delineate neither flight nor failure.

The text of Joyce's *Bildungsroman* seems to imply that the develop-

143

ing artist's notorious misogyny will prove to be still another dimension (and limitation) of his youthful priggishness. The pervasive irony that tinges the hero's scrupulous devotions and gives his aesthetic theory that 'true scholastic stink' surely informs his relations with women – from his mother and Dante Riordan to Emma and the unnamed bird-girl he transfigures on the beach. In a tone of gentle mockery, Joyce makes clear to his audience that Stephen's fear of women and his contempt for sensuous life are among the many inhibitions that stifle this young man's creativity. Before he can become a true priest of the eternal imagination, Stephen must first divest himself of the spiritual-heroic refrigerating apparatus that characterises the egocentric aesthete. Narcissism and misogyny are adolescent traits he has to outgrow on the path to artistic maturity. Not until the epic Ulysses will a new model begin to emerge – one that recognises the need for the intellectual artist to make peace with the mother-lover of his dreams and to incorporate into his masterful work those mysterious breaks, flows, gaps, and ruptures associated with the repressed semiotic flow of male/female desire. □

In a later section, Henke considers the last two pages of *Ulysses*:

■ A flower of Gibraltar and Howth, Molly says 'yes' to Leopold and herself becomes a Bloom. She knows that sexual and marital consent are in this case identical, and her feelings about both suggest a strong attraction to Bloom's epicene personality – a fascination that will not only endure but prevail through sixteen storm-tossed years of bourgeois marriage.

In the androgynous Leopold Bloom/Henry Flower, Molly finds a sympathetic love-object whose nurturant qualities provide a psychological surrogate for the absent mother of childhood abjection. On the unconscious, latent and symbolic level, the man-womanly Bloom satisfies Molly's repressed longing for pre-Oedipal (comm)-union. His penis metaphorically 'flowers' as phallic signifier in a substitution and reversal of the lost maternal breast, in accordance with Freud's formulation that 'when sucking has come to an end, the penis also becomes heir of the mother's nipple.'[12] In the mythic guise of Eve/Persephone, Molly, tasting the seed of forbidden fruit, returns it seasoned with spittle to the mouth of a maternal surrogate, to inseminate the fertile and receptive male with her own mimetically nurturant seed(cake). Molly feeds Bloom with the spittle/seed-cake/Ceres-cake that she herself desires, offers nurture as he sucks her breasts, and symbolically re-enacts the mother/child drama of reciprocal love and psychic valorisation denied her in infancy. At the end of 'Penelope', she tantalises her lover with a poetic pabulum that resuscitates his manhood and wins, in turn, the seminal gift of sexual/phallic/fetishistic completion.

As Joyce's idealised paradigm of the Jewish 'family man', Bloom embodies those Oriental qualities associated in Molly's imagination with the lost Lunita. Molly displays a keen perception of and appreciation for her husband's 'difference' from the others: he is warm, considerate, caring, sensitive, and 'polite to old women'. Her real concern, of course, is that he be polite and loving to her, no matter what her age or physical appearance. She desperately longs for that *heimlich* womb and nurturant presence obliterated from childhood memory by Lunita's untimely desertion. It is Bloom who offers his blossoming mountain flower not only eight full-blown (opiate) poppies, but the unqualified gift of non-judgemental affection associated with mother-love. Enamoured of this dark semitic stranger, a virginal Molly says 'yes' to her solicitous suitor and to the 'awful deepdown torrent' of heterosexual passion that both replicates and redefines the frustrated pulsions of infantile desire.

The emotional gaps in Molly's past engender, throughout 'Penelope', a subversive feminine discourse that defies logocentric boundaries, borders on the margins of hysteria, and, in its melancholic quest for the absent (M)Other, longs to suture the wound of pre-Oedipal separation. In being 'not all', Molly evinces a 'supplementary *jouissance*', a *jouissance* 'of the body ... *beyond the phallus*'.[13] She perpetually seeks to heal the trauma of maternal abjection by re-creating the polyphonous rhythms and lyrical echolalias of semiotic communication. Leopold Bloom serves as a channel, a surrogate, an instrument for the articulation of primordial feminine desire – ruptured in its futile search for an original, oceanic union with the imaginary mother, but temporarily healed in fantasised recollections of erotic joy and orgasmic transcendence shared, at the height of youthful exuberance, with an androgynous son/husband/lover.

Throughout *Ulysses*, sexual identities are indeterminate and poly-morphous, psychologically mobile and perpetually transferable. Joyce's novel mockingly reproduces the Oedipal triangle of 'Daddy-Mummy-Me' only to shatter and disrupt the dictates of its culturally embedded scenario. Molly and Leopold reciprocally occupy comple-mentary subject-positions of beneficent phallic mother and blissfully dependent *infans*. Each oscillates, by turn, between a subjective articulation of polymorphously perverse desire and the valorising role of Lacanian *objet a*. Although Stephen temporarily plays a surrogate son binding Molly and Leopold together as Oedipal parents, this Freudian family romance quickly gives way to a nostalgic mother-child coupling, with the new womanly man and psychologically bisexual woman at its enigmatic nexus. Poldy plays

'Mummy' to a bedsteadfast spouse who takes shape as mythic (M)Other in his own heterogeneous imagination. And Molly, historically in love with an absent female figure, learns to reconstruct the maternal subject-position through, and in relation to, an uxorious spouse.

In the Blooms' unusual conjugal configuration, the patriarchal subject-position of authoritarian Daddy remains conspicuously vacant. It is temporarily occupied by such caricatured males as Major Brian Cooper Tweedy and the indomitable Blazes Boylan. But the voice of authority is radically diffused in the carnivalesque atmosphere of 7 Eccles Street and disrupted by the 'thousand break-flows' of pre-Oedipal (and anti-Oedipal) desire that revel in libidinal viscosity: 'Flows ooze, they traverse the triangle, breaking apart its vertices.'[14] This anarchic ménage brings us, in Deleuzian terms, 'yet another message and another code: everyone is bisexual, everyone has two sexes' in a schizoid world of polymorphously perverse 'desiring machines'.[15] Lunita Laredo and Major Tweedy, Rudolph, Ellen Higgins, Millicent and Rudy Bloom all lie together in the great conjugal bed of psychological filiation.

Both Molly and Leopold handle the Lacanian experience of radical 'lack' by nostalgically endowing one another with theological wholeness and plenitude. Their reveries of salutary presence belong to an always-already absent world of prelapsarian bliss. As Bertha declares in *Exiles*, romantic epiphany 'comes only once in a lifetime. The rest of life is good for nothing except to remember that time' (*E*91). And it is precisely this act of poetic remembering, of re-collecting transitory moments of love and (imaginary) communion and recasting them in aesthetic form, that gives joy, delight, and aesthetic *jouissance* to the psychic horizons of an 'all too human', and all too mortal, physicality. □

Joyce's Irishness, so much an issue to the early hostile reviewers of his work, tended to be overlooked once he had achieved canonical status, although Richard Ellmann's *Ulysses on the Liffey* and, more recently, the work of Seamus Deane stand as honourable exceptions to this rule.[16] MacCabe and Mahaffey's contributions in this guide have both reacted against the long-standing convention of an apolitical Joyce, the high modernist haughtily aloof from the issues of class, nation and cultural identity. Vincent Cheng's study, *Joyce, Race and Empire*, also questions this view, arguing instead that many of the revolutionary qualities of Joyce's stylistic, linguistic and literary innovations can be traced to, and grounded in, his sense of ideological, ethnic and colonial dispossession. In doing so he points out how Joyce was writing in opposition to the British imperialist cultural assumptions of his time. Cheng offers yet another celebration of *Ulysses*, this time as an expression of multicultural solidarity.

■ While nationalism and national pride are certainly essential to any liberation movement and to the formation of a new nation, the particular *forms* of national consciousness and discourse of Nation a society chooses to articulate (from among nationalisms in the plural) are crucial, a matter demanding self-aware cultural scrutiny. It is narratives that, over time, construct the particular forms of national discourses. As Homi Bhabha points out, 'Without such an understanding of the performativity of language in the narratives of the nation, it would be difficult to understand why Edward Said prescribes a kind of "analytic pluralism" as the *form* of critical attention appropriate to the cultural effects of the nation'. Frantz Fanon has argued that 'National consciousness, which is not nationalism, is the only thing that will give us an international dimension', in contrast to what he calls a 'tribal dictatorship' and an 'ethnic dictatorship' which 'claims to speak in the name of the totality of the people';[17] and Bhabha elaborates that it is 'this *inter*national dimension both within the margins of the nation-space and in the boundaries in-between nations and peoples' that our efforts and narratives should be directed at, in our explorations of 'the problematic unity of the nation' and in 'the articulation of cultural difference in the construction of an international perspective.' This requires an awareness of cultural and geographical spaces as 'contact zones', for 'The "other" is never outside or beyond us; it emerges forcefully, within cultural discourse, when we *think* we speak most intimately and indigenously "between ourselves"'.

Bhabha, in his essay on 'DissemiNation: Time, Narrative, and the Margins of the Modern Nation', theorises how the 'imagined community' is simultaneously linked to the issues of essentialism, difference, and narration/narrative – a process which, as we have seen, *Ulysses* illustrates and symptomatises. Bhabha argues for 'Counter-narratives of the nation that continually evoke and erase its totalising boundaries – both actual and conceptual' so as to 'disturb those ideological manoeuvres through which "imagined communities" are given essential identities'. For the 'nation', he notes, 'reveals, in its ambivalent and vacillating representation, the ethnography of its own historicity and opens up the possibility of other narratives of the people and their difference'. *Ulysses* seems to me just this sort of narrative, which – in its cultural specificity and detailed historicity, set as it is in the concrete and material specificities of turn-of-the-century Dublin – enacts symptomatically and voices all the diverse discourses and ideological positions of 1904 Dublin; in its precision of concrete detail and specific representation (each person, each street, each building drawn in such particularised detail, distinct and different, so as to avoid the 'the narrative of national cohesions' signified by 'the many as one'), it attempts to avoid the homogenising of difference; in its presentation of analogies and similarities between those differences and peoples, it suggests possible lines of solidarity and refutes the binary essentialisms of absolute difference.[18] It is thus both universal and particular at the same time, allowing for solidarity/likeness while accepting and respecting heterogeneous difference; it is (perhaps along with *Finnegans Wake*) at once the most materially concrete/specific, *and* the most analogically universal, work imaginable – covering Ireland both vertically and horizontally in its dialogical re-presentation of the conscience of a race as a pluralistic contact zone. Thus, it illustrates what Bhabha advocates (in taking up Abdul JanMohamed and David Lloyd's term) as 'minority discourse':

> Minority discourse ... contests genealogies of 'origin' that lead to claims for cultural supremacy and historical priority. Minority discourse acknowledges the status of national culture – and the people – as a contentious, performative space of the perplexity of the living in the midst of the pedagogical representations of the fullness of life.

That seems to me a fair description of *Ulysses*.

In quoting Walter Benjamin's contention that 'To write a novel means to carry the incommensurable to extremes in the representation of human life. In the midst of life's fullness, and through the representation of this fullness, the novel gives evidence of the profound perplexity of the living' – Bhabha argues for novels of discursive resistance:

> It is from this incommensurability in the midst of the everyday that the nation speaks its disjunctive narrative. It begins ... from that anterior space within the arbitrary sign which disturbs the homogenising myth of cultural anonymity. From the margins of modernity, at the insurmountable extremes of storytelling, we encounter the question of cultural difference as the perplexity of living, and writing, the nation.

Ulysses, a novel steeped 'in the midst of the everyday', displays in its cultural specificity and representational fullness what Seamus Deane calls a 'mirror held up to Culture', disturbing the homogenising myths of a racial/national essence through its representations of a heterogeneous and inevitably pluralistic culture, a narrative space charting, through its detailed representations of the perplexity of living, both the discursive processes of 'writing the nation' and the conscience of a 'race'.

Claude Lévi-Strauss had understood 'the unconscious as providing the common and specific character of social facts ... not because it harbours our most secret selves but because ... it enables us to coincide with forms of activity which are both *at once ours and other*'. Joyce's own study of the unconscious evokes much the same discursive awareness of the interpenetrated nature of the Same/Self and the Other – for, as Foucault argued, 'the history of the order imposed on things would be the history of the Same'. *Ulysses*, through the images revealed in its 'nicely polished looking-glass' of the cultural contact zone that was Dublin in 1904, advocates an acceptance simultaneously of heterogeneity and difference, on the one hand, and, on the other hand, of a potential sameness and solidarity of shared similarities-in-difference – between Irish, Jewish, black, Oriental, Indian English, Boer, paleface, redskin, jewgreek and greekjew – within a multivalent, inter-nationalist perspective, rather than within a binary polarisation that freezes essences into poles of absolute and unbridgeable difference.[19] □

Joyce's texts, particularly *Ulysses*, seem indefatigable in their capacity to generate utopias, whether sexual, political or electronic. The similarity of Joyce's later work to Hypertext has not gone unnoticed, and he seems perfectly at home in Cyberspace. The ideal reader with ideal insomnia and access to the Internet should start here: http://www.2street.com/joyce/.

Jacques Derrida, of all people, has confessed to intimidation at the encyclopaedic ubiquity of Joyce and Joyce scholarship, and its information empire:

■ The intimidation amounts to this: Joyce experts are the representatives as well as the effects of the most powerful project for programming over the centuries the totality of research in the onto-logico-encyclopaedic field. ... A Joyce scholar has the right to dispose of the totality of competence in the encyclopaedic field of the *universitas*. He has at his command the computer of all memory, he plays with the entire archive of culture – at least of what is called Western culture. ...

We can imagine that there will soon be a giant computer of Joycean studies ('operating all this trunk line. ... Book through to eternity junction'). It would capitalise all publications, co-ordinate and teleprogram all communication, colloquia, theses, papers, and would draw up an index in all languages. We would be able to consult it any time by satellite or by 'sunphone', day and night, taking advantage of the 'reliability' of an answering machine. 'Hello, yes, yes, what are you asking for? Oh, for all the occurrences of the word yes in Ulysses? Yes.' It would remain to be seen if the basic language of this computer would be and if its patent would be American, given the overwhelming and significant majority of Americans among the trustees of the Joyce Foundation. It would also remain to be seen if we could consult this computer on the word yes in every language, and if the yes, in particular the one involved in the operations of consultation can be counted, calculated, numbered.[20] □

Derrida's wittily voiced concern for the encyclopaedic ambitions of Joyce's work are echoed and amplified in the following excerpt from Leo Bersani's *The Culture of Redemption*,[21] a study that argues that modern literature's claims to redemptive authority over experience depend on a devaluation of that experience. 'A crucial assumption in the culture of redemption is that a certain type of repetition of experience in art repairs inherently damaged or valueless experience.'[22] The dangers implicit in such claims to mastery, and the complicity of even the most sophisticated of recent theory in this process, are brought out in Bersani's essay 'Against *Ulysses*', a brilliant reading whose elegiac scepticism brings this book to a fitting conclusion.

■ Let us approach *Ulysses* as naively as possible, while admitting that this decision can be little more than a ruse. The ruseful naiveté I have in mind will consist in our pretending not to have any extratextual information about the novel – especially information about Joyce's elaborate scheme of Homeric correspondences and about the geography and history of Ireland's capital city. In saying this, I expose our naiveté as, precisely, a decision: it is only because we know how important Homer and Dublin are in *Ulysses* that we can refer to a reading ignorant of that importance as naive. I do not mean that it is natural to read any novel in a state of cultural ignorance. I do, however, want to suggest that it would not be naive to set about reading *La Chartreuse de Parme, War and Peace*, or *Moby Dick* without, in the cases of Stendhal and Tolstoy, more than a fairly general, non-specialist's knowledge of Napoleon's campaigns in Belgium and Russia, and, for Melville's work, cetological expertise. This also means that the difficulties of these novels cannot in any way be resolved by consulting sources external to them. Our ideally uninformed readers of *Ulysses*, on the other hand, may very well be overcome with embarrassment to discover, upon opening their first work of criticism, that what they had been thinking of quite simply as chapters 8 and 10 are universally referred to as 'Lestrygonians' and 'Wandering Rocks', or that wholly impenetrable passages have in fact the most satisfying transparency to cognoscenti, say, of nineteenth-century records of Gaelic legends or of theatre programs and journalistic *faits divers* in turn-of-the-century Dublin.

Naiveté, then – when it is not the sophisticated and artificial luxury I propose we briefly enjoy – becomes a retrospective judgement: how could I have read *Ulysses* without at least trying to exploit the clue provided by the novel's title, and – what is even more humiliating – how could I have mistaken cryptic or truncated allusions to the minutiae of Dublin life around 1900 for passages of textual ambiguity or complexity? The title itself, in addition to furnishing an important clue, is after all also a clear warning against the perils of innocence: the Latinised version of Odysseus alludes to one of world literature's most resourceful and wily heroes, and – as if that weren't enough – Buck Mulligan draws our attention on the novel's very first page to Stephen Dedalus' 'absurd name, an ancient Greek' (2); the name, that is, of the cunning artificer who both constructed and escaped from Minos' labyrinth.

In short, we have only to glance at the title and read page one of *Ulysses* to be forewarned: trickery and cunning are the novel's first connotations, and the possibility is thus raised from the very start that those qualities not only belong to certain characters within the novel but, much more significantly, that they define an authorial strategy. And in that case naiveté is tantamount to walking into a trap. We would therefore do well to take trickery and cunning as hortative and not merely psychologically predictive connotations: they propose the ideal-reader response to *Ulysses* as one of extreme – or extremely nervous, perhaps even somewhat paranoid – vigilance.

The tensest vigilance will, however, allow us to still approach *Ulysses* with what may at first have seemed like dangerous naiveté. For we may now go on to suspect that the connotative cluster of trickery may itself be part of a superior trickery. Might it be possible that Joyce wastes no time in encouraging us to find the novel more complicated, more devious, than it actually is, and that a comparatively simple and uninformed reading may not be so inappropriate after all? An intentionally or unintentionally naive reading of *Ulysses* can perhaps reveal things about the novel that our inevitable loss of readerly innocence will obscure. Since my emphasis will be mainly on the nature and consequences of the ideally informed reading of *Ulysses*, we should begin by doing justice to the insights of ignorance, the interpretative games to be had from the assumption that *Ulysses* can be read as if it were a nineteenth-century realistic novel.

Those gains are far from negligible. If we were unaware of the avant-gardist claims made for Joyce's novel, we would, I think, have little hesitation in speaking of it as a psychological work, as a novel of character. We might of course be bothered by what an old-fashioned critical discourse has called a disproportion between the technical machinery and the psychological or 'human' content, machinery that frequently obscures our view of what is happening.[23] For it is undeniable that a certain type of story – rather, a story *tout court* – has awakened in us certain desires by which the second half of the novel seems embarrassed and to which the most chic contemporary critics of Joyce implicitly claim to be immune. *Ulysses* is an exceptionally detailed study of character – especially of the character of Leopold Bloom, but also of Stephen Dedalus, Molly Bloom and even of Gerty MacDowell, who appears in only one episode. We know these characters inside out, and both from the inside and from the outside. There is much evidence of how they look to others, and long sections of internal monologue and free indirect style make us all familiar with their most intimate habits of mind. There is even an entire episode – 'Eumaeus' – written in the manner of Bloom, that is, in the style he would presumably use were he to try his hand at writing (a possibility he himself raises in this very chapter). Since the style of 'Eumaeus' also suggests – not unpainfully – why Bloom will always prefer talking to writing, the episode can be considered still another characterising technique. This very late section (it is episode 16) lets the reader know the character even more intimately than before by temporarily turning the narrator into the dummy-double of a ventriloquistic Bloom.

Has any fictional character ever been so completely known? Warm-hearted, commonsensical and unfanatic in politics and religion, a loving son, father, and even husband, full of enterprising (if unrealised and impractical) commercial schemes, slightly but not unappealingly pretentious intellectually, horny and a bit guilty sexually, garrulous but a stylistic outsider in a city of besotted skilled rhetoricians, perhaps a bit tight-fisted by Dublin pub standards (where one unpardonable sin is failing to pay your round), something of a loner (but by no means a rebel or an outcast) with his daydreams of travel in exotic Eastern lands, Bloom is eminently appealing and eminently ordinary. In one of the exchanges that constitute the impersonal catechism of 'Ithaca', Bloom is called 'Everyman or Noman'. In any case, he is a Sweet Man, and if Joyce has inspired a kind of attachment and anecdotal curiosity (about him, about the streets of Dublin) evocative of that affection for Jane Austen which was for so long an obstacle to her being thought of as a serious writer, it is largely because of his success in creating Bloom. The Joyceans are quite a bit raunchier that the 'Janeites', but the extraordinarily prosperous Joyce industry (with organised visits to holy spots in Dublin and Zurich) largely depends, as in the case of Austen, on the by no means unfounded or inconsiderable pleasure of recognition. The Blooms are an identifiable couple, and it is an extraordinary tribute to Joyce's power of realistic evocation that all the fancy narrative techniques of *Ulysses* are unable to dim the vivid presence of Poldy and Molly. For hordes of aficionados, June 16 will always be celebrated as Bloomsday, and it would be not only snobbish but critically wrong to suggest that the innovative power of Joyce's novel lies in a questioning or breakdown of traditional novelistic assumptions about personality.

But there are, from the very beginning, certain knots, or certain gnats, in the narrative, that disturb our relaxed reading and easy appreciation of *Ulysses'* rounded characters. Much of the novel's difficulty, especially in the early sections, is the result not of our having to learn to think about novelistic names (such as Stephen Dedalus or Leopold Bloom) in non-psychological terms, but rather of the uncompromising nature of the mimetic techniques. An 'accurate' rendering of a character's consciousness presumably requires that the narrator do nothing to help us follow the moves of that consciousness. Confronted with characters at once vivid and obscure, the reader may be inspired to take on the exegetical task of reducing the obscurity, of getting to know Bloom, Molly, or Stephen even better by completing their sentences and explaining their allusions. Far from destroying a mimetic effect that may seem to depend on a certain degree of maintained obscurity in the recorded consciousness, exegesis in this case is itself a secondary mimetic technique: a certain type of textual research is experienced as an investigation into real lives.

Thus we are required to complete the portraits of Bloom and Stephen, an activity that includes but is very little threatened by the perception of their absorption into a variety of alien styles and non-representational techniques. Indeed, in Joycean criticism the most sophisticated technical analysis comfortably cohabits with the most naive reading. John Paul Riquelme's intelligent and thorough study of mimetic disruptive techniques in *Ulysses* apparently intensified his affection for Bloom. In the midst of the most trenchant, no-nonsense point-of-view analyses, Riquelme frequently praises Bloom as a man who avoids extremes, one who 'perceives what Boylan is blind to: a basis for human action in concern for others rather than primarily in self-interest'.[24] Is there no relation between elaborate analysis of *Ulysses* as pure linguistic effects and a type of psychological and moral appreciation already made obsolete by the New Criticism of half a century ago? My point is, of course, that the relation is only too clear, and that Joyce's avant-gardism largely consists in forcing his readers to complete the rear-guard action that the novel itself simultaneously performs and elaborately disguises.

Filling in the blanks of consciousness is, however, only part of the game, although none of the more sophisticated moves into which Joyce maneuvers us will seriously undermine the traditional view of human identity that *Ulysses* defends. The novel is full of what has rather curiously been called stylistic intrusion, as if literature were ever anything but just that. Most frequently, these intrusions take the form of discontinuities or inconsistencies of point of view. I have in mind passages where Bloom abruptly begins to think with stylistic resources obviously not his, as well as those other moments when, as Hugh Kenner puts it, 'the normally neutral narrative vocabulary [is pervaded by] a little cloud of idioms which a character might use if he were managing the narrative,'[25] or, finally, when different characters' points of view are briefly merged. The celebrated perspectival jolts and mergers of *Ulysses* include the paragraph in 'Nausicaa' that abandons Bloom's limited angle of vision and takes us on a panoramic tour of the entire Howth neighbourhood, the name distortions in 'Scylla and Charybdis' (which may be Stephen's mental horseplay with his companions' names or the fooling around of a lexically ebullient narrator), and, in 'Sirens', the subtle invasion of Bloom's consciousness by musicalising tics of the dominant narrative style (alliterations, verbal echoes, staccato rhythms).

All of this has made Joyce one of the darlings of that branch of narratology obsessed with origins, with determining where narrators are located, over whose shoulder they may be speaking, from what temporal perspective and in whose voice they address us. In its more ambitious manifestations, this school of literary analysis moves from particular literary works to the devising of a master plan of possible narrative points of view – a model that can then serve in future readings. With a writer as perspectivally shifty as Joyce, we can easily imagine how handy, and how comforting, such pocket codes of narrative perspective can be. Now he's there and now he's not; point-of-view analysis is the literary-criticism version of hide and seek. It is the paranoid response to what might be called the irreducibility of voice in literature to locations and identities.

If point-of-view criticism is intent on getting everything straight, on putting the literary house in order (and there are academic domestic quarrels about where certain pieces of stylistic furniture belong), it can also be titillated by disorder, or perspectival incon-sistencies. Only narratologists truly worth their salt will identify all the traps Joyce sets for us in *Ulysses*. One example: immediately after a passage that quotes Bloom's thoughts about Shakespeare (we know it's Bloom: he wrongly attributes Congreve's 'Music hath charms to soothe the savage breast' to Shakespeare), we find, 'In Gerard's rosery of Fetter lane he walks, greyedauburn' (362). This is an almost exact repetition of one of Stephen's remarks during the Shakespeare discussion in 'Scylla and Charybdis', and so we go rushing back to that episode to make sure we were right to think Bloom wasn't there. He wasn't; but the narrator was, and since he's as free as he wants to be, he has simply dropped this bit of Stephen's speech into the flow of Bloom's consciousness. There are of course cases of much greater ambiguity in Joyce's writing, one of which occurs in the description of Buck Mulligan on the first pages of *Ulysses*: 'He peered sideways up and gave a long slow whistle of call, then paused awhile in rapt attention, his even white teeth glistening here and there with gold points. Chrysostomos. Two strong shrill whistles answered through the calm.' Who says or thinks 'Chrysostomos'? And is it the rhetorically adept Mulligan we are meant to compare to the 'golden-mouthed' father of the early church, St. John Chrysostomos, or is it *Ulysses* itself? As Fritz Senn has written, the word can be taken 'as the translation of a visual impression, as Stephen's internal comment, as the heralding of a new technique characterised often by the sacrifice of the syntactically complete sentence structure, as a reflection on *Ulysses* itself. ... But it *might*, after all, also be the comment of some narrator.' Then there are passages, such as the description of Mulligan's dressing, which appear to mix not only different types of narrative reporting (third-person descriptions, internal monologue, and dialogue) but characters themselves:

> And putting on his stiff collar and rebellious tie he spoke to them, chiding them, and to his dangling watchchain. His hands plunged and rummaged in his trunk while he called for a clean handkerchief. [Agenbite of inwit.] God, we'll simply have to dress the character. I want puce gloves and green boots. Contradiction. Do I contradict myself? Very well then, I contradict myself. Mercurial Malachi. A limp black missile flew out of his talking hands. – And there's your Latin quarter hat, he said. (19)

The two sentences beginning 'God, we'll simply have to dress' and 'I want' seem to be Buck's speech, but with 'Contradiction' we enter what David Hayman has called 'a dead space between thought and action,' a space that may belong to Stephen or to Buck or to both (or is it the narrator's allusion to Whitman?), one in which 'the two individuals are momentarily and magically joined by the narrator whose procedures are more comprehensible on the thematic and analogical levels than on the mimetic.'[26] This ambiguity, I should emphasise, in no way threatens a solidly established difference between Stephen and Buck, just as the playful transposition of the sounds of Stephen's and Bloom's names in 'Ithaca' (they momentarily become 'Stoom' and 'Blephen') is nothing but a momentary lexical joke that has no effect whatever on differences already elaborated for well over five hundred pages by a scrupulously realistic psychology.

Joyce both provokes and soothes our critical paranoia (he provides it with exorcising exercises); the difficulty, or even impossibility, of attribution in *Ulysses* is almost always a local affair, one that takes place against a background of firmly identified and differentiated personalities. Since, for example, we could no more confuse Bloom's voice with Stephen's than we could mistake Gibbon's style for Malory's in the pastiches of 'Oxen of the Sun', the intrusions, confusions, and discontinuities of point of view in *Ulysses* must, I think, be read as an important element in the strategic centring of the narrator's authority. That is, they should be read as part of his aggressively demonstrated superiority to the patterns and models of representation he insists that we recognise and analytically elaborate while he himself partially neglects them

I do not mean by this that the perspectival agitations of *Ulysses* are insignificant. The question of point of view is essentially a question of citation – whose voice is the narrative quoting? – and citation is crucial to the intra- and inter-textual authority of Joyce's novel as a Masterwork. Indeed, Joyce's occasionally grand indifference to consistency of point of view should perhaps be read as a way to redirect our attention from the comparatively trivial quotations of consciousness to what I will call the quotation of essential being. And in this he brings to the mimetic tradition in literature what may be its most refined technique. Consider the first sentence of *Ulysses*: 'Stately, plump Buck Mulligan came from the stairhead, bearing a bowl of lather on which a mirror and a razor lay crossed.' 'Bearing' instead of 'carrying' is part of the 'novelese' characteristic, as Kenner reminds us, of the first episode.[27] Both it and the two adjectives used to describe Buck reflect his particular rhetorical pomposity. But it is not exactly as if Buck had written the sentence; nor do we have an otherwise neutral narrative vocabulary pervaded by 'a little cloud of idioms which a character might use if he were managing the narrative'. Rather, Buck's verbal mannerisms are a necessary part of a wholly objective presentation of him. 'Plump' somewhat deflates 'stately'; it helps us to visualise the character in a way that does not exactly support the vaguer connotations of 'stately'. The sentence is at once seduced by Mulligan's rhetoric and coolly observant of his person. Not that Buck would have been incapable of writing the sentence (which is a rather silly issue for criticism to address at any rate); but in writing it he would already, so to speak, have stepped out of himself, would have performed himself with irony. And we could say that a complete or objective view of Buck can be given neither by a direct quote nor by an analytical description, but only by a self-performance at a certain distance from the performing self. In other words, the sentence objectifies the point of view it takes.

It is this non-perspectival point of view that explains the peculiar and disturbing power of *Dubliners*, where Joyce characterises not only individuals but also a kind of collective consciousness through such objectified subjectivity. This impressive achievement should, I think, be considered in the light of Stephen's definition of beauty in *A Portrait of the Artist as a Young Man*, as well as the references in *Ulysses* to Aristotle's notion of entelechy and the 'form of forms'. In trying to understand what Aquinas means by 'radiance' (or *claritas*) in his enumeration of the 'three things needed for beauty' (*integritas, consonantia, claritas*), Stephen comes to the following solution: 'The radiance of which he speaks is the scholastic *quidditas*, the *whatness* of a thing.'[28] It is as if literature could quote being independently of any particular being's point of view. We would, that is, have the point of view of neither a narrator nor a character; instead we would have the quidditas of Buck Mulligan, and even of Dublin. The individual's or the city's point of view has been purified to its essence, to a whatness ontologically distinct from the phenomenality of having a point of view.

The somewhat comical side of this realisation of Aquinas in narrative techniques of realistic fiction is evident in the following sentence from 'The Boarding House', which describes Protestant Dubliners going to church on a bright summer morning: 'The belfry of George's church sent out constant peals and worshippers, singly or in groups, traversed the little circus before the church, revealing their purpose by their self-contained demeanour no less than by the little volumes in their gloved hands.' An essence of Dublin churchgoing receives expression here not as a result of either a dramatic or an analytic approach; instead the most scrupulously impersonal description manages to raise the object of description to a kind of objectifyingly ironic self-description. The very neatness of the sentence, with its elegantly controlled but somewhat fancified syntax and its concluding succession of nouns each with a single modifier ('self-contained demeanour', 'little volumes', 'gloved hands'), actually speaks the activity itself as a somewhat trivial manifestation of the human taste for ritualised disorder.

But the language also demystifies the very idea of an essentialised self-expression by allowing us to *locate* its transcendental, non-perspectival point of view. If Dublin speaks itself in *Dubliners*, the essentialising voice itself cannot escape having a social and psychological identity. The pitiless quidditas of realistic fiction allows for the dephenomenalising of character only *as* a phenomenon of point of view. Who can repeat Dublin with particular radiance without, however, being able to take another point of view (and another point of view would precisely, however superior it might be, destroy the essentialising repetitions) – who, if not an educated Dubliner or a Dublin schoolteacher, one who, like Stephen in the 'Nestor' episode of *Ulysses*, fully assumes the continuity between his dull-witted student and himself, thereby perhaps plotting his escape from Dublin through his articulated recognition of his own Dublin-ness in art? The schoolteacher can speak only Dublinese (unless – and this is of course the difference between *Dubliners* and *Ulysses* – he borrows voices from other places): we can hear, in the second half of our sentence from 'The Boarding House' those adeptly poised rhythmical designs, so receptive to hyperbole ('revealing their purpose by ... no less than by'), which in *Ulysses* animate the endless recitation of local news in public meeting places. The quidditas of a Dublin church group is, then, itself a kind of secondary or occasional form within the superior, more general form of Dublin-ness. Quidditas here is manifested most profoundly as a kind of respiratory pattern in language, a pattern that then has the potential – associated by Aristotle with entelechy – to engender actualities (fictional characters and events) of the same kind, which repeat it. In Joyce, the Schoolman is reformulated as the schoolteacher; an educated but inescapable provincialism is the social precondition of an art content to give *claritas* to the artist's inherited consciousness.

Claritas is an effect of quotation, although, as I have been suggesting, the quote is at the level of essence and not of existence. Of course in *Ulysses* Joyce does not merely cite Dublin; the novel is an encyclopaedia of references. And this means that voices are always on loan. Several critics have noted the absence of what we would call a personal style in Joyce. Stephen Heath, writing – for the most part brilliantly – as a representative of post-structuralist (and mainly French) readings of Joyce, notes: 'In place of style we have *plagiarism*', and then goes on to speak of Joyce's writing as 'ceaselessly pushing the *signified* back into the *signifier* in order to refind at every moment the drama of language, its production.'[29] I will not linger over the satisfying spectacle of a professor praising plagiarism (high-class plagiarism, true); but the notion of a plagiaristic wandering among signifiers – of the writer as a kind of open switchboard picking up voices from all over – does deserve more attention. For it raises a question that has been of major importance in this book: the authority of literature over the materials it incorporates. In *Bouvard et Pécuchet* we have seen another encyclopaedic novel that appears to indulge in massive quotation. But the intertextuality of *Bouvard et Pécuchet* is highly deceptive: the textual act of quotation is simultaneously a disqualification of the citational process. Flaubert erases our cultural memory at the very moment he awakens it. The mutations of epistemological discourses in *Bouvard et Pécuchet* remove the novel from the cultural history it non-connectedly absorbs. Nor does the work's intratextuality create connective designs or structures; each section repeats a process of solipsistic play that cuts it off from the other sections echoed in the repetition. Finally, not only does the work or art *know nothing*, but in its incommensurability with all cultural discourses of knowledge, it can only exist in a continuous anxiety about its capacity to sustain itself, perhaps even to begin itself.

For Joyce, on the other hand, art is by definition the transcendence of any such anxiety. *Ulysses* is often hard to read, but more than any other work of literature, it is also a guidebook to how it should be read. Actually a guidebook was issued before the novel was published. Partly for reasons beyond Joyce's control (the delay of more than ten years between the publication of *Ulysses* in Paris and its appearance in England and America) and partly because Joyce wanted it that way (he sent the first known schema for *Ulysses* to Carlo Linati in September 1920 – a year before Shakespeare and Co. published the book – and a second schema to Valéry Larbaud in late 1921), *Ulysses* was an object not only of discussion but also of interpretation long before its audiences had access to the complete text. Many readers thus had lessons in reading before they had anything to read. In itself that is sufficient evidence of this great modernist text's need for a reader, of its dependence on a community of comprehension. If the modernist artist refuses to make his work accessible to a mass audience, he is, as Richard Poirier has argued, far from indifferent to being read and understood.[30] Joyce, like Eliot in his notes for 'The Waste Land', helps us on the road to all those recognitions and identifications necessary for the 'right' reading of *Ulysses*: recognitions of the elaborate network of repetitions within the novel, identifications of all the other cultural styles and artifacts alluded to or imitated.

There is in *Ulysses* an intratextuality meant to guide us in our intertextual investigations, to teach us how to leave the novel, and, above all, how to return to it in our exegeses. Frank Budgen records pointing out to Joyce that the word 'yards' would be more accurate than 'crosstree' to designate the spars to which the sails are bent on the schooner Stephen sees in Dublin Bay in 'Proteus'. 'There's no criticism I more value than that,' Joyce answered, and then he went on to say: 'But the word 'crosstree' is essential. It comes in later on [in 'Scylla and Charybidis'] and I can't change it.'[31] The repetition is not one we are likely to notice on a first reading (or perhaps on a second or third reading). It is, however, lying in wait for our recognition, and that seems to have been enough for Joyce. For he knew that even if we missed 'crosstree', at least he made us expect such repetitions, and he therefore had the obligation of providing them for us even if we never see them. The training is given in a series of graduated lessons. Slightly more likely to awaken a memory are such things as Molly's allusion, in 'Penelope', to Gerty MacDowell's unflattering reference to 'flighty' girl cyclists 'showing off what they hadn't got' (466) – Molly remembers an Andalusian singer in Gibraltar who 'didn't make much secret of what she hadn't' (917) – or (farther up on the scale of visibility) the echo, in Bloom's anticipation of his bath in the last lines of 'Lotus Eaters' – he 'saw the dark tangled curls of his bush floating, floating hair of the stream around the limp father of thousands, a languid floating flower' (107) – of the description, in 'Proteus', of the tide at Sandymount Strand: the 'breath of waters' that 'flows purling, widely flowing, floating foamproof, flower unfurling' (62). The words in 'Proteus' could be Stephen's, but the concluding passage of 'Lotus Eaters' is clearly out of Bloom's linguistic range. What might in another writer be taken as coincidence (the recurrence of 'crosstree'), or as forgetfulness (the repetition of Gerty's thoughts in Molly's mind), becomes in *Ulysses* an important sign of the author's virtuosity. It is as if more and more circuits were lighted as we read and reread; the movement forward, from episode to episode, is simultaneously a spatialisation of the text, which is transformed into a kind of electrical board with innumerable points of light connected to one another in elaborate, criss-crossing patterns.

'Circe' condenses the activity of textual remembrance ceaselessly taking place throughout the novel. *Ulysses* is itself the hallucinating subject of 'Circe'; the episode is the book dreaming itself even before it is finished (there are anticipatory echoes of things yet to come, and to some extent it is even Joyce's oeuvre both calling up moments from its past and, in certain word plays, announcing the verbal textures of *Finnegans Wake*). 'Circe' is also a way for us to check our textual memory, to be tested on how well we have read, to find out to what extent *Ulysses* has occupied our mind. Even more: it is a model dream for the ideally occupied, or possessed, reader of *Ulysses*. 'Circe' implicitly defines an absolute limit of readerly absorption. Not only would Joyce's work provide all the terms of our critical activity, it would also be the inexhaustible material of our dreams, in Freudian terms both the daytime residue and the unconscious drives. Before *Finnegans Wake*, Joyce already projects in *Ulysses* the literary textuali-sation of the entire mind, of our day-consciousness and our night-consciousness. In so doing, he unwittingly exposes what may be the secret project behind all talk of the mind or of the world as text:

the successful positing of the Book – or, more accurately, of books, of a certain type of professional activity – as the ontological ground of history and desire.

The 'drives' of the Book are, however, drives without affects. 'Circe' hallucinates the unconscious as word play. The unconscious, it is true, never is anything but word play in literature, and though this should probably be taken as the sign of an incommensurability between mental life and the instruments of literary expression, it has recently authorised interpretations of the unconscious as a structure 'in some way' analogous to that of language. Thus a sublimating bookishness domesticates the unconscious, enacting the very repudiations it purports to analyse as linguistic effects. The violations of logic and linearity, the displacements and the condensations of discourse in which we are inclined to read the operations of unconscious process, are themselves constitutive of the vast sublimating structure of human language. That structure – perhaps thought itself, as Freud suggested – may have evolved as the result of a primary displacement of a wish – a displacement from the untranslatable terms of a drive to so-called linguistic metaphors of desire, metaphors that express drives only on the ground of their self-constitutive negation of drives.

'Circe' is most explicit and, we might say, most Flaubertian in its insistence on the non-referential finality of the signifier in literature. To a certain extent, it counters the mimetic effects I began by emphasising. It is the episode that most openly invites a psychoanalytic interpretation, even as it compels us to acknowledge impenetrable resistance to any such interpretation. As part of a book's hallucinatory play with its own elements, Bloom's presumed masochism, for example, can only be a joke. Bloom's psychology is elaborated in 'Circe' – given the dimension of unconscious drives – as it is nowhere else in *Ulysses*, but the suggestion is that, in writing, psychology can never be anything but farce. A desire with nothing more than a textual past has the lightness and unconstrained mobility of farce. In 'Circe' Joyce exuberantly stages masochism with a kind of wild inventiveness – as if to insist on the profound difference between the mysterious repetition of a painful pleasure, which Freud obscurely posits as the essence of human sexuality in the *Three Essays on the Theory of Sexuality*, and masochism as an occasion for extravagantly varied scenic effects. In 'Circe' the book dreams masochism without pain (or with an inconsequential pain, one that can be erased from one page to the next), and in so doing it appears to leave behind not only the 'burnt up field' of *Ulysses*' own mimetic seriousness but also the devastated terrain of a more general cultural discourse.[32] Toward the other texts it quotes in various ways – especially Sacher-Masoch's

161

Venus in Furs, Krafft-Ebing's *Psychopathis Sexualis*, and Flaubert's *Tentation de St. Antoine*, all textual elaborations of the perverse in human conduct – 'Circe' engages in an extremely intricate operation of what we might call a resublimating desublimation. In this farcical treatment of other cultural discourses, Joyce can be understood as proposing, first of all, that the claim to truth of any cultural artifact is its primary mystification. The farcical here operates as the sign of a desublimated discourse – although it is not the sexual in this case that is revealed as the referent of an allegedly higher discourse. On the contrary: the works that 'Circe' quotes claim, in different ways, to analyse or to represent sexual drives, but, Joyce suggests, the reality those claims disguise is nothing more than the arbitrary play and productiveness of the signifier. The virtuosity of desire as linguistic effects is, I think, meant to lead us to conclude that *language cannot represent desire*.

This, however, does not necessarily diminish the authority of literary language. We will have to look more closely at the resublimating aspect of the operation I have just referred to. First note that the frequently marvellous comedy of 'Circe' is much more ambiguous – even suspect – than I have suggested. There is in Joyce, from *Stephen Hero* to *Ulysses*, a scrupulously serious use of techniques obviously meant to represent characters realistically, as well as the cultivation of a remarkable perspectival strategy suggesting, as we have seen, that we have the essence of a character independent of his or her point of view. Not only does Joyce frequently work within formal conventions inescapably associated with a referential bias in fiction; his departure from familiar techniques of novelistic reporting actually reinforces the illusion of referentiality. The quotation of characters in their essential being, though it violates a certain literalism in realistic point of view, suggests that characters exist outside of their novelistic appearances. The narrator quotes them at a level of reality they are themselves incapable of representing, and this means that the narrative frequently refers to, say, a Bloom or a Mulligan more real than the Bloom or the Mulligan it allows us to see and hear. Thus the reduction of Bloom's depths to verbal farce in 'Circe' is countered by the very passages to which 'Circe' refers us. The novel has already committed itself to illusions of truth, that is, to a belief in novelistic language as epistemologically trustworthy, as capable of recreating the density of human experience, or referring to or carrying more than its own relational play.

This commitment is visible even in episodes that emphasise a purely rhetorical finality. To write is to experience the seductive powers of language itself, the ways in which it turns us away from the objects it designates. But that seduction is of course not limited to writing, and Joyce's interest in a milieu celebrated for its rhetorical performances allows him to represent, as an object of his own novelistic consciousness, the absorption in language that also characterises literary consciousness. The importance of rhetorical virtuosity in Dublin talk is appreciatively recognised by Joyce in the space he gives to such talk and is also exploited as the occasion for dramatising a general epistemological skepticism. Thus the parodies of journalistic and popular literary styles interrupting the nameless narrator's account, in 'Cyclops', of what happened at about 5 P.M. in Barney Kiernan's pub are, in a sense, not really interruptions at all. The entire episode is a comic display of hyperbolic styles, and the nameless one's account, though it enjoys more space than any of the parodic asides, is merely another version of the exaggerating modes of speech (the technique here is 'gigantism') characteristic of the entire episode. And this also means that, though we have a very strong sense of what is happening in this dramatic scene (Bloom is the victim of an antisemitic attack and he makes his famous defence of love as the opposite of hatred), we are perhaps also invited to doubt the validity of the narrative report. Or rather, with his customary ambivalence about such things, Joyce seems anxious both to profit from assumptions about the reliability of reporting he himself continuously exposes as naive and to give a dazzling demonstration of the epistemological finality of the report's language. Similarly, the headlines in 'Aeolus' are not so much intrusions into an otherwise naturalistically rendered dialogue as a reminder that the headline itself is a modern addition to the classical repertory of rhetorical figures in this section's style. If the newspaper increases our knowledge about the world, it also significantly modifies modes of cognition, and the world we get to know better is also inseparable from the journalistic medium that may be offering little more than reports on its own resources. Displays of rhetoric are, then, an important part of *Ulysses*' referential network.

Furthermore, if Joyce somewhat fitfully makes the points I have associated principally with 'Circe', they are not exactly new points. The works of Flaubert and Henry James already make the case for knowledge as a matter of style and for the self as a play of the signifier. What is original in Joyce is the use to which he puts this awareness. James's *The Europeans* – and I recognise the bizarreness of the comparison – might be read in terms not too different from those I have used for 'Circe'. The farce of 'Circe' is a function of the melodramatic associations it evokes. Just when Bloom is to be characterised in depth, he disappears as a self, and a cultural discourse on the perverse in human nature is comically replayed devoid of a referent, as part of the more general comedy of entertaining but epistemologically insignificant mutations in the history of cultural discourse. And, at least in the immediate context of this demonstration in *Ulysses*, there is, so to speak, no one around to be affected. What interests James, on the other hand, is the effect of something like the disappearance of self on human relations. Rather than propose an extreme (and extremely theoretical) skepticism about our ability to report on anything at all, James in *The Europeans* stages a confrontation between characters who expect their inherited vocabulary to correspond to something real in human nature and a woman (Eugenia) who may be nothing but a play of styles. James suggests, with great originality, that Eugenia's lack of self may be the most morally interesting thing about her, while the Wentworths' need to know others severely limits them (they are finally compelled to label Eugenia a liar).

I will make an even more incongruous juxtaposition by suggesting that Beckett is closer to James in this respect than to his friend and compatriot. From *Waiting for Godot* to *Company*, Beckett suggests that, whereas there can no longer be 'characters' in literature, that very deprivation thrown into sharper relief than ever before the infinite geometry of relational play among human subjects. *Godot* demonstrates the inevitability of conversation at a cultural juncture when there may be nothing left to talk about; and the strategies for continuing talk survive the absence of psychological subjects. And *Company*, even after the elimination of a human other, performs a solipsistic sociability inherent in the grammar of language itself. (Sociability in Joyce is a function of realistically portrayed characters and not, as in Beckett, the fascinatingly anachronistic remnant of the disappearance of such characters.) Beckett's authentic avant-gardism consists in a break not only with the myths fostered by cultural discourse but, more radically, with cultural discourse itself. The mystery of his work is how it is not only sustained but even begun, for intertextuality in Beckett (the echoes of Descartes and Malebranche in the early works, for example) is not a principle of cultural continuity (as it is in Joyce, in spite of the parodic nature of the repetitions) but the occasion for a kind of psychotic raving. Cultural memories exist in the minds of Beckett's characters like fossils belonging to another age, like instruments no one knows how to use anymore. Beckett's work remembers culture as Lucky remembers the structure of a logical argument in *Godot*: they are played like the broken records of language and consciousness.

Joyce, for all his parodic intentions, rejuvenates the Homeric myths that, somewhat above the characters' heads, give an epic dimension to a prosaic day in Dublin's life. Thus *Ulysses*, however crookedly and mockingly, resuscitates Odysseus, and Joyce's ambivalent argument against the mimetic seriousness of literature, unlike

Beckett's or Flaubert's, actually works to increase literature's authority, to realise a dream of cultural artifacts as both unconstrained by and superior to life, superior by virtue of the intertextual designs they silently invite us to disengage. The resublimation of cultural discourse in 'Circe' is a function of the episode's intertextuality. Joyce ultimately 'saves' the other texts that 'Circe' parodistically quotes, and he does this simply by putting them into relation with 'Circe'. Joycean parody simultaneously 'scorches' the other texts to which it refers and reconstitutes them as cultural artifacts within the intertextual designs woven by *Ulysses*. Intertextuality is, of course, not a phenomenon peculiar to *Ulysses*; what is peculiar is the novel's use of the intertext as a redemptive strategy. The Joycean intertext rescues Western literature from the deconstructive effects of the intertext itself. The parodistic replays of Homer, Shakespeare, and Flaubert – not to speak of all the authors quoted in 'Oxen of the Sun' – are neither subversive of nor indifferent to the fact of cultural inheritance; rather, Joyce relocates the items of that inheritance with *Ulysses* as both their centre and belated origin.

This is very different from Flaubert's insistent demonstration of art's indifference to its sources. There is no pastiche in *Bouvard et Pécuchet*, which means that Flaubert never advertises his authority over other cultural texts. Flaubert's novel is deliberately monotonous and narrow, as if it couldn't do anything with the mass of human knowledge it incorporates except to submit all of it to the same, tirelessly repeated stylistic operation. The originality of *Bouvard et Pécuchet* is identical to its epistemological and cultural incompetence. In a sense, the artist is revealed (and this remark might not have displeased Flaubert) as somewhat stupid: no matter what is presented to him, he reacts with the same stylistic reflex, with a cliché. And, as I argued earlier, the writer's limited authority, even his political effectiveness, depends on this stripping away of all authority, on the recognition of the work of art as an impotent discourse. The work's solipsistic existence in the margins of history undermines, or at least helps to delay, the inevitable complicity of all art in a civilisation's discourse of power.

Beckett, and not Joyce, would be the most attentive reader of the Flaubert I have been discussing. The very variety of stylistic designs in *Ulysses* reveals Joyce's designs on culture. Far from transmuting all his cultural referents into a single, recognisably Joycean discourse, Joyce scrupulously maintains the distinctness of innumerable other styles *in order to legitimise misquoting them*. The accuracy is not merely a referential scruple, just as the inaccuracies are far from being mere sloppiness. We have to recognise the sources of *Ulysses* if we are to acknowledge its superiority to them. *Ulysses* indulges massively in quotation – quotation of individual characters, social groups, myths, other writers – but quoting in Joyce is the opposite of self-effacement. It is an act of appropriation, which can be performed without Joyce's voice ever being heard. It is as if Joyce were quoting Western culture itself in its quidditas – except that the whatness of all those cultural referents is designated not as the essential property of the referents themselves but rather as a consequence of their being (mis)quoted. Joyce miraculously reconciles uncompromising mimesis with a solipsistic structure. Western culture is saved, indeed glorified, through literary metempsychosis: it dies in the Joycean parody and pastiche, but, once removed from historical time, it is resurrected as a timeless design. Far from contesting the authority of culture, *Ulysses* reinvents our relation to Western culture in terms of exegetical devotion, that is, as the exegesis of *Ulysses* itself.

Beckett, on the other hand, babbles culture, as if its cultural memories afflicted the work of art – afflicted it not because they stifle its originality but because they infect it like foreign or prehistoric organisms. The difficulty of art in Beckett is in no way connected to the encyclopaedic nature of the work's intertextual range; rather it is the function of an art alienated from culture, the consequence of Beckett's extraordinary effort to stop remembering, to begin again, to protect writing from cultural inheritance. As his late work suggests, the most refined stage of Beckett's artistic consciousness is identical to a moving back, to a return to that stage of difficulty which, he may feel, he left too early: the stage at which the writer is paralysed by the insurmountable problem of description, of saying what he sees. It is perhaps only at this stage that the writer discovers the nature of writing; 'ill seen, ill said' defines nothing less than the essence of literature.

Ulysses is a novel curiously unaffected by its most radical propositions. Perhaps because the realistic psychology of its characters is barely affected by – to quote Heath again – Joyce's 'ceaselessly pushing the signified back into the signifier in order to refind at every moment the drama of language, its productions' (this remark, however problematic we may find it today, actually does describe *The Europeans*), this pushing never engenders any oppositional pressures. To put it schematically, the finality of the signifier is at once posited and ignored. We have, however, learned from other writers that literature's greatest ruse may be to insist that language perform the function of knowledge that the writer's special intimacy with language has taught him radically to doubt. This is the ruse of a reflexive 'I' conscious of an aberrant consciousness of both its inner and outer worlds, and yet skeptical of that very consciousness of error.

For the epistemological nihilism that may be the consequence of our sense of the human mind as a language-producing mechanism (linguistic signifiers can proliferate independently of what they signify and what they refer to) is itself the event of a linguistic consciousness, and the most daring move of all in this 'prison house of language' may be to insist that language give us the truth it falsely claims to contain.

I will name three writers who make this insistence: Proust, Lawrence, and Bataille. One can hardly imagine more different artists, and yet all three share a sense of the implausibility *and* the necessity of forging a correspondence between language and being. In his foreword to *Women in Love* Lawrence writes that the 'struggle for verbal consciousness should not be left out in art. It is a very great part of life. It is not superimposition of a theory. It is the passionate struggle into conscious being' of the writer's 'unborn needs and fulfilment'. This Lawrentian struggle – the word is repeated five times in one short paragraph – is perhaps not too far from what Bataille calls, in his foreword to *Le Bleu du ciel*, the 'intolerable, impossible ordeal [that alone] can give an author the means of achieving that wide-ranging vision that readers weary of the narrow limitations imposed by conventions are waiting for'. 'An anguish to which I was prey' was, we remember, at the origin of the 'freakish anomalies' of *Le Bleu du ciel*. Thus Bataille announces his identification with his frenetically restless narrator Troppmann, and in so doing he argues, from the very start, for an abdication of the novelist's mastery of his material. *Le Bleu du ciel* – like *Women in Love* and, to a certain extent, *A la recherche du temps perdu* – has trouble settling on its own sense, and this is how these works revolutionise the practice of writing novels. They have to be performed before any technique for dominating their sense has been worked out. Most important, the struggles and ordeals of which Lawrence and Bataille speak are incorporated into the very work of their writing, with the result that their fiction is compelled to abdicate any authority for resolving the dilemmas it poses, any superior point of view that might justify a broader cultural claim for art as a vehicle of truth.

The freakish anomalies of *Ulysses*, far from threatening the author's control of his material, are the very sign of that control. Consider 'Oxen of the Sun', which may be the most difficult and the most accessible episode of the novel. Once we have identified all the referents in this virtuoso pastiche of prose styles from Sallust to modern slang, what else does the episode give us? How does its language enact its sense? While the narrator is engaging in this stylistic tour de force, several of the characters – including Stephen and Bloom – are sitting around drinking and talking in a maternity hospital, where Mrs. Purefoy is going through the final moments of a long, hard labour. With some help from a letter Joyce wrote to Frank Budgen as he was working on 'Oxen of the Sun', critics have proposed a series of parallels between the evolution of English prose and (1) biological gestation and birth, (2) the development of the embryonic artist's prose style, (3) faunal evolution, and (4) Stephen's rebirth as an artist. The episode may be the most extraordinary example in the history of literature of meaning unrelated to the experience of reading and to the work of writing. What Joyce obviously worked on was a series of brief pastiches aligned in chronological order. The characters and plot of *Ulysses* provide the material for the pastiche, although Joyce wants to think of the relation between the stylistic exercise and its anecdotal context in more organic terms. And so we have a series of imitative fallacies. In what way is the historical transformation (which is of course not a development or the maturation of an organism) of English prose styles 'parallel' or 'analogous' to (and what do these words mean here?) the biological development of an embryo in a womb? Also the beginnings of a modern writer's work obviously in no way resemble Anglo-Saxon; the transformation of an individual prose style reflects an experience of language wholly unrelated to the reasons for the difference between Dickens and the *Morte d'Arthur*. Finally, the idea of a significant connection between Mrs. Purefoy's gestation or the history of English prose styles to Stephen's emergence as an artist is so absurd that it is difficult even to find the terms in which to object to it.

Now I may of course be taking all these analogies too seriously, and Joyce's letter to Budgen, characteristically manages both to sound quite earnest and to strike a comic note: 'Bloom is the spermatozoon, the hospital, the womb, the nurse, the ovum, Stephen the embryo.'[33] (He even adds: 'How's that for High?') Joyce's shifty tone suggests a wager: 'let's see how much I can be credited for, and, in the worst of cases (if my critics are uncomfortable enough with these analogies), it can always be argued that I proposed them with tongue in cheek.' It is true that the 'Oxen of the Sun' analogies are not the sort of thing looked at too closely by the most sophisticated of Joyce's admirers, but they have, for example, led Richard Ellmann to suggest that 'Mrs. Purefoy has laboured and brought forth a Purefoykin, English has laboured and brought forth Stephen', and even to say that 'Mrs. Purefoy's oncoming baby is paralleled by the outgoing Stephen' (he leaves the hospital before Bloom, who entered first and was 'hospitably received by the nurse' – who is, according to Joyce, the 'ovum'), Stephen who, with his friends, can also be thought of, as they rush from the hospital to a pub, as 'the placental outpouring ... (it is the afterbirth as well as an ejaculative spray).'[34]

Such criticism is itself a joke, but my point is that it is not unauthorised by the novel (not to speak of Joyce's suggestions for reading the novel) and that authorisation is itself a moment of significance in the story of how literature has been thought about. If the history of philosophy can no longer measure approximations to truth but must instead be satisfied with chronicling the mutations of fictions, and if hermeneutics can no longer provide a science of interpretation but itself becomes a stage in the history of the forms of intelligibility, 'Oxen of the Sun' might be seen as one of the contributions to the literature section of such a history. Joyce initiates us to a radical separation of interpretation from the phenomenology of reading. The announced correspondences and meanings of *Ulysses'* episodes can be thought of as a way not of elucidating the novel's sense, but of forcing us to see that *sense is a series of ingenious jokes on the signifier*. It is the very prose styles of 'Oxen of the Sun' that are parodied by their repetition in Mrs. Purefoy's womb. And the idea of Stephen's literary or spiritual birth in this chapter is a magnificently irresponsible way of understanding the insignificant role he plays in the episode, as well as of interpreting the possibility (suggested by Kenner)[35] of his having slugged Mulligan (and thus repudiated the sterile past connected with Mulligan) in the interval between episodes 9 and 14.

The Lawrentian (and, as I have shown elsewhere, the Mallarmean)[36] attempt to coerce language into an espousal of the moves of an individual consciousness – moves that an impersonal linguistic coherence necessarily 'skips', to which such coherence is inherently alien – is rejected in 'Oxen of the Sun' as an insidious fallacy. And yet a whole set of conventional psychological and moral significances coexists quite comfortably in Joyce with a radical skepticism concerning the validity of any move whatsoever beyond the line of the signifier. (This cohabitation is quite familiar to us today. The Lacanians' ritualistic repetition of the word *significant* as the key to Lacan's radical rethinking of the Freudian unconscious has, for example, in no way affected the normative status, in their thought, of the psychologically and morally specific referent of a phallocentric heterosexuality.) The perception of human reality as a language effect has generally had the curious consequence of forestalling, of leaving no terms available for, the criticism of psychological, moral, and social orders elaborated by the quite different view – now seen as epistemologically naive – of language as essentially descriptive of a pre-existent real. The rhetorical criticism associated with Derrida and, more properly, de Man has much to say about the deconstructive effects of the figural on political or moral assertions, and very little to say about the strategic nature of its own analytic enterprise. The

169

decision to treat history as rhetoric must itself be deconstructed – which is of course to say reconstructed – as a profoundly reactionary move: it deliberately ignores how network of power can be independent of the subversive effect presumably inherent in their own discursive practices. The resistance of language to its own performance provides insufficient friction to curtail the operational efficiency of even the most 'mystified' (but powerful) linguistic performances. Foucault, it seems to me, had the great merit of seeing that effects of power are indifferent to their rhetorical legitimacy, and that a predominantly rhetorical analysis of a society's discursive practices therefore runs the risk of collaborating with those coercive intentions, even while ceaselessly demonstrating their inescapably (but on the whole ineffectually) self-menacing nature.

Ulysses substitutes for the interpretative ordeals posed by such writers as Lawrence, Mallarmé, and Bataille a kind of affectless busyness, the comfortable if heavy work of finding all the connections in the light of which the novel can be made intelligible but not interpreted. The experimentalism of *Ulysses* is far from the genuine avant-gardism of *Women in Love*, *Le Bleu du ciel*, or almost any of Beckett's fictions. The inter-textual criticism invited by *Ulysses* is the domestication of literature, a technique for making familiar the potentially traumatic seductions of reading. Even more: *Ulysses* eliminates reading as the ground of interpretation; or, to put this in other terms, it invites intertextual elucidations as a strategy to prohibit textual interpretations. In much contemporary criticism, reading no longer provides a hermeneutical ground of interpretative constraint. This is not to say that there should be or ever was one legitimate interpretation of each text, but rather that – in what we might call the critical progeny of *Ulysses* – texts are made intelligible only by the intra- and inter-textual clues they drop. *Ulysses* is a text to be deciphered but not read. Joyce's schemes already provide a model of interpretive nihilism. They propose, with a kind of wild structural neatness, meanings so remote from our textual experience as to suggest that there is no other basis for sense than the 'line' that can be drawn between two textual points. The exegetical work to be done is enormous, but is has already been done by the author and we simply have to catch up with him.

If criticism always rewrites the texts to which it somewhat deceptively adheres, Joyce minimises the losses inevitably incurred by literature in its critical appropriation by directing the appropriating process. In a sense, the unhappy destiny of the literary work is that it cannot avoid being read. However much the writer may work to create the ideal reader for his text, a certain inattentiveness in the reading of texts defeats that work, thus saving us from such totalitarian projects.

We perhaps sensitise ourselves to effects that the author is either unwilling or unable to include among those to which he would have us respond by the uneven rhythm of our reading, by a certain laxity in our responses, a willingness to miss things that can become an escape from the image into which the text would transform us. *Ulysses* allows for no such laxity, and rather than bother – as, say, Stendhal does in his anxious and intricate effort to forge the sensibility worthy of reading him – with seductive conversionary tactics, the Joycean text escapes from the reader's dangerous freedom merely by insisting that it be read with an excruciatingly close attention and a nearly superhuman memory. It asks that we be nothing but the exegetical machine necessary to complete its sense. *Ulysses* is constantly proposing homework, work we can do outside the text (checking Dublin geography, rereading Homer, Dante, Goethe, Shakespeare, Arnold, the theosophists, Gaelic legends), and in thus insisting on how much it needs us, it also paradoxically saves itself from us. The texture of Joyce's novel is entirely remarkable in that it is at once dense and empty; it imprisons us by the very moves that eject us from the text, and it insists on an uninterrupted attention not exactly to itself but to its instructions for its own further elaboration. *Ulysses* promises a critical utopia: the final elucidation of its sense, the day when all connections will have been discovered and collected in a critical Book that would objectively repeat *Ulysses*, which, in being the exegetical double of its source, would express the quidditas of Joyce's novel, would be *Ulysses* replayed as the whole truth of *Ulysses*.

Finally – and perhaps not so strangely – the very nihilism I have referred to goes along with a promise of salvation. Not only does *Ulysses* keep its conservative ideology of the self distinct from its increasing emphasis on the finality of language's productiveness; not only does it display a perspectival technique that brings to psychological realism the prestige of a Thomistic confidence in art's ability to radiate with the essence of things; Joyce's novel also refers us to a mind purified of 'impossible ordeals' or 'struggles' and elevated to the serene and redemptive management of its cultural acquisitions. Where *Ulysses* really leads us is to Joyce's mind; it illuminates his cultural consciousness. At the end of the reader's exegetical travails lies the promise of an Assumption, of being raised up and identified with the idea of culture made man. Joyce incarnates the enormous authority of sublimation in our culture – of sublimation viewed not as a non-specific eroticising of cultural interests but as the appeasement and even transcendence of anxiety.

Ulysses is modernism's monument to that authority, although – in what I take to be the most authentic risk Joyce takes in producing this monument – it also alludes to the anxiety from which we escape in our exegetical relocation of the work itself within the authorial consciousness at its origin. I am referring to certain moments in the representation of Bloom's solitude – not to his social solitude as a Jew in Ireland, or even to his estrangement from Molly, but rather to a kind of cosmic lack of linkage, a singleness that can be rendered only by images of his floating in interplanetary space. In one of the moral clichés to which this presumably revolutionary novel has given rise, Stephen's coldness and inability to love are often opposed to Bloom's warmth and concern for others. But Stephen's solitude is psychological (it includes his estrangement from his father and his unshakable sense of a crime against his mother); Bloom's aloneness is metaphysical. Furthermore, Stephen is as sociable and loquacious a boozer as all the other characters we meet in the editorial offices of the *Freeman* or in Barney Kiernan's pub; he too spends his day in talk and even plots his oratorial effects (in 'Scylla and Charybdis'), and (in 'Aeolus') he blushes with pleasure ('his blood wooed by grace of language and gesture') as he listens to the rhetorical flourishes in J. J. O'Molloy's recitation of the lawyer Seymour Bushe's 'polished period' describing 'the Moses of Michelangelo in the vatican'. If, in 'Ithaca', both Bloom and Stephen are said to be comforted by the spectacle of 'the heaventree of stars hung with humid nightblue fruit' when they move from the house to the garden, it is Bloom who meditates on 'the parallax or parallactic drift of so-called fixed stars, in reality ever-moving wanderers from immeasurably remote eons to infinitely remote futures' and who, alone after Stephen leaves, feels 'the cold of interstellar space, thousands of degrees below freezing point on the absolute zero of Fahrenheit, Centigrade or Reaumer: the incipient intimations of proximate dawn'. And in the de Quincey passage from 'Oxen of the Sun', which J. S. Atherton rightly sees as 'a most remarkable example of Joyce's 'power of combination', 'Bloom gazes at the triangle on the label of the bottle of bass until it becomes a 'triangled sign upon the forehead of Taurus' – combining lingam and yoni in one symbol, which itself replicates the underlying symbol of the chapter, and placing it in the depths of space.[37]

It is the relentlessly tedious 'Ithaca', with its nearly unreadable scientific expositions of such things as the many uses and virtues of water and the recent restrictions on water consumption in Dublin (when Bloom turns on a faucet), which, precisely because of the impersonality of its technique, becomes a kind of Pascalian meditation on the lack of connectedness not only between human beings but also between the human and the cosmos. We might of course also be tempted to see in the lostness of Bloom an image for the historical situation of Ireland itself: a country with no consensus about its past, little hope for its future, and cut off, both physically and culturally, from the rest of Europe. The anxiety that *Ulysses* massively struggles to transcend – however we choose to understand its origins – is that of disconnectedness. It is perhaps here that Joyce's dependence on his readers is most pronounced, for it is their intra- and extra-textual work that reconstitutes his mind as the serene repository of the resources of our language and culture. From this perspective it hardly matters if the Homeric correspondences are, to say the least, not always exact or that the pastiches of 'Oxen of the Sun' are not always very close to their originals. *Ulysses* is composed as a model of the cultural fragmentation it represents in various ways. Furthermore, Joyce's authority depends on the idiosyncratic nature of the culture he reconstructs; *Ulysses* gives us back our culture as his culture.

For authors, the anguish of paternity is experienced as an uncertainty about the property of their work, about who owns it and if it is indeed their own. 'Fatherhood, in the sense of conscious begetting,' Stephen announces in 'Scylla and Charybdis', 'is unknown to man.' It is 'on that mystery and not on the madonna which the cunning Italian intellect flung to the mob of Europe the church is founded and founded irremovably because founded, like the world, macro and microcosm, upon the void. Upon incertitude, upon unlikelihood' (170). In our tireless elucidation of *Ulysses*, we certify Joyce's paternity, we bring his work back to him, we eliminate what Stephen describes as the natural enmity between father and son by showing how the book gives birth to its author. Exegesis reveals that *Ulysses* signifies Joyce's multitudinous stylistic and structural intentions; it demonstrates that the work glorifies its creator just as Christ – concentrating and purifying in his person a universal human truth – glorifies the Father. And for the worthy disciples of *Ulysses* – which we should now be able to recognise as modernism's most impressive example of the West's long and varied tribute to the authority of the Father – there are of course enormous rewards. *Ulysses* does not restore cultural continuities presumably broken by the modern age. Indeed, in a manner consistent with its nihilistic indifference to any relation between our experience of reading it and those concealed structures it signifies, Joyce's novel asks only that we reconstruct the structurally coherent fragments of Joyce's own cultural consciousness. It is not Western culture that matters, but the coherence of a particular broken version of it. Joyce is faithful to our humanist tradition at a deeper level, in his re-enactment of its assumptions and promise that the possession of culture will transcend anxiety and perhaps even redeem history.

Intertextual criticism is the practical activity that testifies to our espousal of a cultural ethos of the redemptive authority and mastery of art; it is, in the case of *Ulysses*, the imitation that allows us to join Joyce in a community built on identifications and recognitions. Verbal consciousness in *Ulysses* is not – as it is in Lawrence and Bataille – a process of clarification repeatedly menaced by the personal and social pressures antagonistic to all clarifications; rather it is a conquest the multitudinous forms of which are disguised but never threatened by the novel's textures. The community in Ulysses and its exegetes is redemptive in its failure to acknowledge any operative relation between experience – of this text or of reality – and the forms of intelligibility it proposes. It is the *Vita Nuova* in which Joyce thrillingly proposes that we spend our life with him. The call is very hard not to heed. Even in writing 'against *Ulysses*', we can only feel a great sadness in leaving it – to stop working on *Ulysses* is like a fall from grace. □

BIBLIOGRAPHY

All page references within the text are to James Joyce, *A Portrait of the Artist as a Young Man*, edited with an introduction and notes by Seamus Deane (Harmondsworth, Penguin Books, 1992), and to James Joyce, *Ulysses: Annotated Student's Edition*, with an introduction and notes by Declan Kiberd (Harmondsworth, Penguin Books, 1992).

References to Joyce's other works are as follows. The abbreviated form used is shown in brackets.

The Critical Writings of James Joyce, ed. Ellsworth Mason and Richard Ellmann (New York, Viking, 1959) *(CW)*.

Dubliners (Harmondsworth, Penguin Books, 1992) *(D)*.

Exiles (London, Jonathan Cape, 1952) *(E)*.

Letters of James Joyce, Vol. I edited by Stuart Gilbert (London, Faber and Faber, 1957), Vols II and III ed. Richard Ellmann (London, Faber and Faber, 1964).

Finnegans Wake (London, Faber and Faber, 1964) *(F)*.

Stephen Hero (London, Jonathan Cape, 1956) *(S)*.

Derek Attridge (ed.), *The Cambridge Companion to James Joyce* (Cambridge, Cambridge University Press, 1990).

Derek Attridge and Daniel Ferrer, *Post-Structuralist Joyce: Essays from the French* (Cambridge, Cambridge University Press, 1984).

Harry Blamires, *The New Bloomsday Book* (London, Routledge, 1988).

Morris Beja (ed.), *'Dubliners' and 'A Portrait of the Artist as a Young Man: A Casebook* (London, Macmillan, 1993).

Leo Bersani, *The Culture of Redemption* (Yale University Press, 1990).

Harold Bloom (ed.), *James Joyce's 'Ulysses': Modern Critical Interpretations* (New York and Philadelphia, Chelsea House, 1985).

Frank Budgen, *James Joyce and the Making of Ulysses* (Oxford, Oxford University Press, 1972).

Vincent J. Cheng, *Joyce, Race, and Empire* (Cambridge, Cambridge University Press, 1995).

Robert H. Deming (ed.), *James Joyce: The Critical Heritage* (London, Routledge and Kegan Paul, 1970).

Jacques Derrida, *'Ulysses* Gramophone: Hear Say Yes in Joyce', in *Acts of Literature*, ed. Derek Attridge (London, Routledge, 1992).

Richard Ellmann, *James Joyce* (Oxford, Oxford University Press, 1983).

Richard Ellmann, *Ulysses on the Liffey* (London, Faber and Faber, 1972).

Stuart Gilbert, *James Joyce's 'Ulysses'* (Harmondsworth, Peregrine Books, 1963).

S.L. Goldberg, *The Classical Temper: A Study of James Joyce's 'Ulysses'* (London, Chatto and Windus, 1969).

Suzette Henke, *James Joyce and the Politics of Desire* (London, Routledge, 1990).

Hugh Kenner, *Dublin's Joyce* (Guildford, Columbia University Press, 1987).

Hugh Kenner, *Joyce's Voices* (London, Faber and Faber, 1978).

Hugh Kenner, *Ulysses* (London, George Allen and Unwin, 1980).

Karen Lawrence, *The Odyssey of Style in 'Ulysses'* (Princeton, Princeton University Press, 1981).

Harry Levin, *James Joyce* (New York, New Directions, 1941 (reprinted 1960)).

A. Walton Litz, *The Art of James Joyce: Method and Design in 'Ulysses' and Finnegans Wake* (London, Oxford University Press, 1964).

David Lodge, *After Bakhtin* (London, Routledge, 1990).

Colin MacCabe, *James Joyce and the Revolution of the Word* (London, Macmillan, 1979).

Colin MacCabe (ed.), *James Joyce: New Perspectives* (Brighton, The Harvester Press, 1982).

Vicki Mahaffey, *Reauthorising Joyce* (Cambridge, Cambridge University Press, 1988).

Vladimir Nabokov, *Lectures on Literature* (London, Pan Books, 1983).

Willard Potts (ed.), *Portraits of the Artist in Exile: Recollections of James Joyce by Europeans* (New York, Harcourt Brace Jovanovich, 1986).

John Paul Riquelme, *Teller and Tale in Joyce's Fiction: Oscillating perspectives* (Baltimore, Johns Hopkins University Press, 1983, p. 202).

Bonnie Kime Scott, *Joyce and Feminism* (Brighton, Harvester Press, 1984).

Fritz Senn, *Joyce's Dislocations,* ed. John Paul Riquelme, *Perspectives* (Baltimore, Johns Hopkins University Press, 1984).

Thomas F. Staley (ed.), *'Ulysses' Fifty Years* (Bloomington, Indiana University Press, 1974).

Thomas F. Staley, *An Annotated Critical Bibliography of James Joyce* (Hemel Hempstead, Harvester, 1989).

Edmund Wilson, *Axel's Castle* (New York, Charles Scribner's Sons, 1931).

NOTES

INTRODUCTION

1 Jeri Johnson, *Ulysses* (Oxford: Oxford University Press, The World's Classics, 1993), introduction p. xvii.

2 John Paul Riquelme, *Teller and Tale in Joyce's Fiction: Oscillating perspectives* (Baltimore: Johns Hopkins University Press, 1983), p. 202.

3 Hugh Kenner, *Ulysses* (London, George Allen and Unwin, 1980), p. 5, n. 11.

CHAPTER ONE

1 *In Letters of James Joyce*, ed. Richard Ellmann, vol. 2 (London, Faber and Faber, 1962), pp. 371–2.

2 ibid., pp. 372–3.

3 Ezra Pound 'At Last the Novel Appears', *Egoist*, iv, No. 2 (February 1917), pp. 21–2. Quoted in *James Joyce The Critical Heritage*. Vol. 1, ed. Robert H. Deming (London: Routledge and Kegan Paul, 1970), p. 83.

4 *The Critical Heritage*, p. 85

5 Ibid., p. 92

6 Ibid. pp. 86–8

7 Ibid. p. 167

8 Virginia Woolf, 'Modern Fiction', in *The Common Reader*, first series (New York: Harcourt, Brace and World, 1953), pp. 154–5.

9 Ford Madox Ford, 'A Haughty and Proud Generation' *Yale Review*, xi, (July 1922), pp. 714–7. Quoted in *The Critical Heritage*, pp. 128–9.

10 July 20th 1919, *Letters*, 1:129

11 Letter to Carlos Linati, September 1st 1920.

12 Source: Valéry Larbaud, 'James Joyce', *Nouvelle Revue Française*, xviii, (April 1922), pp. 385–405. Excerpts included in *The Critical Heritage*, pp. 252–62.

13 Source: T. S. Eliot, '*Ulysses*, Order and Myth,' *Dial*, November 1923, pp. 480–3. Also in *Critical Heritage*, Vol. 1, pp. 268–71.

14 Ezra Pound, 'James Joyce et Pécuchet', *Mercure de France*, clvi (June 1922), pp. 307–20. Quoted in *Critical Heritage*, Vol. 1, pp. 263–7.

15 Source: Arnold Bennett, 'James Joyce's *Ulysses*', *Outlook* (London) (29th April

1922), pp. 337–9. Excerpted in *Critical Heritage*, Vol.1, pp. 219–22.

16 Source: Wyndham Lewis 'An Analysis of the Mind of James Joyce', in *Time and Western Man* (London: Chatto and Windus, 1927), pp. 91–130.

CHAPTER TWO

1 See A. Walton Litz, 'Pound and Eliot on *Ulysses*: The Critical Tradition', in Thomas F. Staley, ed. '*Ulysses' Fifty Years* (Bloomington, Indiana University Press, 1974), pp. 5–18. See also Jeri Johnson's introduction to the World's Classics edition (Oxford, 1993), p. xviii.

2 Harry Levin, *James Joyce*, (New York, New Directions, 1941, repr. 1960), pp. 65–6.

3 Richard Ellmann, *James Joyce* (Oxford University Press, 1983), p. 616.n.

4 Source: Frank Budgen, *James Joyce and the Making of Ulysses* (Oxford University Press, 1972), pp. 18–22.

5 Hugh Kenner, *Ulysses*.

6 Edmund Wilson, *Axel's Castle* (New York, Charles Scribner's Sons, 1931).

7 Source: Harry Levin, *James Joyce: A Critical introduction*, (New York, New Directions, 1960), pp. 49–54.

CHAPTER THREE

1 Richard Ellmann, *James Joyce*, (Oxford: Oxford University Press, 1982), pp. 296–7.

2 Hugh Kenner, 'The *Portrait* in Perspective', in *Dublin's Joyce* (Guildford, Columbia University Press, 1987), pp. 109–33.

3 Gorman V–iii, VII–i, VII–iii, VII–vi. See also Theodore Spencer's introduction to Stephen Hero.

4 Stanislaus Joyce, 'James Joyce: A Memoir', *Hudson Review*, II. 4, p. 496.

5 Budgen, p. 107.

6 – You want me, said Stephen, to toe the line with those hypocrites and sycophants in the college. I will never do so.

– No. I mentioned Jesus.

– Don't mention him. I have made it a common noun. They don't believe in him; they don't observe his precepts...' *S141/124*.

7 Compare the opening sentence: 'Eins within a space, and a wearywide space it wast, ere wohned a Mookse', F152. Mookse is moocow plus fox plus mock turtle. The German 'Eins' evokes Einstein, who presides over the interchanging of space and time; space is the Mookse's 'spatialty'.

8 Joyce's names should always be scrutinised. Simon Moonan: moon: the heatless (white) satellite reflecting virtue borrowed from Simon Peter. Simony, too, is an activity naturally derived from this casually businesslike attitude to priestly authority.

9 'The Theme of Ulysses', *Kenyon Review*, XVIII (Winter, 1956), pp. 36, 31.

10 'A Comic Principle in Sterne–Meredith–Joyce' (Oslo, 1954), p. 22.

11 *James Joyce* (Norfolk, Va., 1941), pp. 58–62.

12 'Technique as Discovery', *Hudson Review*, I (Spring, 1948), pp. 79–80.

13 'How to Read a Novel' (New York, 1957), p. 213.

14 'The Role of Structure in Joyce's 'Portrait', *Modern Fiction Studies*, IV (Spring, 1958), p. 30. See also Herbert Gorman, *James Joyce* (London, 1941), p. 96, and Stuart Gilbert, *James Joyce's Ulysses* (London, 1930), pp. 20–2.

15 William T. Noon, S. J., *Joyce and Aquinas* (New Haven, Conn., 1957), pp. 34, 35, 66, 67. See also Hugh Kenner, 'The *Portrait* in Perspective', *Kenyon Review*, X (Summer, 1948), pp. 361–81.

16 James Joyce's *Ulysses*, p. 22.

17 Richard Ellmann concludes that whether we know it or not, 'Joyce's court is, like Dante's or Tolstoy's, always in session' (*James Joyce* [New York, 1959], p. 3).

18 Norman Friedman considers it a 'tribute to Joyce's dramatic genius that a Catholic can sympathise with the portrayal of catholic values in the novel which the hero rejects' ('Point of View in Fiction', *PMLA*, LXX [December, 1955] pp. 11–84). But this is not to say that the Catholic readers are right, or that we need not make up our minds about the question.

19 *Modern Fiction Studies*, IV (Spring, 1958), pp. 72–99.

20 See, for example, J. Mitchell Morse's defence of a fairly 'straight' reading of *Ulysses*, based largely on Gorman's reading of Joyce's *Notebooks* ('Augustine, Ayenbite, and *Ulysses*', PMLA, LXX [December, 1955], p. 1147, n. 12).

21 Ed. Theodore Spencer, 1944. Only part of the MS. survives.

22 See Denis Donoghue's 'Joyce and the Finite Order', *Sewanee Review*, LXVIII (Spring, 1960), pp. 256–73. 'The objects [in *Portrait*] exist to provide a suitably piteous setting for Stephen as sensitive Plant; they are meant to mark a sequence of experiences in the mode of pathos. ... The lyric situation is insulated from probes, and there is far too much of this cosseting in the Portrait ... Drama or rhetoric should have warned Joyce that Stephen the aesthetic needed nothing so urgently as a correspondingly deft eiron; lacking this, the book is blind in one eye' (p. 258). Joyce would no doubt reply – I think unfairly – that he intended Stephen as both alazon and eiron.

23 One reviewer of *Stephen Hero* was puzzled to notice in it that the omniscient author, not yet purged in accordance with Joyce's theories of dramatic narration, frequently expresses biting criticism of the young Stephen. The earlier work thus seemed to him 'much more cynical', and 'much, much farther from the principles of detached classicism that had been formulated before either book was written'. How could the man who wrote Stephen Hero go on and write, 'in a mood of enraptured fervour' a work like *Portrait*? (*T.L.S.*, 1 February 1957, p. 64).

It is true that, once we have been alerted, signs of ironic intention come rushing to our view. Those of us who now believe that Joyce is not entirely serious in the passages on aesthetics must wonder, for example, how we ever read them 'straight'. What did we make out of passages like the following, in those old, benighted days before we saw what was going on? The lore which he was believed to pass his days brooding upon so that it had rapt him from the companionship of youth was only a garner of slender sentences from Aristotle's Poetics and Psychology and a Synopsis Philosophiœ Scholasticœ ad mentem divi Thomœ. His

178

thinking was a dusk of doubt and self-mistrust, lit up at moments by the lightnings of intuition ...' 'In those moments the world perished about his feet as if it had been [with] fire consumed: and thereafter his tongue grew heavy and he met the eyes of others with unanswering eyes for he felt that the spirit of beauty had folded him round like a mantle and that in reverie at least he had been acquainted with nobility. But, when this brief pride of silence upheld him no longer, he was glad to find himself still in the midst of common lives, passing on his way amid the squalor and noise and sloth of the city fearlessly and with a light heart' (opening pp. of Chap. V). If this is not mockery, however tender, it is fustian.

24 Source; From Wayne C. Booth, *The Rhetoric of Fiction* (1961), pp. 324–36

25 Source: Vladimir Nabokov: *Lectures on Literature* ed. Fredson Bowers (London, Pan Books, 1983), pp. 285–90.

26 Source: Cleanth Brooks, *A Shaping Joy: Studies in the Writer's Craft* (London: Methuen, 1971), p. 83.

CHAPTER FOUR

1 London, Macmillan, 1979.

2 Roland Barthes, *Image-Music-Text* (London and Glasgow, Fontana, 1977), pp. 145–6.

3 For this see also Catherine Belsey, *Critical Practice* (London, Methuen, 1981), and for a dissenting view see David Lodge's essay on 'Classic Realism' in *After Bakhtin*.

4 Margaret Schlauch, 'The Language of James Joyce', in *Science and Society*, Vol. 3, pp. 482–97.

5 The definition of a meta-language is taken from Tarski's classic article on the semantic conception of truth: Alfred Tarski, 'The semantic conception of Truth' in *Readings in Philosophical Analysis*, eds H. Feigl and W. Sellars (New York, 1949), pp. 52–84.

6 Letter to Harriet Shaw Weaver, 11 July, 1924.

7 MacCabe, *Op. cit.*, pp. 2–4.

8 Stephen Heath, *The Nouveau Roman: A Study in the Practice of Writing* (London, 1972), p. 22.

9 MacCabe cites Booth here.

10 MacCabe, *Op. cit.*, pp. 67–8.

11 The sirens are not described in the *Odyssey* although they sit 'in a meadow piled high with the mouldering skeletons of men, whose withered skin still hangs upon their bones'.

12 Karl Marx and Friedrich Engels, *The German Ideology* (London, 1965).

13 Nietzsche provides a symptomatic example of the conflation between music and voice in this period. *The Birth of Tragedy* is written as a defence of Wagner, and Bernard Pautrat, in his book on Nietzsche, remarks that 'Throughout this period, music is considered as a sort of ideal voice, the pre-eminent mode of expression against which all other voices could be judged and evaluated.' Pautrat, *Versions du soleil: Figures et système de Nietzsche* (Paris, 1971), p. 46. Nietzsche's texts also contain, however, another conception of writing which is in contradiction with the search for a pure mode of expression (cf. Pautrat pp. 48–122). Joyce himself would appear to have shared this belief in sound (music) as the true expressive medium in his youth: 'He read Blake and Rimbaud on the values of letters and even permuted and combined the five vowels to construct cries for primitive emotions' (SH, p. 37). Later, however, he was to say that Rimbaud, although he had the artistic temperament, was 'hardly a *writer* at all' (letter to Stanislaus Joyce about 24 September, 1905).

14 Walter Benjamin, *Charles Baudelaire: A Lyric Poet in the Era of High Capitalism* (London, 1973), p. 96.

15 cf. *Portrait*, p. 108.

16 'The Prelude' (1805), XI, 278–315.

17 Jean Laplanche and Serge Leclaire, 'The Unconscious: A Psychoanalytic Study', in *Yale French Studies*, 48, 1972, pp. 118–78.

18 Sigmund Freud, 'The Interpretation of Dreams', Pelican Freud Library, 4, pp. 671–2.

19 David Lodge, *After Bakhtin* (London, Routledge, 1990).

20 David Lodge, *The British Museum is Falling Down* (Harmondsworth, Penguin Books, 1980).

21 James Joyce, *Ulysses*, p. 1.

22 Claudia Jameson, *Lesson in Love*, Mills & Boon, 1982, p. 76.

23 *Readings in Russian Poetics*, p. 188. My account of Bakhtin's discourse typology is based mainly on this extract from Bakhtin's first book, *Problems of Dostoyevsky's Art* (1929), later revised and expanded as *Problems of Dostoevsky's Poetics* (1963).

CHAPTER FIVE

1 Hélène Cixous, 'The Laugh of the Medusa', trans. Keith and Paula Cohen, *Signs*, 1, (1976), pp. 875–93. See also *The Exile of James Joyce* (New York, David Lewis, 1972).

2 Sandra Gilbert and Susan Gubar, 'Sexual linguistics: gender, language, sexuality'. *New Literary History* 16 (1985), 515–43. Quoted in Karen Lawrence, 'Joyce and Feminism', in Derek Attridge (ed.), *The Cambridge Companion to James Joyce* (Cambridge, Cambridge University Press, 1990), p. 237.

3 Vicky Mahaffey, *Reauthorising Joyce* (Cambridge, Cambridge University Press, 1988), pp. 96–8, 102–3, 178, 187–91.

4 'His master's voice? The questioning of authority in literature', in *The Modern English Novel: The Reader, the Writer and the Work*, ed. Gabriel Josipovici (New York, Harper and Row, 1976), p. 126.

5 J. Hillis Miller, 'Ariadne's Thread: Repetition and the Narrative Line', pp. 57–77; and 'Ariachne's Broken Woof', pp. 44–60.

6 *Gyn/Ecology*, p. 400.

7 Suzette Henke, *James Joyce and the Politics of Desire* (London, Routledge, 1990), pp. 72–82, 121–4.

8 Simone de Beauvoir, *The Second Sex*, pp. 166–7.

9 cf. Bonnie Kime Scott, *James Joyce*, p. 88.

10 See Hugh Kenner, *Dublin's Joyce*, p. 123.

11 See Hélène Cixous, *The Exile of James Joyce*, p. 498.

12 Sigmund Freud, 'Anxiety and the Instinctual Life' in *New Introductory Lectures in Psychoanalysis*, trans. and ed. James Strachey (New York, Norton, 1965).

13 Jacques Lacan, 'God and the Jouissance of The Woman', in *Feminine Sexuality: Jacques Lacan and the école freudienne*, ed.

Juliet Mitchell and Jacqueline Rose (New York, Norton, 1982), pp. 144–5.

14 Gilles Deleuze and Félix Guattari, *Anti-Oedipus: Capitalism and Schizophrenia*, trans. Robert Hurley, Mark Seem and Helen R. Lane (Minneapolis, University of Minnesota Press, 1983) p. 67.

15 Ibid., p. 69.

16 Richard Ellmann, *Ulysses on the Liffey* (London, Faber and Faber, 1972); Seamus Deane, 'Joyce the Irishman', in *The Cambridge Companion to James Joyce*.

17 When 'the so-called national party behaves as a party based on ethnic differences', Fanon argues, it 'becomes, in fact, the tribe which ... claims to speak in the name of the totality of the people ... [and] organises an authentic ethnic dictatorship. We no longer see the rise of a bourgeois dictatorship, but a tribal dictatorship' (*Wretched*, p. 183).

18 As David Lodge argues in *Anomalous States: Irish Writing and the Post-Colonial Movement*: '*Ulysses*'s most radical movement is in its refusal to fulfil either of these demands [i.e. individual and stylistic totalisations] and its correspondent refusal to subordinate itself to the socialising functions of identity formation. It insists instead on a deliberate stylisation of dependence and inauthenticity, a stylisation of the hybrid status of the colonised subject as of the colonised culture, their internal adulteration and the strictly parodic modes that they produce in every sphere.' (p. 110).

19 Vincent J. Cheng, *Joyce, Race and Empire* (Cambridge, Cambridge University Press, 1995), pp. 246–8.

20 Jacques Derrida, 'Ulysses Gramophone: Hear Say Yes in Joyce' in *Acts of Literature* ed. Derek Attridge (London, Routledge, 1992), pp. 281, 286.

21 Leo Bersani, 'Against *Ulysses*' in *The Culture of Redemption*, pp. 157–77.

22 *Ibid.*, p. 1.

23 See S.L. Goldberg, *The Classical Temper: A Study of James Joyce's 'Ulysses'* (London, Chatto and Windus, 1969).

24 John Paul Riquelme, *Teller and Tale in Joyce's Fiction: Oscillating perspectives* (Baltimore, Johns Hopkins University

180

Press, 1983), p. 202.

25 Hugh Kenner, *Joyce's Voices* (London, Faber and Faber, 1978), p. 17.

26 Fritz Senn, *Joyce's Dislocutions*, ed. John Paul Riquelme, (Baltimore, Johns Hopkins University Press, 1984), p. 141.

27 Kenner, *Joyce's Voices*, pp. 69–70.

28 *A Portrait*, p. 231.

29 'Ambiviolences: Notes for reading Joyce', in *Post-Structuralist Joyce*, pp. 33, 57.

30 See Richard Poirier, 'The Difficulties of Modernism and the Modernism of Difficulty, *Humanities in Society*, 1 (Spring 1978).

31 Frank Budgen, *James Joyce and the Making of 'Ulysses'*, p. 56.

32 In a letter to Harriet Shaw Weaver, Joyce spoke of the 'scorching' effect of his writing: 'each specific episode, dealing with some province of artistic culture ... leaves behind it a burnt up field', *Letters*, 20 July, 1919, 1:129.

33 Joyce, *Letters*, letter to Frank Budgen, 20 March, 1920, 1:139–40.

34 Richard Ellmann, *Ulysses on the Liffey* (London, Faber and Faber, 1972), pp. 136–9.

35 Kenner, *Joyce's Voices*, p. 40.

36 In Leo Bersani, *The Death Of Stéphane Mallarmé* (Cambridge, Cambridge University Press, 1982).

37 J.S. Atherton, 'The Oxen of the Sun', in *James Joyce's 'Ulysses': Critical Essays*, ed. Clive Hart and David Hayman (Berkeley, University of California Press, 1974), p. 3331.

ACKNOWLEDGEMENTS

The editor and publishers wish to thank the following for their permission to reprint copyright material: Chatto & Windus (for material from *Time and Western Man*); Oxford University Press (for material from *James Joyce and the Making of Ulysses*); New Directions (for material from *James Joyce: A Critical Introduction*); Columbia University Press (for material from *Dublin's Joyce*); University of Chicago Press (for material from *The Rhetoric of Fiction*); Pan Books (for material from *Lectures on Literature*); Methuen (for material from *A Shaping Joy: Studies in the Writer's Craft*); Macmillan (for material from *James Joyce and the Revolution of the Word*); Cambridge University Press (for material from *Reauthorising Joyce* and *Race and Empire*); Routledge & Kegan Paul (for material from *James Joyce and the Politics of Desire*); Yale University Press (for material from *The Culture of Redemption*).

Every effort has been made to contact the holders of any copyrights applying to the material quoted in this book. The publishers would be grateful if any such copyright holders whom they have not been able to contact, would write to them.

John Coyle is a lecturer in English Literature at the University of Glasgow.

INDEX

9155